# THE TWO AMERICAN POLITICAL SYSTEMS

## Society, Economics, and Politics

### CREEL FROMAN

*University of California, Irvine*

Prentice-Hall, Inc., Englewood Cliffs, New Jersey 07632

*Library of Congress Cataloging in Publication Data*

Froman, Creel
    The two American political systems.

    Bibliography: p. 207
    Includes index.
    1. United States—Politics and government.  2. United
States—Economic conditions.  3. Property—United States.
4. Income distribution—United States.  I. Title.
JK271.F767 1984      320.973     83-19242
ISBN 0-13-934902-2

Editorial/production supervision and
   interior design: Kate Kelly
Cover design: Ben Santora
Manufacturing buyer: Ron Chapman

Printed in the United States of America

10  9  8  7  6  5  4  3  2  1

ISBN 0-13-934902-2

Prentice-Hall International, Inc., *London*
Prentice-Hall of Australia Pty. Limited, *Sydney*
Editora Prentice-Hall do Brasil, Ltda., *Rio de Janeiro*
Prentice-Hall Canada, Inc., *Toronto*
Prentice-Hall of India Private Limited, *New Delhi*
Prentice-Hall of Japan, Inc., *Tokyo*
Prentice-Hall of Southeast Asia Pte. Ltds., *Singapore*
Whitehall Books Limited, *Wellington, New Zealand*

This book is dedicated to all of us
who have ever thought
that there *must* be *something* more to politics
than what we have heretofore been taught.

# CONTENTS

# PREFACE

The study of politics, like the study of all human activity, is more complex than is sometimes thought. It requires observation, the careful collection of facts, and *inferences* about what those facts, assembled together, mean. Most of us can agree on the facts, although facts present their own peculiar problems. There are obviously so many possible facts that researchers choose, given their general orientation, those they think are relevant and important.

In general, the study of American politics has proceeded within a particular orientation. The democratic creed, the substance and function of which will be carefully explored in the following pages, is taken as the foundation of observation, data collection, and inference. Two major consequences of this strategy—a very limited one from this author's point of view—need mentioning: (1) the role of ideology itself is frequently unexamined; and (2) the connection between economics and politics is little explored.

Chapter 6, a key chapter in this book, suggests that the only alternative available to political scientists is to demonstrate, as reasonably as possible, the validity and usefulness of the inferernces they make in assembling the facts in order to provide a coherent *understanding* of the political system. One does not *prove* the existence of a concept such as power—one infers it from the data presented.

What this means, then, is that the study of politics is very much like story-telling, at least in those books that attempt to provide an overall understanding of the political process. Individual researchers, of course, can simply concentrate on collecting selected facts without making inferences as to how those facts are to be interpreted. But in order to give *meaning* to those facts, one must give them a broader interpretation. And what makes the analysis of politics a kind of storytelling is the *inferences* that have to be made about the forces that hold the selected facts together. Further, these inferences may also guide the researcher in selecting the facts themselves to be studied.

The democratic creed provides a particular set of forces from which inferences are made. In general, these forces have to do with the "will of the people" as expressed through elections. In the story you are about to read, it is suggested—and demonstrated as well as I am able—that the motive force of politics lies elsewhere. And what this means is that the whole story changes; for we see the cast of characters in the story considerably enlarged, the setting broadened to include economic data, and a totally different understanding of American politics emerging.

All stories are composed of five basic ingredients: (1) forces (motives), moving (2) characters, in a particular (3) setting, to (4) action, resulting in (5) outcomes. Politics is no different. It is an activity, a real-life, on going activity of people with motives performing actions in settings that produce outcomes.

Both the story of American politics that you are about to read, and the one it is meant to replace, contain these same five ingredients. But this account differs significantly from the usual version of American politics—the one specified by the democratic ideology. The normal account of American politics that is given in civics courses in high school and elsewhere is an idealized account, not of what takes place in politics, but of what would be nice to believe takes place.

There are a number of reasons why the story of American politics is usually told in an idealized fashion, reasons that we shall carefully explore in this book. But this account you are about to read differs in *every* respect from the usual story: the motives are different, the characters are different, the setting is different, the action is different, and the outcomes are different.

The telling of this new story will proceed in the following way: Chapter 1 introduces you to motives; Chapter 2 to the setting; Chapters 3 and 4 to the characters; Chapters 5, 6, 7, and 8 to action; and Chapters 9, 10, and 11 to outcomes. Chapter 12 then provides a number of summary propositions that trace the development of the story from beginning to end; and the Epilogue discusses the very important issue of what, if anything, citizens can do about the political world in which they find themselves.

There is also another feature of stories, particualrly political stories, that should be mentioned, since it concerns the kind of reaction you might have in reading what follows. All stories raise moral questions of good and bad, whether or not the author is conscious of raising them or not. This story is no exception to this general rule—although the question of how we might feel about the story itself is dealt with here quite explicitly.

Stories can vary widely with respect to what is good and what is bad: they can present sympathetic people activated by bad motives (Bonnie and Clyde, for example), bad people activated by bad motives, good outcomes coming from bad motives (Adam Smith), bad outcomes coming from good motives (what we all feel when we really foul something up), and so on. Hardly anything is all good or all bad, even though we might like to think otherwise, and even though it would certainly simplify our understanding of things if it were true.

The contrast between the story you are about to read and the normal story of U.S. politics is one of this book's most salient features. The democratic ideal smothers U.S. politics under a blanket of idealized justice, equality, and fairness. Any story that tries to remove this blanket is likely not only to reveal unsettling events that are inconsistent with what we have been led to believe, but also to evoke a strong desire to reject the story itself. I will have a good deal to say about this problem as we go along, but it is important to be aware of it and not be discouraged by it. You *will* feel uncomfortable about what you learn in the following pages. Some of the data may appear to be so outrageous compared to what you thought were the facts that you will refuse to believe them. U.S. politics is usually treated as a romance, where good wins out over evil. This version suggests that politics is more complicated that that; we are dealing with real people in real situations in which the stakes are very high indeed.

For some of you the whole tenor of this story may seem so tragic that you will read it only reluctantly. I can do nothing but encourage you to continue anyway. There is, as the book itself points out, a lot to be gained by seeing the world as it really is, if only to be in a better position to make it more like the world of one's fantasies. Conversely, there is a great deal to be lost in believing that the fantasy actually represents the real world in which we live.

I am one of those people to whom this book is dedicated. I have always felt that there *must* be *something* more to politics than what I had thought, taught, and even wrote about. The road that led me to the writing of this book was long and circuitous, and involved a number of intellectual stops and starts. I offer this book as a sort of beginning, hoping that others may find something here worth looking into further. As a professional political scientist, I share a strong concern with others in my field for the correct understanding of U.S. politics, and share with many the agonies of finding that enough has not yet been established, let alone even explored.

So I dedicate this book to all who, like myself, have profoundly regretted their inability to assemble a coherent picture of what is really going on in politics. This book indicates the directions in which I feel it would be fruitful to travel, and the conclusions that one may already draw. I would like to think that others might share this sense of direction when they arrive at the end.

# ACKNOWLEDGMENTS

Stan Wakefield, Social Science Editor of Prentice-Hall, and his staff have considerably expedited the publication of this book. Kate Kelly and Barbara Bernstein ably handled the production process.

Roger Schaefer, Texas Tech University, Robert Pecoralla, New York University, Terrance Jones, University of Missouri, and Eugene A. Mawhinney, University of Maine read the manuscript for Prentice-Hall and contributed valuable suggestions and comments.

My father, an economist, and I spent many fruitful hours of discussion while this book was being written. I profited enormously from his comments. It is partly as a consequence of these discussions that I felt Chapter 6 should be added.

Both my mother and father made the writing of this book possible in ways in which they are probably not even aware.

My daughters, Lizzie and Katrina, have always been a constant source of inspiration and purpose.

Jill has the knack of making me feel that what I do is important.

# CHAPTER ONE
# POLITICS
# AND PROPERTY
## *An Introduction*

It is common to treat American politics as though it were all of a piece. Democratic politics, after all, concerns the relationship between governmental institutions and the people; and the almost exclusive concern of those who write about American government and politics is in terms of their democratic features. This is especially true for high-school and even college textbooks, although less so for newspapers and magazines. Textbooks serve as materials for indoctrination into social, economic, and political systems of this country (that is, they introduce and reiterate the prevailing ideology), whereas the print media are more attuned to "the news," inside stories, and what, presumably, is "really" happening. Societies are composed of large groups of people who must somehow live together without excessive violence and conflict. One of the most important roles a society performs is to provide its members with a common way of looking at things, a "conventional wisdom," a prevailing idea structure that helps to hold it together. This socialization into the way in which the political system is *said* to operate, its ideology, is especially relevant for the young, although repetition also helps to reinforce the ideas even for long-time members.

The usual way of acquiring an understanding of how American politics functions is to study the institutions of government and the formal (and to some extent the informal) political processes that link the government to the populace.

This usually entails a discussion of the Constitution, the presidency, Congress, and the Supreme Court, the bureaucracy (to a lesser degree), elections, political parties, public opinion, and, perhaps, a short introduction into the role of interest groups.

## TWO KINDS OF PERSONS

This emphasis on institutions and the relationship of the general public to them might be a fine way to do things if all people were the same—that is, if they had approximately the same amount of influence and power, or even potential influence and power. It would also simplify our task enormously: we would have but one political system to study. Indeed, the idea that all people in a democracy are more or less the same is derived from the democratic *ideal* of equality and is the major rationale for describing American politics as a single system. The general argument is that, in a democracy, the "will of the people" prevails through the voting mechanism. But all people are not the same. In fact, aside from the usual inequalities of race, age, sex, wealth, and so on, there are, literally, two kinds of persons in the United States. Let us explore this a little further.

### Individual Persons

The Fifth Amendment to the U.S. Constitution contains, among other stipulations, the following: "No person shall be . . . deprived of life, liberty, or property, without due process of law . . ."; and the Fourteenth Amendment contains a similar provision designed to extend the language of the Fifth Amendment regarding national rights to the several States: "No State shall . . . deprive any person of life, liberty, or property, without due process of law; nor deny to any person within its jurisdiction the equal protection of the laws."

Now, on one level, this sounds as it should be. Neither the national government nor the state in which a person resides can deprive any person of life, liberty, or property without due process of law. What could be more fair? The answer is that, as a procedure, nothing could be more fair, assuming, of course, that the laws by which persons are deprived of life, liberty, or property are themselves just, and—the corollary of this—that the laws by which persons are not deprived of life, liberty, or property (that is, the laws that protect these rights) are also just. The Constitution does not say that persons cannot be deprived of life, liberty, or property, nor that they should not be. In fact deprivations of this sort are quite common: taxes (depriving people of property), war (depriving people of life), and legislation against falsely shouting "fire" in a crowded theater (depriving people of liberty). The Constitution states only that if persons are so deprived, due process must be followed—that is, actions must be taken legally, and must be within the scope of the Constitution as interpreted by the courts. If the laws depriving persons of life, liberty, and property are unjust in their *con-*

*tent,* however, they could still meet the *procedural* requirement of due process while being unjust in their effects. And if laws that protect life, liberty, or property are unjust, then due process undoubtedly works against those who would like to change them. It is clear, then, that the questions of due process and equal protection, important as they are, are utterly dependent upon the content of the laws that are legislated, and how they are interpreted and enforced.

It is vitally important that laws be just and that the procedures for carrying out those laws be just. These are ideals to which we can all subscribe, and most of us would like to believe that that is how the law functions in the United States. Whether or not the laws and procedures are in fact just, however, is quite a different matter from how we would like things to be. And, since the Fifth and Fourteenth Amendments refer to "persons," the question of justice is going to be especially complicated and difficult to unravel if there is more than one kind of person in the United States.

The question of who is a person seems trivial. In fact, it may not even have occurred to you that it is a question at all. We are all persons. At the same time, however, we are also aware of certain differences between people that determine how they are treated socially, economically, and politically, that have influenced, and continue to influence, how the ideals of equality and due process are carried out. For example, it took another constitutional amendment, the Thirteenth, to end slavery, and another provision of the Fourteenth Amendment to end the constitutionally directed practice of counting slaves as three-fifths of a person in apportioning congressional seats and Electoral College electors. (Untaxed Indians, however, were still excluded from personhood.) Another amendment, the Nineteenth, granted women the right to vote (thus modifying their status as persons); and the Twenty-sixth Amendment lowered the voting age from 21 to 18 (thus extending certain rights to those 18 or over but excluding those under 18). It is relevant, also, to point out that the Equal Rights Amendment, which would have extended equal rights to women, and which was passed by the necessary two-thirds vote in each house of Congress, fell short of the required ratification by three-fourths of the states and thus failed to become part of our Constitution. Controversies regarding child labor, the treatment of the insane and others judged incompetent, and whether or not a fetus is a person, and the continued discrimination (whether legal or illegal) against blacks, women, Indians, and Latinos are still important matters affecting one's status as a person.

## Corporate Persons

These are questions, however, of the rights of individual persons and the extent to which justice and equality are extended to people as *individuals.* That all individual persons *should* be treated equally is a fundamental tenet of American ideology that never has been true in practice and never will be. (No one argues, for example, that 12-year-olds should be allowed to vote.) Sex, race, religion, and ethnic background have always been social, political, and economic criteria affecting equality and justice, and will undoubtedly, and regrettably, continue to be. So too are the privileges that come from wealth, income, educa-tion, status, position, and power.

But the main point is not that due process of law and equal protection of the laws are potential guarantees only to the extent that laws themselves provide for equality and justice, nor that the concept of "person" varies with the kinds and types of individuals. The main point concerns the social creation of an entirely new kind of "person" who is not a person at all in the sense in which we usually use the word. The concept of a "person" has become elastic not only in deciding how individual human beings are to be treated, but also how certain forms of wealth are to be treated. Early in the nineteenth century, at the beginning of the Industrial Revolution, *corporations* were defined as persons by the Supreme Court (*Bank of Augusta* v. *Earle,* 1839) and thus were granted the privileges and immunities of individual persons under the Fifth and, eventually, Fourteenth Amendments of the Constitution. This was neither a question of expanding nor restricting the rights of individuals as persons, but rather of creating a whole new class of persons who were not single individuals but groups of individuals associ-ated together for business purposes. Hence, according to the interpretation of the Supreme Court, one cannot deprive a corporation of life, liberty, or property without due process of law. Not only does this ruling reveal the esteem in which corporations are held and the status given them in our political system, but it also protects certain "persons" who have, since the initial decisions, become ex-tremely wealthy and powerful, much wealthier and more powerful than individu-als.

There are, then, two kinds of persons in the United States: individuals and corporations. As a consequence, given that politics is the relationship between governmental institutions and "the people" (that is, "persons"), there are two political systems in the United States: the corporate political system and the indi-vidual political system.

Our focus in this book will be on the structures of the two political systems, the different ways in which they operate, and the points at which they come to-gether. American politics is not all of a piece, a single thing. It comes in *two* pieces. In our description and analysis of these two political systems we shall, in addition, link the political with the economic and the social; we shall explore how the three normally separate social sciences, political science, economics, and sociology, come together to provide us with a more coherent picture of the way in which a country, in this case the United States, carries out many of its most important activities.

## TRADITIONAL ANALYSES OF U.S. POLITICS

Most books on politics and government attempt to describe what the institutions of government are and how they function. To the extent they tell us anything at all about what politics is, they are vague notions about "power" or who "wins," and say little or nothing about what, fundamentally, the exercise of power is all about, or what, in particular, there is to win and what winning means. If they do tell us anything about motives, it is almost always in terms of what the *participants* report their motives to be. Given the fact that political language tends to be highly rhetorical and serves to justify, in terms of the conventional wisdom, the actions of those engaged in politics, what the participants tell us concerning their motives must always be viewed with suspicion if not outright cynicism.

As a result of this lack of understanding of what politics is all about, most analyses of American politics concentrate on the *processes* of government, how the institutions are structured, and how they presumably go about their business. Seen from this "process" perspective, government and politics appear as a vast morass of institutions, elected and appointed officials, departments and agencies, court decisions, interest groups and citizen activities, political parties, public opinion, and the like. What the study of government, given this more or less contentless approach, seems to lack is a focus telling us what *motivates* government activity. What is needed is some indication of the *content* of the motivation, what the major overriding interest is in government: what it is that government provides and protects. Our answer to this question is that what lies behind the social, economic, and political systems of this country (or for that matter any country) is control over its resources, which means, ultimately, control over property, its uses (production, profit, opportunity), and its benefits—i.e., wealth and income.

Not only does the economic, social, and political history of the United States make this clear, but it has been stated quite unequivocally by major public figures, sometimes in unguarded moments, sometimes explicitly. President Coolidge was accustomed to saying that "the business of America is business"; and Charles Wilson, secretary of defense under President Eisenhower suggested that "what's good for General Motors is good for the country." A more recent version of this kind of forthrightness occurred in 1982 when President Reagan's budget director, David A. Stockman, in an interview with the *Atlantic Monthly,* explained the "trickle-down" aspect of the administration's "supply-side" economic program, in which the tax policies would simply redistribute wealth to the rich, much of it in the form of advantages for corporations. But we have a much more august authority than David Stockman, or even Calvin Coolidge or Charles Wilson, to explain the generating force that lies behind politics and government; we have a major Founding Father and fourth president of the United States, James Madison.

## MADISON AND PROPERTY

At the end of the Constitutional Convention in 1787, which had met to revise the Articles of Confederation (the loose and weak governmental structure adopted at the end of the Revolutionary War), there was a good deal of controversy surrounding the newly drafted Constitution. There were two major groups in conflict, as we shall learn from Madison. On one side were those who wanted a stronger central government that would honor the large debts incurred during the Revolutionary War and afterwards, and that would help to establish a certain economic security for those who owned most of the property. On the other side were the small landholders, engaged mostly in subsistence farming, and unpropertied laborers in the commercial towns and cities. These latter two groups, of course, represented the overwhelming majority of American citizens. Approval by nine of the original thirteen states was required for ratification; and although most of the smaller states acted rapidly, the larger states, where conflicts between debtor farmers and the landed aristocracy and commercial interests were particularly vehement, found themselves embroiled in considerable disagreement. The outcome of the vote for ratification was therefore quite uncertain. For example, just a year earlier, in Massachusetts, in what has become known as Shays's Rebellion, a group composed mostly of poor farmers threatened with mortgage foreclosures had marched on the courthouse in the town of Northampton and were finally dispersed by the state militia. This uprising, occurring as it did during a major depression in which economic hardship was severe and widespread, was clearly a sign of the times and a portent of further violent unrest. Indeed, the prospect of a major clash between, essentially, the poor and the more well-to-do is considered to be one of the principle factors that prompted the call for a Constitutional Convention in the first place.

Alexander Hamilton, a leading political figure in the state of New York, a signer of the Constitution, and later our first secretary of the treasury under President Washington, initiated the idea of publishing a series of articles in various New York newspapers designed to urge the adoption of the new Constitution. To help him in this project he called on James Madison from Virginia, and John Jay from New York. The result of this collaboration was what has now become known as *The Federalist Papers*. One of the most celebrated of these is Federalist Paper No. 10, written by James Madison. It is considered to be a brilliant argument that lays out the advantages of the new Constitution, especially concerning the benefits of establishing a large republic with powers going beyond those provided for in the Articles of Confederation, and the better control of what he calls "factions." What interests us, however, is the candid nature in which Madison pleads the case of *property rights* (a feature, by the way, that is usually ignored in United States government texts). When reading the following document, then, be alert for this aspect of his argument.

### The Size and Variety of the Union as a Check on Faction

*To the People of the State of New York:* Among the numerous advantages promised by a well-constructed Union, none deserves to be more accurately developed than its tendency to break and control the violence of faction. The friend of popular governments never finds himself so much alarmed for their character and fate, as when he contemplates their propensity to this dangerous vice. He will not fail, therefore, to set a due value on any plan which, without violating the principles to which he is attached, provides a proper cure for it. The instability, injustice, and confusion introduced into the public councils, have, in truth, been the mortal diseases under which popular governments have everywhere perished; as they continue to be the favorite and fruitful topics from which the adversaries to liberty derive their most specious declamations. The valuable improvements made by the American constitutions on the popular models, both ancient and modern, cannot certainly be too much admired; but it would be an unwarrantable partiality, to contend that they have as effectually obviated the danger on this side, as we wished and expected. Complaints are everywhere heard from our most considerate and virtuous citizens, equally the friends of public and private faith, and of public and personal liberty, that our governments are too unstable, that the public good is disregarded in the conflicts of rival parties, and that measures are too often decided, not according to the rules of justice and the rights of the minor party, but by the superior force of an interested and overbearing majority. However anxiously we may wish that these complaints had no foundation, the evidence of known facts will not permit us to deny that they are in some degree true. It will be found, indeed, on a candid review of our situation, that some of the distresses under which we labor have been erroneously charged on the operation of our governments; but it will be found, at the same time, that other causes will not alone account for many of our heaviest misfortunes; and, particularly, for that prevailing and increasing distrust of public engagements, and alarm for private rights, which are echoed from one end of the continent to the other. These must be chiefly, if not wholly, effects of the unsteadiness and injustice with which a factious spirit has tainted our public administrations.

By a faction, I understand a number of citizens, whether amounting to a majority or minority of the whole, who are united and actuated by some common impulse of passion, or of interest, adverse to the rights of other citizens, or to the permanent and aggregate interests of the community.

There are two methods of curing the mischiefs of faction: the one by removing its causes; the other, by controlling its effects.

There are again two methods of removing the causes of faction: the one, by destroying the liberty which is essential to its existence; the other, by giving to every citizen the same opinions, the same passions, and the same interests.

It could never be more truly said than of the first remedy, that it was worse than the disease. Liberty is to faction what air is to fire, an aliment without which it instantly expires. But it could not be less folly to abolish liberty, which is essential to political life, because it nourishes faction, than it would be to wish the annihilation of air, which is essential to animal life, because it imparts to fire its destructive agency.

The second expedient is as impracticable as the first would be unwise. As long as the reason of man continues fallible, and he is at liberty to exercise it, different opinions will be formed. As long as the connection subsists between his reason and his self-love, his opinions and his passions will have a reciprocal influence on each other: and the former will be objects to which the latter will attach themselves. The diversity in the faculties of men, from which the rights or property originate, is not less an insuperable obstacle to a uniformity of interests. The protection of these faculties is the first object of government. From the protection of different and unequal faculties of acquiring property, the possession of different degrees and kinds of property immediately results; and from the influence of these on the sentiments and views of the respective proprietors, ensues a division of the society into different interests and parties.

The latent causes of faction are thus sown in the nature of man; and we see them everywhere brought into different degrees of activity, according to the different circumstances of civil society. A zeal for different opinions concerning religion, concerning government, and many other points, as well of speculation as of practice; an attachment to different leaders ambitiously contending for pre-eminence and power; or to persons of other descriptions whose fortunes have been interesting to the human passions, have, in turn, divided mankind into parties, inflamed them with mutual animosity, and rendered them much more disposed to vex and oppress each other than to co-operate for their common good. So strong is this propensity of mankind to fall into mutual animosities, that where no substantial occasion presents itself, the most frivolous and fanciful distinctions have been sufficient to kindle their unfriendly passions and excite their most violent conflicts. But the most common and durable source of factions has been the various and unequal distribution of property. Those who hold and those who are without property have ever formed distinct interests in society. Those who are creditors, and those who are debtors, fall under a like discrimination. A landed interest, a manufacturing interest, a mercantile interest, a moneyed interest, with many lesser interests, grow up of necessity in civilized nations, and divide them into different classes, actuated by different sentiments and views. The regulation of these various and interfering interests forms the principal task of modern legislation, and involves the spirit of party and faction in the necessary and ordinary operations of the government.

No man is allowed to be a judge in his own cause, because his interest would certainly bias his judgment, and, not improbably, corrupt his integrity. With equal, nay with greater reason, a body of men are unfit to be both judges and parties at the same time; yet what are many of the most important acts of legislation, but so many judicial determinations, not indeed concerning the rights of single persons, but concerning the rights of large bodies of citizens? And what are the different classes of legislators but advocates and parties to the causes which they determine? Is a law proposed concerning private debts? It is a question to which the creditors are parties on one side and the debtors on the other. Justice ought to hold the balance between them. Yet the parties are, and must be, themselves the judges; and the most numerous party, or, in other words, the most powerful faction must be expected to prevail. Shall domestic manufactures be encouraged, and in what degree, by restrictions on foreign manufactures?

are questions which would be differently decided by the landed and the manufacturing classes, and probably by neither with a sole regard to justice and the public good. The apportionment of taxes on the various descriptions of property is an act which seems to require the most exact impartiality; yet there is, perhaps, no legislative act in which greater opportunity and temptation are given to a predominant party to trample on the rules of justice. Every shilling with which they overburden the inferior number, is a shilling saved to their own pockets.

It is in vain to say that enlightened statesmen will be able to adjust these clashing interests, and render them all subservient to the public good. Enlightened statesmen will not always be at the helm. Nor, in many cases, can such an adjustment be made at all without taking into view indirect and remote considerations, which will rarely prevail over the immediate interest which one party may find in disregarding the rights of another or the good of the whole.

The inference to which we are brought is, that the *causes* of faction cannot be removed, and that relief is only to be sought in the means of controlling its *effects*.

If a faction consists of less than a majority, relief is supplied by the republican principle which enables the majority to defeat its sinister views by regular vote. It may clog the administration, it may convulse the society; but it will be unable to execute and mask its violence under the forms of the Constitution. When a majority is included in a faction, the form of popular government, on the other hand, enables it to sacrifice to its ruling passion or interest both the public good and the rights of other citizens. To secure the public good and private rights against the danger of such a faction, and at the same time to preserve the spirit and the form of popular government, is then the great object to which our inquiries are directed. Let me add that it is the great desideratum by which this form of government can be rescued from the opprobrium under which it has so long labored, and be recommended to the esteem and adoption of mankind.

By what means is this object attainable? Evidently by one of two only. Either the existence of the same passion or interest in a majority at the same time must be prevented, or the majority, having such coexistent passion or interest, must be rendered, by their number and local situation, unable to concert and carry into effect schemes of oppression. If the impulse and the opportunity be suffered to coincide, we well know that neither moral nor religious motives can be relied on as an adequate control. They are not found to be such on the injustice and violence of individuals, and lose their efficacy in proportion to the number combined together, that is, in proportion as their efficacy becomes needful.

From this view of the subject is may be concluded that a pure democracy, by which I mean a society consisting of a small number of citizens, who assemble and administer the government in person, can admit of no cure for the mischiefs of faction. A common passion or interest will, in almost every case, be felt by a majority of the whole; a communication and concert result from the form of government itself; and there is nothing to check the inducements to sacrifice the weaker party or an obnoxious individual. Hence it is that such democracies have ever been spectacles of turbulence and contention; have ever been found incompatible with personal security or the rights of property; and have in general been as short in their lives as they have been violent in their deaths. Theoretic politicians, who have patronized this species of government, have erroneously supposed that by reducing mankind to a perfect equality in their political rights, they would, at the same time, be perfectly equalized and assimilated in their possessions, their opinions, and their passions.

A republic, by which I mean a government in which the scheme of representation takes place, opens a different prospect, and promises the cure for which we are seeking. Let us examine the points in which it varies from pure democracy, and we shall comprehend both the nature of the cure and the efficacy which it must derive from the Union.

The two great points of difference between a democracy and a republic are: first, the delegation of the government, in the latter, to a small number of citizens elected by the rest; secondly, the greater number of citizens, and greater sphere of country, over which the latter may be extended.

The effect of the first difference is, on the one hand, to refine and enlarge the public views, by passing them through the medium of a chosen body of citizens, whose wisdom may best discern the true interest of their country, and whose patriotism and love of justice will be least likely to sacrifice it to temporary or partial considerations. Under such a regulation, it may well happen that the public voice, pronounced by the representatives of the people, will be more consonant to the public good than if pronounced by the people themselves, convened for the purpose. On the other hand, the effect may be inverted. Men of factious tempers, of local prejudices, or of sinister designs, may, by intrigue, by corruption, or by other means, first obtain the suffrages, and then betray the interests, of the people. The question resulting is, whether small or extensive republics are more favorable to the election of proper guardians of the public weal; and it is clearly decided in favor of the latter by two obvious considerations:

In the first place, it is to be remarked that, however small the republic may be, the representatives must be raised to a certain number, in order to guard against the cabals of a few; and that, however large it may be, they must be limited to a certain number, in order to guard against the confusion of a multitude. Hence, the number of representatives in the two cases not being in proportion to that of the two constituents, and being proportionally greater in the small republic, it follows that, if the proportion of fit characters be not less in the large than in the small republic, the former will present a greater option, and consequently a greater probability of a fit choice.

In the next place, as each representative will be chosen by a greater number of citizens in the large than in the small republic, it will be more difficult for unworthy candidates to practise with success the vicious arts by which elections are too often carried; and the suffrages of the people being more free, will be more likely to centre in men who possess the most attractive merit and the most diffusive and established characters.

It must be confessed that in this, as in most other cases, there is a mean, on both sides of which inconveniences will be found to lie. By enlarging too much the number of electors, you render the representative too little acquainted with all their local circumstances and lesser interests; as by reducing it too much, you render him unduly attached to these, and too little fit to comprehend and pursue great and national objects. The federal Constitution forms a happy combination in this respect; the great and aggregate interests being referred to the national, the local and particular to the State legislatures.

The other point of difference is, the greater number of citizens and extent of territory which may be brought within the compass of republican than of democratic government; and it is this circumstance principally which renders factious combinations less to be dreaded in the former than in the latter. The smaller the society, the fewer probably will be the distinct parties and interests composing it; the fewer the distinct parties and interests, the more frequently will a majority be found of the same party; and the smaller the number of individuals composing a majority, and the smaller the compass within which they are placed, the most easily will they concert and execute their plans of oppression. Extend the sphere, and you take in a greater variety of parties and interests; you make it less probable that a majority of the whole will have a common motive to invade the rights of other citizens; or if such a common motive exists, it will be more difficult for all who feel it to discover their own strength, and to act in unison with each other. Besides other impediments, it may be remarked that, where there is a consciousness of unjust or dishonorable purposes, communication is always checked by distrust in proportion to the number whose concurrence is necessary.

Hence, it clearly appears, that the same advantage which a republic has over a democracy, in controlling the effects of faction, is enjoyed by a large over a small republic—is enjoyed by the Union over the States composing it. Does the advantage consist in the substitution of representatives whose enlightened views and virtuous sentiments render them superior to local prejudices and to schemes of injustice? It will not be denied that the representation of the Union will be most likely to possess these requisite endowments. Does it consist in the greater security afforded by a greater variety of parties, against the event of any one party being able to outnumber and oppress the rest? In an equal degree does the increased variety of parties comprised within the Union, increase this security. Does it, in fine, consist in the greater obstacles opposed to the concert and accomplishment of the secret wishes of an unjust and interested majority? Here, again, the extent of the Union gives it the most palpable advantage.

The influence of factious leaders may kindle a flame within their particular States, but will be unable to spread a general conflagration through the other States. A religious sect may degenerate into a political faction in a part of the Confederacy; but the variety of sects dispersed over the entire face of it must secure the national councils against any danger from that source. A rage for paper money, for an abolition of debts, for an equal division of property, or for any other improper or wicked project, will be less apt to pervade the whole body of the Union than a particular member of it; in the same proportion as such a malady is more likely to taint a particular county or district, than an entire State.

In the extent and proper structure of the Union, therefore, we behold a republican remedy for the diseases most incident to republican government. And according to the degree of pleasure and pride we feel in being republicans, ought to be our zeal in cherishing the spirit and supporting the character of Federalists.

PUBLIUS

The substance of Madison's Federalist No. 10 is as follows. I will take the liberty of annotating it, using direct quotes where appropriate. I will follow, except for a reversal of the first and second points, the same order in which Madison makes his argument.

1. "Complaints are everywhere heard from our most considerate and virtuous citizens [meaning those, like Madison himself, who are wealthy landowners] that our governments are too unstable, that the public good is disregarded in the conflicts of rival parties, and that measures are too often decided, not according to the rules of justice and the rights of the minor party, but by the superior force of an interested and overbearing majority." Remember that this is a time of serious depression when the vast majority are poor farmers barely eking out a living, many with mortgages to pay off, and that the "minor party" to which Madison refers are the well-to-do property owners and creditors.

2. "A well-constructed Union" will help "to break and control the violence of faction."

3. "By a faction, I understand a number of citizens, whether amounting to a majority or minority of the whole [Madison later points out that a minority faction isn't a serious problem], who are united and actuated by some common impulse of passion, or of interest, adverse to the rights of other citizens, or to the permanent and aggregate interests of the community." The "permanent and aggregate interests of the community" refer, of course, to what those in authority determine they are, and in this context clearly include Madison himself and other large property holders.

4. From what does faction spring? Answer: "the diversity in the faculties of men, from which the rights of property originate." Be perfectly clear what Madison is saying here: that the *rights* of property originate in the diverse faculties of men to acquire it.

5. "The protection of these faculties is the first object of government." Little could be more clear than that!

6. "From the protection of different and unequal faculties of acquiring property, the possession of different degrees and kinds of property immediately results; and from the influence of these on the sentiments and views of the respective proprietors, ensues a division of the society into different interests and parties." Here Madison is very candid about what the basic conflict in society is all about, and in point 5, what government is all about.

There are haves and have-nots, and it is the first object of government to see to it that the situation is preserved.

7. "The most common and durable source of factions has been the various and unequal distribution of property. Those who hold and those who are without property have ever formed distinct interests in society."

8. "The inference to which we are brought is, that the *causes* of faction cannot be removed, and that relief is only to be sought in the means of controlling its *effects*." (Italics in the original.) What Madison is now saying is that the Union must be constructed in such a way as to prevent a majority from ruling, to "break and control the violence of faction" (see point 2 above).

9. "When a majority is included in a faction, the form of popular government, on the other hand, enables it to sacrifice to its ruling passion or interest both the public good and the rights of other citizens. To secure the public good and private rights against the danger of such a faction, and at the same time to preserve the spirit and the form of popular government, is then the great object to which our inquiries are directed." Again, the same point. The energies of the Constitutional Convention were directed toward establishing a form of government that would make it very difficult, hopefully even impossible, for the majority to rule when their wishes are contrary to those of the wealthy.

10. "By what means is this object attainable? Evidently by one of two only. Either the existence of the same passion or interest in a majority at the same time must be prevented, or the majority, having such coexistent passion or interest, must be rendered, by their number and local situation, unable to concert and carry into effect schemes of oppression." Majorities must not only be prevented from ruling, obstacles must be put in their way to thwart their even *coming together*.

11. Madison then goes on to reject what he calls "pure democracy" (direct democracy) on the grounds that "such democracies have ever been spectacles of turbulence and contention; have ever been found incompatible with personal security or the rights of property."

12. "Theoretic politicans, who have patronized this species of government, have erroneously supposed that by reducing mankind to a perfect equality in their political rights, they would, at the same time, be perfectly equalized and assimilated in their possessions, their opinions, and their passions." Equality of political rights, then, is to be rejected on the grounds that economic equality is neither desirable (point 11) nor attainable (due, as we have already seen, to the inherent differences in the faculties of men to acquire property). It should be noted that points 11 and 12 represent a very important admission by a Founding Father of the Constitution of Madison's stature. *Political equality* is *rejected* even as an *ideal*.

13. "A republic, by which I mean a government in which the scheme of representation takes place, opens a different prospect, and promises the cure for which we are seeking. Let us examine the points in which it varies from pure democracy, and we shall comprehend both the nature of the cure and the efficacy which it must derive from the Union." A republican form of

government, a representative democracy, such as that established in the Constitution to be adopted, is the remedy Madison seeks to prevent majorities from ruling.

14.    "The two great points of difference between a democracy and a republic are: first, the delegation of the government, in the latter, to a small number of citizens elected by the rest; secondly, the greater number of citizens, and greater sphere of country, over which the latter may be extended." It is clear that Madison and his confreres wanted to avoid a democracy, and in its place, establish a republic.

15.    "The effect of the first difference is, on the one hand, to refine and enlarge the public views, by passing them through the medium of a chosen body of citizens, whose wisdom may best discern the true interest of their country, and whose patriotism and love of justice will be least likely to sacrifice it to temporary or partial considerations." Elected representatives will be less likely to follow the will of the people, tempering what the people want with "wisdom," "patriotism," and "love of justice" in the "true interest" of their country.

16.    Madison then goes on to argue that a large republic will make it even more likely that a majority will not form. "Extend the sphere and you take in a greater variety of parties and interests; you make it less probable that a majority of the whole will have common motive to invade the rights of other citizens."

17.    The advantage of a republic, then, "consists in the substitution of representatives whose enlightened views and virtuous sentiments render them superior to local prejudices and to schemes of injustice." The bias here, as elsewhere throughout the text, is clearly evident in Madison's choice of words for those he favors, the property owners ("enlightened," "virtuous"), and those he doesn't favor, those who would be likely to compose a majority faction ("prejudice," "injustice").

18.    And now, the pièce de résistance to Madison's argument, what he really wants to avoid, what he really thinks "factions" are all about: "A rage for paper money, for an abolition of debts, for an equal division of property, or for any other improper or wicked project, will be less apt to pervade the whole body of the Union."

Let there be no mistake about it. Politics is about property; government is to protect property; those who wish change are engaged in a "wicked" project and are to be impeded. Whether you agree or disagree with Madison's side of the issue is not the point. The point is that Madison is making a very forthright and candid statement with respect to what politics is all about—i.e., property.

## DEMOCRACY VS. REPUBLIC

One of the additional facts we learn from Madison's Federalist essay is that it was not the intention of the Constitutional Convention to establish a democracy for the United States, but rather what he calls a "republic." It must be remembered that in 1787, Western European countries, including England, from which most of our population at this time had come, were monarchies. Indeed, it was the monarchy of England from which the colonies had separated themselves during the Revolutionary War. Although there were the beginnings of some form of representation in councils advisory to the king in both England and Sweden, this period in the eighteenth century marks a rapid increase in challenges to the king's absolute authority by the rising commercial and mercantile classes. The French Revolution, for example, was only five years away. It was a new era of business and trade, and those interested in commercial ventures were rapidly growing in number. The world of Western Europe was changing, and the nascent United States was a part of that heritage of change.

## Greek Democracy

Those assembled at the Constitutional Convention, then, who represented the large landholders and the commercial and financial communities, were interested in establishing something other than a monarchy as a government. Indeed, all of the colonies had some form of representative government already. But the Constitutional Convention had few models to choose from. The idea of democracy originated in Greece in the time of Plato and Aristotle. In the democracy of the early Greek city-states (Athens being the most prominent), those of means (the very small percentage of the population who owned property, in what were already very small city-states) would get together in the *agora,* or marketplace, to discuss the pressing issues of the day. The word "democracy" comes from the word *demos,* meaning people; and democracy means, literally, rule by the people. A form of representative government, with elections, was not practiced by the Greeks.

## Democracy in the American Republic

When Madison speaks of the difference between a democracy and a republic, what he has in mind is this difference between direct rule by "the people" (however narrowly or broadly defined), and rule by representatives of "the people" who, presumably, *re-present* the wishes of others. What Madison forthrightly suggests is that representatives are to serve as a buffer against those in the community who might want to change the system of property rights or attempt to redistribute wealth from rich to poor. Political equality is to be eschewed because it will lead to efforts to change the existing inequalities in wealth and property. It is perfectly clear, also, that a system of direct democracy would be impractical in a country as large as the United States (even at that time) and in an era when the only means of transportation was by foot or horseback. In order for direct democracy to work, the governmental region must be very small in size and with few people, small enough that all eligible participants could meet conveniently in one place. This did in fact occur in some very small towns and villages in the United States, but it was certainly not feasible as a form of state or national government.

The republican principle of representative democracy, then, was the only practical solution. Besides, as Madison so deftly points out, it is essential that such a principle be followed in order to preserve the existing property arrangements. "Factions," that is, majorities (or minorities) seeking "improper or wicked purposes" (defined by Madison as tampering with existing distributions of property) were to be "controlled," "broken" if necessary. Representatives were expected to be drawn from the more well-to-do classes whose interests would lie in the preservation of property rights regardless of what a majority of common citizens might wish. In addition, Madison clearly argues at the end of his essay that the interests of the property owners would be better served by a large republic rather than a group of smaller ones (as was the case under the Articles of Confederation), again to avoid what he saw as the pitfalls of "factious" majorities.

The barriers to majority rule erected by the Founding Fathers were indeed formidable. There was to be an executive branch, with a president and vice-president, elected not directly by the people but by the indirect method of an electoral college, a procedure we still have to this day, though its workings have been somewhat modified by the political party system. All other executive officials were to be, and still are, appointed.

The legislative branch was to consist of two houses of Congress. The Senate was not elected by the people at all, but by state legislatures, a system that was not changed until the adoption, in 1913, of the Seventeenth Amendment, which provided for direct election of senators. Only the House of Representatives was to be chosen by direct vote.

The judicial branch was to consist of a Supreme Court and other national courts as the circumstances required, all to be appointed, not elected.

In all, then, sixty-seven people served in elective positions when our government was first established in 1789 (an indirectly elected president and vice-president, and sixty-five members of the House of Representatives). The present-day number of elected officials is hardly much more. Out of a population of approximately 225 million, there are 537 elected officials (one president, one vice-president, 100 senators and 435 representatives). All other members of the national government are appointed, over 3.5 million of them. We were then, and are still, clearly a republic, not a democracy; although in popular usage the terms democracy or representative democracy have come to describe our system of government.

There are two reasons why it is important for us to dwell on the distinction between a democracy and a republic. The first has to do with the expectations that people develop when they believe they live in a democracy, and the cynicism that develops when these expectations are not fulfilled. Americans, in general, are imbued with the idea that they live under a democratic government. The key words and ideas, in this perspective on our governmental system, are that the ultimate source of power lies with "the people," that the majority rules, that all "persons" have certain inalienable rights (enumerated in the first ten amendments to the Constitution), and that we live in freedom, liberty, justice, and equality.

None of these ideas concerning American government are true in any absolute sense, nor could they be. They are, at best, *ideals* that have become part of our understanding of how American government is supposed to function. As Madison has so clearly shown, however, the Constitution establishes neither economic equality nor political equality, nor was it ever intended that it do so. Consequently, people run into all kinds of frustrating experiences, depending in part on whether they are black or white, rich or poor, and so on, which clearly belie the fundamental tenets of democracy. Many of these people are led to believe that such frustrations are their own fault, because, in addition to the ideals listed above, it is also part of the American ideology to believe that this is a land of opportunity and that anyone who works hard can succeed. It therefore follows that those who do not succeed have no one to blame but themselves. That the system itself may have something to do with who succeeds and who does not, that, in fact, the system was designed primarily to protect property rights, as Madison has informed us, is rarely told as part of the story. When, therefore, people run into situations where the ideals of democracy are not met, they are left with little, if anything, to hold on to.

The second reason for stressing the difference between a democracy and a republic is that we are also led to believe that the presumed relationship between the government and the people results in one, and only one, political system. This expectation is also false. There are two kinds of "persons" in the United States, and although differences between and among individual persons are extremely important in explaining how people will be treated by the government, the difference between individual persons and corporate persons may even be more important. There are *two* American political systems. One, the individual political system, is not what we are led to believe it is; and the second, the corporate system, is rarely discussed and is certainly not a part of the public's common understanding of American government. It is, in fact, for all practical purposes, hidden. That this is so is remarkable, given the share of the economic assets it holds and its impact on government decisions. We shall have much more to say about this in the chapters that follow.

# CHAPTER TWO
# SOCIETY, PROPERTY, AND POLITICS

Politics is concerned with the governmental aspects of the relationships of "persons" to property. By "property" is meant not simply land, although ownership of and control over land can certainly be political issues. At the time of Madison these were two of the most important issues with which the government had to deal. The United States was an agricultural economy (as were all economies in the world during this period), and land was the most important resource. Ownership and control over land were not only the chief domestic issues, they were also the most important foreign policy issue. The American Revolution was fought over whether the British or the colonists were to control the territory. In addition, in its policy of territorial expansion, the United States in the eighteenth and nineteenth centuries was busy against the French, the British, the Spanish, and the Indians in its acquisition of land, mostly through war, but also by purchase. Florida, Texas, New Mexico, Arizona, and California were taken from the Spanish. Much of the Midwest was obtained from the French in the Louisiana Purchase; British and French garrisons that remained in the Midwest had to be routed. And, of course, the Indians, the original holders of land, had to be displaced and for all practical purposes exterminated. (It is estimated that fifteen-sixteenths, or 94 percent, of the Indian population had been eliminated during the seventeenth, eighteenth, and nineteenth centuries.) The control of territory was, and still continues to be, a central issue in both domestic and foreign policy.

But property also means *anything* that can be owned and controlled. Land is one of these things, but so too are people (slaves), places of business, homes and buildings, money, stocks and bonds, bank accounts, personal possessions and equipment. Indeed, the meaning of "property" can be extended to include all forms of wealth, and this is the meaning that will be employed in this book. The study of the relationships that people have to property—and to each other, as conflicts arise concerning its disposition—will be our central focus.

Lest the distribution, control over, and use of property, and the relations between "persons" and government that ensue, be construed as too narrow a definition of politics, we should be reminded that, in a larger sense, the most significant form of "property" all of us possess is our own "person." This extension of the notion of "property" is not as farfetched as it may at first appear, and the law itself seems to be moving further and further in this direction. To give but one example, much of the current controversy over abortion concerns this very question: who, the woman herself or the state, is to control a woman's body? Corporations as physical entities (land, plant, and equipment) are also "persons" in this *physical* sense, as were slaves, and as indeed are all individuals.

## SOCIAL PROPERTY AND POLITICAL POWER

Politics, then, in this more inclusive definition of "property," encompasses control over our physical being, our actions, and our relations with others. But these matters, in turn, are related to the question of wealth and income, and in two directions: (1) how our physical and social characteristics affect our ability to acquire property (in Madison's sense); and (2) how our acquisition of property, and the amount and extent of our holdings, enhance our power vis-à-vis the political system. Personal characteristics such as race, sex, and age, as we shall see, are directly related to the ability to acquire property, as are social characteristics such as education and occupation. And, again as we shall see, the acquisition of property is directly related to political clout.

Indeed, it would be a very peculiar world if this were *not* so, if ownership and control over material resources were not related to how well one does in the political system. Although strong pressures in our ideology encourage us to believe that the vote is the great leveler in democracies (republics) and that other resources, especially wealth, should be irrelevant, not only does all of the evidence lead to a contrary conclusion in practice, there is also a good deal of data to indicate that wealth is important in elections themselves. This is true not only with regard to who is likely to vote in elections (in general, the greater one's wealth, status, and education, the more likely one is to go to the polls), but also in the selection of candidates, in the funding of their campaigns, and in the general and specific stands such candidates are likely to take on issues. This is why most political science texts that deal primarily in questions of "civics," the rights and duties of citizens, and the "shoulds" and "oughts" of American politics, usually have a very hollow ring to them and are unable to tell us how American politics actually functions. These texts simply do not make sense given the world we *do* live in. To argue what the role of members of Congress ought to be tells us nothing whatsoever about how they are selected, the commitments they make, the sources of funding they receive, and how they go about their everyday business. In addition, such texts are likely to *assume* a relevant relationship between the voting process and public policy outcomes without exploring the empirical foundations of that assumption. Much of what is contained in this book is just such an exploration. That is, we shall be interested in examining how public policy is arrived at *without* assuming from the outset that the major answer lies in the electoral process.

Some examples of the connections between "persons" as physical and social beings, the ability to acquire property, and political influence will reveal the importance of viewing most, if not all, of what happens in politics in quite concrete, material terms. That the *language* used by those who engage in politics may stray from the tangible, personal benefits that are actually at issue should come as no surprise to us, given the desire we all have of seeing our actions as highly moral and laudatory. A distinction must be made between how political activity is *justified* and how it may be *explained:* that is, the reasons people give for what they do may be quite self-serving and have little to do with the *causes* of their actions. These causes may not be at all congruent with the democratic ideology that leads us to expect political activities to be related to the "will of the people" and what is in the "general interest." This is not to say that politicians frequently lie to us, although we need only remember the Watergate scandals to refresh our memories in this regard. It is to say, rather, that when asked about a particular policy, it is more consistent with the democratic creed to give a justification, an answer that places the policy in question in a praiseworthy moral context of good intentions, than it is to talk about the actual pressures one is being subjected to. Newspaper journalists, for a number of interesting reasons, seem more concerned than are political scientists in going beyond the stated intentions and ferreting out the causal linkages of public policy making, even if their stories fly in the face of the democratic ideology.

To the extent, however, that political science is interested in explaining what motivates political activity, the consensus seems to be that, ultimately, all decisions benefit some people more than others, that there are winners and losers, and that the personal motivation of gain, however justified, is at the heart of economics (the profit motive) and politics (who gets what, when, and how). Although this is not the same thing as specifying the *content* of politics, *what* the winners gain, it does at least give a hint that people are fighting over *something*. As Madison clearly tells us, this "something" is property.

Political issues involve what people can and cannot do with their property, which includes, in our enlarged definition, their own "person." Property as wealth and income provide persons (corporate and individual) with augmented opportunities, privileges, and advantages. This is exactly why they are so important. As a consequence, even the most trivial examples of political regulation (traffic laws, for example) can become enmeshed in factors involving how society values or disvalues people with different personal and social characteristics, which, in turn, is intimately related to matters of wealth and income. Whether we like it or not, and whether or not such attitudes are "justified," people do care about how others dress, talk, look, and behave. Americans are especially enamored of the productive capabilities of others, which helps to explain the high esteem in which corporations as the major productive units of society are held. But the idea of being productive, and what that means in the economic and social systems, is also a criterion for the evaluation of individuals.

## Social Status and Law Enforcement

The political-law enforcement-judicial system is far from exempt in taking into account, and not even consciously or deliberately, the physical appearance and "status" (determined to a large degree by property considerations) of those who fall within its jurisdiction. When I am driving I sometimes see beat-up cars and trucks pulled over to the side of the road for what is obviously a traffic violation involving faulty or unsafe equipment. I also notice that the person driving the car is poor and often Mexican-American or black. It occurs to me that no one would drive such a vehicle unless he or she had to. It requires money to purchase a new-model automobile, and it requires money to keep it in good working order. Although I can see the danger to others (as well as to those in the car) in driving what amounts to a piece of junk, I am also acutely aware that those who cannot afford more expensive property are heavily penalized by the existing laws.

Similarly, how drunk-driving charges are handled, both by the police and the courts, can depend in crucial ways (including the ability to afford a good lawyer) on one's social class, skin color, occupation, the neighborhood one is driving in, and other matters related to "property" in the larger sense. Indeed, crime in the United States is defined almost exclusively in terms of street crime, such as robbery and assault, which are strongly associated with poverty, while "white-collar crime" (fraud and illegal business practices, for example) is treated as something quite apart, and with significantly lesser penalties. Gerald Ford's first act as president was to "pardon" Richard Nixon for actions that had not yet even been established by the courts as crimes, white collar or otherwise, thus preventing criminal charges from even being brought against him.

An example from the business world will also help to make the same point. In 1983, the president of American Airlines was involved in a civil—not a criminal—suit for trying to make a deal with the president of Braniff Airlines in which their two companies would jointly raise fares by 20 percent on lines providing competing service to and from Dallas-Fort Worth. The complaint charged that the president of American Airlines "unlawfully attempted joint and collusive monopolization" in violation of Section 2 of the Sherman Antitrust Act. The courts and the public treat firms that engage in price fixing, which results in higher profits, far differently from the way they do people who are less well situated in society, who also desire to increase their profits by what is called theft, even though both activities are clearly efforts to take other people's money illegally. The question here is not whether Richard Nixon or the president of American Airlines *should* be treated differently from "common criminals." Perhaps you agree they should be, that there is something so different in the status and worth of these people that they merit special treatment under the law. The point is that they *are* treated differently.

## Economic Status and Law Enforcement

Not only, then, is it possible to enlarge the definition of property to include things other than wealth and income (social and personal "assets" and "liabilities," for example), but one can also see how social and personal "property" is related to the acquisition or nonacquisition of economic property and how economic property is related to political influence. As a remedy against young males who do not register for the draft, the Reagan Administration has enacted two punishments, both of which operate more severely against the poor: (1) ineligibility for federally sponsored financial aid in colleges and universities (guaranteed student loans, Pell Grants, work-study, and other special programs for students from disadvantaged backgrounds); and (2) denial of entry into federally assisted job-training programs. Such measures are "peculiar," not only because they fall disproportionately on those who have a demonstrated need for educational and job-training assistance, i.e., the poor, but also because the new laws, to be *effective,* would have to assume it was known that those who are refusing to register are those who need such assistance, facts that are nowhere in evidence.

We will be concerned in this book primarily with the more common view of property, as Madison used the term, which includes tangible wealth and income. But we will also be concerned with the broader notions of "property" that we have just raised: personal and social characteristics of persons that are related to wealth and income; and how such asset accumulation is translated into political power. Economic and political power are not unrelated to what might be called "social power" (race, sex, age, education, occupation, and status being the most important), nor, of course, are they unrelated to each other.

By and large, then, we can talk about wealth or property, and the relationships that people have to wealth and property, in three different but overlapping ways. *Economics* is concerned with the existence and distribution of wealth and income, the direct relationship of people to property, and what is done with that property. *Sociology* is concerned with the relationships that people have to each other, a very important one of which is based on control of resources, including property. And *political science* is concerned with the role of government in the relationships that people have to property and to each other. Not only, however, do conventional political discussions, which describe political institutions from a process point of view, frequently fail to tell us what James Madison told us, that the principle focus of politics and government is property, they also usually fail to see the close relationships political science, economics, and sociology have with each other. They fail to see that each discipline is concerned with a somewhat different aspect of the relationships among people, property, and government. One can know very little about politics if one does not also know something about the economy and the society. Hence, we shall emphasize the relationships of "persons" to property and wealth, and to each other, drawing from sociology and economics as well as from political science to aid us in an understanding of politics and government.

## THE FUNCTIONS OF SOCIETY

The basis of people's relationship to property, of whatever kind, has its roots in both individuals and in societies. Let us explore this a bit further.

There are, at the most basic level, two primary tasks that individuals must perform to stay alive. One requires action of a positive sort: making a living and *providing* for oneself and one's family. This function entails the acquisition and use of property, whether it be perishable and consumable property, such as food, or more permanent property such as shelter, clothing, and tools. In other words, human beings are constantly faced with the need to *gain,* at least enough to keep themselves alive. The second task is negative: avoiding losses and *protecting* oneself and one's property and family from harm.

Both of these tasks are, at the minimum, survival needs: providing and protecting; acquiring and defending property. We all want to be free from the possibility of aggression and from want. Human beings may desire a good deal more than this, but they cannot achieve it if they are not able to survive.

People find that these individual survival needs can often be met better when they live in groups. A large number of people living together can achieve what are called "economies of scale": savings in time, effort, and resources that come with increasing size. Numbers aid in defense and in the activities connected with making a living. One of the most important features of groups is the "division of labor," or "specialization." Some members of the society can concentrate their efforts on hunting, fishing, and food gathering, others on defense, still others on crafts, food production and preparation, building shelters, caring for the young, making clothing, treating the ill and wounded, religious practices, and so on. Each person need not perform all of the tasks required for survival or for other individual needs. He or she need do only some of them, both for himself or herself and at the same time for others. In turn, others do things that help those with other specializations.

Societies, large groups of people living together, have the same basic needs as do individuals: defense and the organization of productive activities leading to economic and physical well-being. The key, here, especially for societies, but also for families and small groups, is the idea of integration. Societies are *organized*; and the social, economic, and political relationships to property become more or less solidified within this organization. Some types of property within any particular society, for example, may be viewed as privately owned; other kinds of property may be thought of as public. There will also be rules about how property is amassed, how it is controlled, and how it changes hands. Societies differ a good deal with regard to the specific content of such rules of property—but rules there will be. Indeed, the legal-judicial system of societies concerns itself mostly with just such questions, both in criminal and in civil law.

## INEQUALITIES IN THE DISTRIBUTION OF PROPERTY

When societies are small there is not much possibility for the productive benefits of economies of scale to come to the fore. Most individuals will live pretty much at a subsistence level, and the distribution of well-being tends to be fairly equal. Food, clothing, shelter, and defense are about the same for everyone, with perhaps only slight variation. It is when a society begins to get larger and the economies of scale lead to a surplus, or what may be seen as a surplus, that the possibility of gross inequalities in the distribution of property arises.

With increasing size, individual members also become more anonymous, and their economic well-being becomes less important to those who see an opportunity to increase their own economic welfare. The question then becomes: if it is possible to either assume that the basic needs of people are being met, or not to care whether they are being met or not, how is a surplus to be distributed? Some individuals will try to gain for themselves and their families a share of this surplus; or, given the size of the population and the reduced social constraints involved in either knowing or caring what is happening to others, some will simply try to do better than they are now doing.

This is a perfectly understandable trait in individuals who live in societies large enough where no one can know everyone else, or even a very large percentage of them. Why not live better rather than worse? Certainly most of the people reading this book would rather live better than worse. Indeed, most of the people reading this book already live better than most people in the United States, and undoubtedly look forward to improving their present position.

Through a number of processes, political, economic, social, and military, inequalities in the distribution of property appear. Unlike smaller societies where economies of scale cannot produce much of a surplus, where individuals and families are well integrated into the social system, and where, as a consequence, what is produced is more or less equally shared, larger societies tend to divide up into those individuals doing better than the average, those more or less at the average, and those below the average. The proportion of people in each of these categories will vary widely from society to society, depending on its technological development.

In a large agrarian society, which was the dominant form of social organization before the Industrial Revolution, and which characterizes most societies even today, inequalities are likely to be very large, producing nobles and peasants, large landholders and serfs. Slaves may be introduced into the society, or labor imported for the purposes of doing the least desirable tasks. Civilizations, in fact, have always been built by imported labor, whether we are talking about the Greeks, the Romans, the Egyptians, the societies during the European Middle Ages, or even present-day nations. The French have their Arabs and Portuguese; the Swiss have Italians and Yugoslavians; the English those from India and Pakistan and the West Indies; and the Americans have blacks, Puerto Ricans, and Mexicans (and before that waves of immigrants from Ireland, Italy, Poland—in fact from the four corners of the world).

## INEQUALITIES AND IDEOLOGY

But inequalities are not just a product of the importation of labor (whether as slaves or as workers). Inequalities also arise internally, as individuals see economic opportunities and seize them. These individuals develop relationships with others, most particularly with each other, and form close associations with the government and the military, to protect what they see as belonging to them. Justifications for these inequalities are established to legitimize differences in the ownership and control over wealth and property, whether these justifications be called "the divine right of kings," "hard work," "the faculties of men" (Madison), "survival of the fittest" (Social Darwinism), or what-have-you. Where you have inequalities, you also find in the *ideologies* of societies ideas, concepts, beliefs, and values that support and make lawful those inequalities. One also finds, therefore, that the institutions of authority within the society— that is, the police, the military, and the government—will have as one of their most important tasks the protection of property rights. Those who have more than others will desire, at the minimum, to hold on to what they have, if not to get more, and will be able to purchase protection within the society to do just that.

If we look at American society in terms of how it is organized economically, socially, and politically, we find much evidence that social, political, and economic relations are based on the unequal distribution of property. We find that American society is *stratified* according to wealth and income. And not only do individuals vary widely in the amount of property they own and control, but "persons" other than individuals are also centers of great concentrations of wealth.

The source of American ideology concerning the ownership, control, disposition, and protection of property comes from those who, like Madison, Jefferson, Adams, Hamilton, and others, were major controllers of property. And it is this ideology, based on property, that is transmitted, via the schools and families, to new members of society, the most important of these being children.

Hence, although it is useful to view a society in terms of the general functions it performs for individual people, it must also be kept in mind that a society is not an undifferentiated mass. It is, rather, composed of definite component parts that are stratified according to wealth and income. In addition, besides individual variations in status and position within our society, we have also seen that there are corporate "persons" as well as individual persons. Not to overly anticipate what is to follow, the power of certain groups within a stratified society will be greater than other groups. When we speak of "society," then, we must be careful to distinguish between its general functions of organization and protection on the one hand, and the ways in which it is organized so that some people have more property and some have less. This distinction will make us more sensitive to how certain groups within the larger society control the *content* of the whole society's ideology, determine its legal rules and procedures for settling conflict, and receive an unequal share of its benefits.

## FORMS OF SOCIAL CONTROL

Societies are large aggregates of people who live together and must somehow function as an organized unit. Individuals pay a price for living in society, although, as we have also seen, they gain the benefits of economies of scale and the division of labor. Both the productive capacities of society and the ability of individuals to protect themselves may be increased. The price paid is that there must be some agreed-upon rules under which people are to live, and individuals will be expected to conform to these rules. This is, indeed, one of the major functions of *government*: to promulgate and enforce society's laws. What the rules are will be strongly related to the power relationships within the society, which, in turn, will be related to the relationship of people to property. But whatever the rules are, society will have to devise means to enforce them. In some cases this will mean individual people applying what is called "social pressure" on others. In other cases, those in which we are most interested, enforcement will involve government.

### Voluntary Compliance

In general there are two major ways by which societies exercise control over individuals. The first is what may be called *voluntary compliance*. It is obviously easier to insure order within a society if the people themselves comply with the rules because they either want to or because they know they ought to. In order to insure voluntary compliance, the rules must be taught and people must think they are right and just (or, in the event they do not think so, they obey them anyway, perhaps out of fear of what will happen if they do not). The teaching of rules, then, and the value of obeying rules (or the fear of not obeying them) must be part of what members of a society learn. What this learning process is called depends somewhat upon what one thinks of the rules. It might be called simply "learning," or "socialization," or "acculturation," or, what is considered to be a more sinister word, "indoctrination." Whatever it is called, this process entails the purposeful attempt within the society to instill in its members a knowledge of, and, if possible, a positive feeling toward, certain rules, norms, values, beliefs, and attitudes. We shall call this process "training" in ideology: the attempt to impart to everyone the same values, beliefs, and attitudes. In principle, the more homogeneous the population is with respect to its ideology, the easier it will be to insure order within a society.

### Forced Compliance

Recall from Federalist No. 10 that Madison suggested that this goal is impossible, that certain interests in property would naturally divide a population, and that this was exactly why government was needed. Indeed, Madison was quite correct. It *is* impossible to succeed 100 percent in giving to all citizens the same opinions. This failure gives rise to the second form in which society imposes order: *forced compliance*. If people will not comply voluntarily, and if the rules, values, and beliefs of the society are considered important (and they most certainly will be by at least some members of the society, and especially those who have most at stake in their adoption), then a mechanism of forced compliance is required.

Government will be established to fulfill a number of functions. One function of government is to protect the society from external danger and aggression. Another is to legislate and make legal certain rules. Another is to aid in the process of teaching, inculcating, socializing, and indoctrinating the population (whether immigrant or native born) into the rules, values, and beliefs of the society. In the event indoctrination fails, government will insure that the rules are followed through enforcement procedures. Voluntary compliance is desired— but forced compliance will be employed if need be. And, since the ideology is created essentially by those who have the most to gain by general compliance with the rules—that is, those who own and control a disproportionate share of property—both the ideology and the government, in the processes of indoctrination, rule making, and enforcement, will be strongly on the side of those with the most to gain by the rules and the most to lose from violations of the rules.

Indoctrination and enforcement of an ideology are characteristic of *any* society, not just that of the United States. Every society requires some form of organization—the larger the society the more elaborate this organization is likely to be. And every society desires order within and among its organized parts. Chaos and potentially severe conflict would result if this were not the case. Indeed, one way of interpreting what happened during our Civil War is in terms of just such a breakdown in a common ideology, in this case the question of whether black human beings were to be considered as a form of property that white human beings could own and control. The *content* of the ideology may, and does, vary from society to society—but the need for an ideology is present in all large social organizations. In addition, all societies will develop systems of relationships of people to property, which also may vary from society to society (the USSR and the United States, for example); but ownership and control of property will be the central political issue, regardless of what the ideology is. In fact, much of the ideology will *concern* the "proper" relationship of people to property, and will produce a system of stratification in which some people (usually a small percentage of the total) own and control a vastly disproportionate share of what there is to own and control. It is, then, to a consideration of property and wealth, its amount and distribution, that we now turn.

# CHAPTER THREE
# CORPORATE WEALTH
# AND ECONOMIC POWER

Data on the distribution of property and wealth in the United States is not easy to come by, especially on a year-to-year basis. Hence, much of the data presented in this chapter is a compilation from various sources and from various calendar years. Although the current dollar value of property usually increases annually (partially due to inflation), its relative distribution among the various sectors changes very little in the short run. For this reason, even though some of the data goes back as far as 1964, there is little reason to suspect that the percentage distributions assigned to each category have changed much. In addition, a good deal of the data was collected in the 1970s, making it relatively recent.

Our first task is to present information on the total value of wealth and assets in the United States. This data comes from a research report of The Conference Board's Division of Economic Research, under the direction of John W. Kendrick, and was published in 1976. As with other references in this book, a full citation will be found in the Bibliography, listed alphabetically by author.

Assets are divided essentially into two types: *tangible assets* (the value of structures, equipment, inventories, and land), which, together with the value of gold reserves and net foreign assets (that is, the value of assets owned abroad by American citizens or corporations minus the value of assets owned by foreign citizens or foreign corporations in the United States), equals what is called *Net National Worth*; and *financial assets* (the value of money and various credit market instruments). These figures together (tangible assets plus financial assets, plus some other smaller categories), represent the total value of assets (*Gross National Wealth*), whether they be owned by individuals, business, government (federal, state, and local), or foreigners. The total value of assets in the United States in 1973 was $9,922,200,000,000, or nearly $10 trillion. Table 3–1 shows the distribution of all assets by category, and gives us some idea of the relative importance of the different kinds of assets. The table merits close scrutiny.

It is also of interest to us to see how United States assets are divided among the personal (individual), business, and government sectors (plus the small percentage representing net foreign assets). Table 3–2 presents this data.

What the figures from Table 3–2 tell us is that of the total Gross National Wealth of nearly $10 trillion in 1973, 40.1 percent is to be found among individual and family households, 37.3 percent is located in business, and 21.7 percent are assets held by government. Personal property and business property assets are about equal in size, with government assets being about one-quarter of their combined total.

Tables 3–1 and 3–2 give us a very rough sketch of the total size of property in the United States and how it is distributed between the three major sectors of

**TABLE 3–1   Asset Position of the United States, 1973 (billions of dollars)**

| | | | |
|---|---:|---:|---:|
| *National Net Worth* | | | 4,719.1 |
| Tangible assets | | 4,657.2 | |
| structures | 1,042.1 | | |
| equipment | 2,202.1 | | |
| inventories | 564.6 | | |
| land | 848.4 | | |
| Gold reserves | | 11.7 | |
| Net foreign assets (213.7 − 163.5) | | 50.2 | |
| *Financial assets* | | | 5,039.6 |
| Savings | | 1,457.2 | |
| demand deposits and currency | 296.0 | | |
| time and savings accounts | 703.1 | | |
| insurance and pension reserves | 458.1 | | |
| Credit market instruments | | 2,974.8 | |
| corporate shares | 896.7 | | |
| corporate bonds | 274.4 | | |
| government obligations | 612.1 | | |
| mortgages | 429.8 | | |
| other | 788.8 | | |
| Security and trade credit | | 261.6 | |
| Other | | 346.0 | |
| Gross Domestic Wealth | | | 9,758.7 |
| Assets owned by foreigners | | | 163.5 |
| *Gross National Wealth* | | | 9,922.2 |

SOURCE: Kendrick, 1976, p. 14.

**TABLE 3–2 Percentage of Gross National Wealth by Sector (1973)**

| | |
|---|---|
| Individual | 40.1 |
| Business | 37.3 |
| Government | 21.7 |
| Net foreign assets | 0.9 |

SOURCE: Kendrick, 1976, p. 30.

society: individuals, business, and government. What we need to do now is to explore in much greater detail how property is distributed within the two seemingly equal groups which form the basis of the two political systems that we are describing: individuals and business. We shall find a great many surprises as we explore this data, as neither sector is as homogeneous as we might think.

## THE DISTRIBUTION OF BUSINESS PROPERTY

When the Constitution was adopted in 1788 and George Washington was installed as our first president in 1789, the United States was still primarily an agricultural country, farming occupying the time and efforts of about 95 percent of the population. Over 50 percent of those employed still worked and lived on farms until well after the Civil War. But the Industrial Revolution was underway by the beginning of the nineteenth century, and by the end of that century was firmly implanted, employing over half of the labor force and becoming the major center of American wealth. This trend continued until the Great Depression of the 1930s; and then, following World War II, another revolution took root: what has now come to be known as the Postindustrial Revolution. Manufacturing declined as a percentage of total Gross National Product; and other business corporations, emphasizing white-collar work, grew quickly in number, until today only about 3 percent of the population makes its living in agriculture, about 31 percent in industry, and the other two-thirds of the population now work in what are called "service industries," comprising, primarily, utilities, communications, transportation, retail trade, and finance.

It was during the nineteenth century also that the business form known as a "corporation" became more and more prevalent, and larger and larger in size. There are, essentially, three types of business enterprises: proprietorships (individual or family-owned small businesses); partnerships (two or more persons going into business together); and corporations, an economic unit that requires a somewhat more lengthy description.

Corporations are a very special form of business enterprise. The major characteristic that distinguishes them from proprietorships and partnerships is that they are permitted to issue stock. Stocks are certificates of ownership, and issuing them allows the incorporated company to raise money, mostly for expansion. Corporations, then, can grow far beyond the size of the limited financial resources of those who originate them. Indeed, there is no limit to their size, nor to their assets, nor to the number of stockholders who may become partial owners.

A second feature of corporations is that the owners (that is, the stockholders) are liable for the debts of the corporation only to the extent of their shares in the company. Legal action by creditors against the corporation, in case of bankruptcy, for example, is limited to the value of the stock, and owners have no further liability. Their own personal assets in the form of bank accounts and other securities may not be touched. This is known as "limited liability." (The British use the abbreviation "Ltd." instead of "Inc." to designate their licensed corporations.) The reason for this provision is obvious. Investors would be reluctant to buy stock in a large corporation over which they had no control if their own personal assets were also at stake.

As of 1977, the total number of all forms of business establishments in the United States was 14,740,000. The number of each type of firm, their total sales, and average sales per firm are given in Table 3–3.

Of the 14,740,000 businesses in the United States, a little over 11 million of them (77%) are proprietorships. But of the $4 trillion 678 billion in total sales of all firms, these 77 percent do only 8 percent of sales, averaging about $35,000 in sales per firm. Partnerships account for only 8 percent of all firms, doing 4 percent of all sales, and averaging $156,982 in sales per firm. Corporations, however, constituting 15 percent of all business enterprises, account for $4 trillion 103 billion in sales (88%), averaging nearly $2 million in sales per firm. Clearly, although proprietorships and partnerships constitute the vast majority of all business units (85%), they account for a small percentage of sales (12%).

But this is just the beginning of the story. As with almost all of the findings in this book, we discover not only a pyramid shape among business enterprises in general (a small percentage of units, in this case corporations, doing most of the sales), but we also find pyramids within pyramids. Ninety percent of all corpora-

**TABLE 3–3   Type of Firms and Their Sales (1977)**

|  | TOTAL NO. OF FIRMS | TOTAL SALES (BILLIONS) | AVERAGE SALES PER FIRM |
|---|---|---|---|
| Proprietorships | 11,346,000 | $  394 | $    34,726 |
| Partnerships | 1,153,000 | 181 | $  156,982 |
| Corporations | 2,241,000 | 4,103 | 1,830,879 |
|  | 14,740,000 | $4,678 |  |

SOURCE: Heilbroner and Thurow, 1982, p. 34. Reprinted by permission of Prentice-Hall, Inc.

tions do less than $1 million in sales (the average for corporations is $2 million), and 10 percent of all corporations account for 88 percent of all corporate sales (recall that, to begin with, all corporations already accounted for 88 percent of all business sales). Eight hundred corporations (each with assets of over $500 million) employ one-third of the total labor force in the country, as many people as all of the other 14 million business firms combined. Two corporations, American Telephone and Telegraph (AT&T) and Exxon, have as much wealth as all of the over 11 million proprietorships put together.

Business corporations are usually subdivided into sectors or types, depending upon the kind of business they are engaged in. Table 3–4 shows these sectors, together with the percentage of national income generated by each. National income is roughly equivalent to Gross National Product, subtracting depreciation and indirect business taxes.

Table 3–4 shows the overall importance of the industrial sector, accounting for one-third of total national income (40% when business alone is considered). But even the contribution of one-third of the nation's national income underrepresents the importance of the industrial sector to the economy. Industry employs nearly one-third of all full-time business employees, and accounts for nearly one-half of total business sales, about one-half of all capital expenditures, nearly one-half of all corporate profits, and 98 percent of nongovernmental expenditures for research and development (Blumberg, 1975, p. 20). If the industrial sector of the economy is in difficulty, it is usually the case that the economy itself is in serious trouble.

Government, to which we shall devote a separate discussion, is the next most important, with a contribution of 16 percent to total national income, followed by: the wholesale and retail trades; services (the most important compo-

**TABLE 3–4    Percentage of National Income, 1972**

|  | PERCENTAGE OF BUSINESS | PERCENTAGE OF TOTAL |
|---|---|---|
| Industrial (manufacturing and mining) | 39.4 | 33.2 |
| Transportation, utilities, and communications | 9.3 | 7.9 |
| Wholesale and retail trade | 17.6 | 14.8 |
| Services | 15.2 | 12.8 |
| Finance, insurance, and real estate | 13.6 | 11.5 |
| Agriculture, forestry, and fishing | 3.8 | 3.2 |
| Rest of world | 0.9 | 0.8 |
| Total business | 100.0 | 84.1 |
| Goverment |  | 15.9 |
| Total |  | 100.0 |

SOURCE: U.S. Department of Commerce, Survey of Current Business, July 1973, Table 1.11, reprinted in Blumberg, 1975, p. 21.

nents of which are medical and health services, nonprofit organizations, and private educational services, public education being located in the government sector); finance, insurance and real estate; transportation, utilities, and communication; and lastly, agriculture.

The concentration of wealth in a small percentage of companies is also very high in several of these sectors, most notably in industry, finance, insurance, transportation, communications, and utilities. For example, in the nation's most important sector, industry, of total sales by the 468,000 industrial firms in 1978 of $1,497,000,000,000 ($1 ½ trillion), the largest 500 industrial corporations accounted for $1,219,000,000,000 of the total. In percentages, this means that one-tenth of 1 percent of all industrial firms did 81 percent of all sales. Two one-hundredths of 1 percent, or 100 firms, did 50 percent of sales in the industrial sector (Helibroner and Thurow, 1982). If we look at the control of assets, we find that the top 100 firms account for 54.9 percent of the total. Seventy-seven firms control 50 percent. Only ten firms control 20.6 percent, or slightly more than one-fifth of the total. In addition, the concentration of assets among the top 100 firms has been increasing during the last 30 years, from 39.8 percent in 1950, to 46.4 percent in 1960, to 52.3 percent in 1970, to 54.9 percent in 1976 (Dye, 1979, p. 22).

The concentration of assets is similar in the transportation, communications, and utilities sector. Of the total number of 67,000 firms, 20 corporations (0.02 of 1%) control 50.7 percent of the assets. American Telephone and Telegraph alone accounted for 23.3 percent.

Of the 14,659 banks in the country, 29 (0.2 of 1%) control 50.3 percent of all banking assets. Three banks, Bank of America, Citicorp, and Chase Manhattan, account for 18 percent. In insurance, 8 companies control 50 percent of all insurance assets, with 3 corporations (Prudential, Metropolitan, and Equitable) accounting for 33 percent.

Summarizing these data on assets (derived from Dye, 1979, pp. 20–25): in industry, banking, insurance, transportation, communications, and utilities, representing nearly two-thirds of all business assets in the country, 50 percent of the assets are held by 134 corporations. As a rough figure, then, derived from the data on the concentration of assets throughout the business community, we can say that of the 37.3 percent of the total national wealth of nearly $10 trillion held by business in the United States (the other 40.1% being held by individuals, 21.7% held by government, and 0.9% representing net foreign assets), one-half is controlled by approximately 200 corporations, or 0.0014 of 1 percent of the 14,740,000 business enterprises in the country.

It is undoubtedly by now intuitively obvious why we are so interested in the concentration of ownership and control of property by individuals, businesses, and government. Our interest should also be clear from our discussion of Madison's Federalist No. 10: it is the first principle of government to protect those who have property, even when, as Madison may not have foreseen, those ''persons'' who have it are corporate persons. Nevertheless, it may be useful at this point, even though we have not yet completed our survey of the distribution of business wealth, nor yet tackled the question of the distribution of individual wealth, to say a few words about the importance of property and how it is distributed.

## The Power of Property

In the first place, property is what there is of economic value, and how much one has of it determines how well one lives in a material sense. No matter how clear it is that material well-being is not the only value that human beings may hold, there is no doubt that most of us, if not all of us, are directly interested in how well we live. At the minimum it is what keeps us alive. Beyond this point it is what makes us more or less able to live comfortably. In this sense, then, ownership and control of property is *power,* the ability to translate needs and desires for material well-being into reality. It is, after all, in this raw sense of ''power'' that most of us exist. Nearly all of us have limited incomes and limited wealth, limited in the sense that what we might like to have is beyond our means to buy it. We may adjust our tastes to fit our budget, a compromise we of necessity adopt, at least most of the time. On the other hand, there is no doubt that given greater resources all of us would find ways to spend it.

Although this is an obvious definition of power, it is by no means trivial. The satisfaction of our creature comforts may not bring happiness—that is not the province of material well-being in any case. But most of us would not mind being better off. An interest in material well-being, then, is a value that we share in common. And, given that the total material resources at any given time are limited (although they may be increased or decreased over time), how they are distributed will affect how well some people are doing as opposed to others. Given any other value than perfect equality in material well-being, a value that even the most egalitarian are not likely to propound, if only from a realistic knowledge of what is possible (should an unemployed person receive as much as a physician, for example?), any other position will inevitably mean that some people are wealthier than others, and some are poorer. Some may, in fact, be vastly wealthier than others; and some may live in the most dire poverty. Ownership and control of property, then, limited at any given moment in time, will permit some people to have a greater share of what the material world has to offer, to exercise power over the physical circumstances of their lives.

## The Social Consequences of Property Ownership

As important as individual power over material existence is, however, it is only the beginning of the ways in which the control and ownership of property creates power. Human beings also tend to evaluate others, at least at first meeting, by their material circumstances. This is obviously why those in similar financial circumstances are likely to live together. We prefer to associate with those who are approximately in the same circumstances as we are, at least most of us do most of the time. Society, then, tends to be spatially and socially segregated on the basis of differences in ownership and control over wealth. This stratification, more or less rigid in terms of the social barriers of neighborhood and social class, is also reinforced by the kinds of opportunities that are available to people, given their financial resources. It determines such things as whether or not people complete high school, attend college, complete college, go on to graduate school, medical school, or law school. It therefore determines people's occupations and their positions in society. These factors, in turn, determine how much money people are likely to make and what stratum of society they reach. The circle is complete. Those who have are able to pass on these advantages to their children. Those who have not can offer little to their children.

Opportunities to improve one's position, then, will obviously be affected by where one starts. If one is poor, black, and from a family that has a low educational level and that does not value staying in school, one must make a supreme effort to achieve the same level as someone who is raised by parents who are college educated and who take a strong interest in how well their children are doing in school. The opportunities to realize one's potential, or even just to find out what it is, are partly determined by what financial resources are available, whether one has to work to help support the family, whether one finds books, magazines, and newspapers at home, and other such seemingly trivial, but in the long run very important, aggregate of factors.

It must also be remembered that at any given time the number of well-paying positions is limited. Not everyone can be a physician, lawyer, or corporation executive. Assuming, then, that someone does improve his or her position, and assuming for the moment that the number of higher-level positions are more or less fixed (after all, someone must work in factories and mines, fix cars, and do maintenance work), moving up may very well mean that someone else has to move down. Even assuming that this process operates on the principle of merit (and there are good reasons for believing that it does not), merit means that some people will be rewarded and that others will not. Life, like some courses in college, is sometimes graded on a curve. There is a certain percentage of A's, B's, C's, D's, and F's. That is what stratification means. Some people will be evaluated highly, and many will not. Whether we approve of it or not, the criterion for this evaluation is usually that value which all of society holds in common: the possession of and control over property.

## PRICES AND MARKET COMPETITION

Besides material comfort, opportunity for self-realization, education, position, and status, which are already a good deal, the fact that business wealth is highly concentrated in a handful of corporations has enormous implications for our society. Power is obviously more important when it is concentrated; it provides leverage on what everyone is more or less interested in. Therefore, when 200 corporations control half of the business wealth of the nation, their policies and actions affect all of us—especially the prices they set on the goods we buy.

Prices determine the amount of money we pay for goods and services; and hence, along with taxes (the price we pay for government), they determine the standard of living of individual consumers. It is therefore important to know how prices are set by business firms, especially the large corporations. (Recall that in the industrial sector, for example, 800 corporations collect 81 percent of all revenues, and that 100 firms account for over 50 percent of all sales.) Consumers have little control over pricing, especially pricing set by large corporations; and this is one of the reasons why people complain so much about taxes (the other major price on consumers). They feel that they should have more control over the price of government than the price of what they buy in the private sector.

Americans are accustomed to thinking that they live in an economy with a high level of competition among sellers. This, indeed, is one of the fundamental tenets of the American business creed, and is greatly lauded by all. Competition, when it in fact takes place, keeps prices low, since consumers tend to buy what they need at the lowest prices; and if firms want to make more money by increasing their share of the market, they need only lower their prices.

There are a number of assumptions underlying the concept of competition among business firms, the most important being that in order to have competitive markets there must be a large number of sellers, so large that no one seller has an impact on the price of the product being sold. In other words, what any one firm supplies to the market should have such a small impact on the total supply available that prices neither rise nor fall if any particular seller decides not to participate and leaves the market entirely. This same idea, by the way, should also apply to individual consumers. If any one buyer leaves the market, there should be so many buyers that the loss of any individual would have no effect on total demand. Except for certain specialized markets, national defense being a prime example, the competitive principle among buyers in fact holds true. The situation among most sellers, however, is far from being competitive.

## Type of Markets

Economists divide markets into three basic types: competitive, oligopolistic, and monopolistic, depending upon the number of firms within the market who act as sellers.

*Competitive markets* are characterized by a large number of sellers. The typical example is in agriculture, where the number of wheat producers, for example, is so large that no single producer can affect to any appreciable degree the total amount of wheat produced and therefore cannot affect its price.

*Oligopolistic markets* are those in which there are a small number of sellers who control a large percentage of the market; examples include automobiles, steel, and chemicals. In fact, as we shall see, most of the markets involving the largest proportion of expenditures on consumer goods, and nearly all of the markets in the industrial sector, are oligopolies.

*Monopolistic markets* occur where there is but one seller. The utility industry is perhaps our best example of a monopoly, in which a single water, electric, gas, or telephone company supplies all of a particular good to a particular city or region.

### Price Tactics

*Price* is the amount of money spent for a particular good or service, and the prices consumers pay for what they buy determine their standard of living. If prices rise, and the amount of money consumers have to spend remains the same or rises more slowly than the increase in prices (for example, during inflation), then consumers are able to buy less with their money. Or, if prices are higher than they "ought to be" (a point we will explore later in this chapter), then consumers are again in a situation where their money buys less.

In competitive markets, in theory, prices are determined by what consumers demand and the supply of the good or service being demanded. Individual sellers are so numerous that no single firm can affect the price of the good or service it sells. In oligopolistic or monopolistic markets, however, this relationship of individual firms to the market no longer holds true. Sellers in these markets are able to affect price because they provide such a large proportion of the supply being demanded. Hence, consumer demand and the supply of a particular good are no longer the sole determinants of prices. Individual firms, being so large, can themselves set prices (a practice called *administered pricing* by economists). This works in the following way.

*Administered pricing.*    Assume, in an oligopolistic market, that four firms control 60 percent of the supply of a particular good (a not atypical situation). Assume that one of the firms wishes to increase its share of the market by lowering its price. The other firms have no alternative but to reduce their price—either that or lose a share of the market to the firm reducing its price. This sounds fine for consumers, but it is not a rational strategy for business firms. If the firms reduce their price, they find themselves in exactly the same situation as before (at least in the short run), except that prices received for goods sold are lower for everyone. Assuming further that the costs of production have remained the same, profits have therefore been reduced, for all firms, including the firm that originally reduced its prices. It is possible, in the long run, that such a price reduction would stimulate a greater demand for the good on the part of consumers, and that eventually all firms would move back up to the same profit level on the basis of an increased demand; but the firms do not know this in advance, and some markets are what economists call *inelastic*, meaning that the demand for an item is not solely related to its price. Necessities and near necessities fall into this category, for example.

*Collusion.* In any case, in order not to risk losing profits, in either the short or long run, firms in oligopolistic markets will be very reluctant to compete with each other over prices. The result could very well be lower profit levels for everyone. This mutual agreement on prices does not even require that the firms collude with each other, although *collusion* may be involved, either in price setting or in dividing up the share of the market that each individual firm will take. Collusion may also involve such tactics as taking turns "winning" contract bids to supply a particular good to buyers, as occurred in the 1960s in a famous case involving General Electric's and Westinghouse's sales of electrical equipment to the government; this is a very tempting form of alliance among business firms in oligopolistic markets. Business firms are interested in *stability* as well as profit, and indeed find that the stability of their markets leads to profit and certainly reduces risk. But whatever the situation with respect to collusion, it is simply rational for firms in oligopolistic markets not to compete with one another over prices. Rather, competition may take the form of the use of brand names, or what is called *product differentiation* (trying to make one's product slightly different from the others, or competing on such intangible factors as "prestige" or "status").

## MARKET CONCENTRATION

The best situation for businesses to be in, then, is that of a monopoly where they have *no* competitors. The next best situation is to be in an industry where there are few sellers controlling the major proportion of the market (oligopoly). In these markets, firms will have some control over the prices that consumers pay and will not be solely at the mercy of market forces.

We like to think that risk taking is a fundamental experience in business. But if we stop to think about it, risk is something anyone would like to avoid, especially when money is involved. Risk taking may be necessary for the launching of *new* businesses; but older, well-established firms are likely to try to reduce the dangers of risk, especially since they are likely to have so much at stake. So attractive, in fact, is the low-risk, high-profit position of firms in which a relatively few sellers dominate market share, that we might propose a general law of economics: *Business will, wherever possible, tend toward oligopolistic markets.*

Economists measure the extent of market concentration by what they call *concentration ratios,* which represent the percentage of the market controlled by the largest four firms in any particular industry. This percentage is based either on sales, or on what is called *value added,* which means, essentially, the difference in price between what the firms receive in revenues and the costs of what they had to buy to produce the product (hence the "value added" from the beginning of production to the final sale). Table 3–5 gives the market share of some of the largest industries in the country, in some cases represented by less than four firms. Table 3–6 provides the same data for the thirty-eight industries ranking highest in four-firm concentration in 1972.

With respect to the extent of concentration in the industrial sector, Fusfield concludes: "A very large proportion of U.S. manufacturing industries are dominated by a relatively few large sellers. When adjusted to account for local and regional market patterns, about one-third of all value added in manufacturing is

**TABLE 3–5    Oligopoly in Some Important American Industries**

| MARKET AND LEADING FIRMS | APPROXIMATE MARKET SHARE (PERCENT) |
|---|---|
| Motor vehicles (3 firms) | |
| General Motors, Ford, Chrysler | 70–75 |
| Petroleum refining (4 firms) | |
| Standard Oil (N.J.) (now Exxon), Texaco, Gulf, Mobile | 40–50 |
| Iron and steel (4 firms) | |
| U.S. Steel, Bethlehem, Armco, Republic | 50–60 |
| Industrial chemicals (4 firms) | |
| Du Pont, Union Carbide, Dow, Monsanto | 60–70 |
| Aluminum (3 firms) | |
| Alcoa, Kaiser, Reynolds | 80–90 |
| Copper (3 firms) | |
| Anaconda, Kennecott, Phelps-Dodge | 60–70 |
| Metal containers (2 firms) | |
| American Can, Continental Can | 80–90 |
| Aircraft (3 firms) | |
| Boeing, McDonnell-Douglas, General Dynamics | 80–90 |
| Aircraft engines (2 firms) | |
| General Electric, United Aircraft (now United Technologies) | 90–100 |
| Drugs (4 firms) | |
| American Home Products, Merck, Pfizer, Lilly | 70–80 |
| Soaps and related products (3 firms) | |
| Proctor and Gamble, Colgate, Lever | 60–70 |
| Dairy products (3 firms) | |
| Borden, National Dairy, Carnation | 60–70 |
| Automobile tires and tubes (3 firms) | |
| Goodyear, Firestone, Uniroyal | 70–80 |
| Television broadcasting (3 firms) | |
| CBS, NBC, ABC | 80–90 |

Source: *Economics: Principles of Political Economy* by Daniel R. Fusfeld. Copyright © 1982 Scott, Foresman and Company. Reprinted by permission.

**TABLE 3–6  Selected Data for 38 Industries Ranking Highest in Value-Added Concentration, 1972**

| Industry | PRIMARY DATA | |
| | FIRST-4 COMPANY VALUE ADDED CONCENTRATION RATIO | NUMBER OF COMPANIES |
| --- | --- | --- |
| Electron tubes, receiving type | 94 | 21 |
| Tanks and tank components | 94 | 18 |
| Primary lead | 93 | 12 |
| Hard surface floor coverings | 93 | 18 |
| Flat glass | 91 | 11 |
| Motor vehicles and car bodies | 92 | 165 |
| Cereal breakfast foods | 91 | 34 |
| Turbines and turbine generator sets | 91 | 59 |
| Electric lamps | 91 | 103 |
| Primary batteries, dry and wet | 91 | 30 |
| Chewing gum | 89 | 15 |
| Small arms ammunition | 89 | 57 |
| Household refrigerators and freezers | 89 | 30 |
| Sewing machines | 89 | 72 |
| Household laundry equipment | 86 | 20 |
| Tire cord and fabric | 85 | 9 |
| Cigarettes | 84 | 13 |
| Chocolate and cocoa products | 83 | 39 |
| Primary aluminum | 83 | 12 |
| Cathode ray television picture tubes | 82 | 69 |
| Gypsum products | 81 | 44 |
| Electrometallurgical products | 79 | 27 |
| Photographic equipment and supplies | 79 | 555 |
| Woven carpets and rugs | 78 | 64 |
| Organic fibers, noncellulosic | 78 | 36 |
| Household vacuum cleaners | 78 | 34 |
| Vehicular lighting equipment | 78 | 46 |
| Reclaimed rubber | 77 | 19 |
| Mineral wool | 77 | 66 |
| Carbon and graphite products | 77 | 58 |
| Blended and prepared flour | 76 | 115 |
| Chewing and smoking tobacco | 76 | 28 |
| Pressed and molded pulp goods | 75 | 32 |
| Vitreous china food utensils | 75 | 32 |
| Carbon black | 74 | 11 |
| Tires and inner tubes | 74 | 136 |
| Calculating and accounting machines | 74 | 74 |
| Aircraft engines and engine parts | 74 | 189 |
| Medians | 83 | 34 |

SOURCE: Farkas and Weinberger, p. 16. Reprinted by permission of the Conference Board.

produced in industries with concentration ratios over 70 percent. Almost 80 percent of value added is from industries with concentration ratios over 40 percent. The average degree of concentration in American industry is about 60 percent. Only 12 percent of value added in U.S. manufacturing is from industries in which the top four firms hold less than 30 percent of the market'' (p. 355).[1]

One of the reasons why the high concentration of oligopoly in American business is of such interest to us is that prices and taxes are the two major areas of spending by American families and individuals. We all complain about high prices, but we also complain, perhaps even more vociferously, about high taxes. As was pointed out earlier, our complaints about taxes are frequently louder because we think that we have some control over them. We tend not to think about controlling prices in the same way. Given that both are prices, however, and that consumer prices affect us even more than do taxes, this emphasis on taxes is misplaced, especially since the ability of firms to control prices violates the fundamental American belief in market competition. For a very large percentage of the U.S. economy, however, price competition is a fiction.

## PROFITS AND COSTS

The aim of business is to make a profit—that is, at the end of a business year, to have revenues from sales exceed costs. Indeed, this profit motive is usually stated more strongly: the goal of business is to *maximize* profits. "Maximize," however, is too strong a word, given the fact that business firms, like almost anything else, are complex entities that seek more than one goal. Nevertheless, business is interested in the largest profits possible, considering the number of complicating factors (the long run versus the short run being one of them, for example).

Business firms in monopolistic and oligopolistic markets make more profits, on the average, than businesses in more competitive markets. While the level of profit depends upon such factors as reducing costs and becoming more "efficient" (either by introducing new technologies or by reducing the costs of materials or labor), it is enhanced when the capricious forces of consumer demand and the number of sellers in a particular market are, at least in part, controlled. A rational firm will want to reduce the risks of doing business and to assure itself of an acceptable level of profit. Let us investigate a little more fully what this entails.

### Fixed and Variable Costs

All business firms face what economists call *fixed costs,* those of land (or rent), capital, and labor. Over the long run these costs may be changed, but in the short run they are fixed. In addition, businesses face what are called *variable*

[1]From *Economics: Principles of Political Economy* by Daniel R. Fusfeld. Copyright © 1982 Scott, Foresman and Company. Reprinted by permission.

*costs,* including decisions regarding the organization of their business, how often to change the design of their product, whether or not to engage a large sales staff, how much to spend on advertising, and so on. In competitive markets, revenues are determined by the total supply of the product or service provided by the entire industry, and the consumer demand for the product or service. Obviously business people are in a much better position to guarantee profits if they can control these forces.

### Advertising

Oligopoly and monopoly are the response to the question of controlling supply, and in part also to the question of controlling demand, mostly through *advertising.* American business spends over $40 billion a year in advertising. In strictly competitive markets, represented by a very large number of very small producers, it would not be rational for firms to advertise (except, in some instances, for purely informational purposes). Wheat growers, for example, do not spend money advertising their product. In noncompetitive markets, however, where price can be controlled by the sellers, the costs of advertising, as well as a number of other costs, can simply be absorbed into the price of the good or service being sold. Recall, also, that although wheat is probably more or less the same, the major function of advertising is to convince us that a Chevrolet is not a Ford.

## THE GROWTH OF FIRMS

Profits in competitive markets, then, are subject to the whims of the marketplace and entail risk and uncertainty. It is obviously much better to be in a situation in which profits are more certain, less risky, and even higher. Firms, therefore, have *growth* as one of their goals, to become large enough to have an impact on total supply, and hence to at least partially control price, thereby ensuring some control over profit.

Growth of individual firms can take place in three ways. First, the entire industry can grow, due to greater consumer demand. This could take place either through the establishment of more small firms, or the same firms could simply become larger. Second, individual firms could grow through more efficient methods of production and thus be able to lower costs and compete more favorably with other firms. And third, individual firms could grow by eliminating some of the competition, either through various business practices (usually referred to as "unfair business practices"), or, more importantly, through *mergers.*

### Mergers

The evidence that a greater share of the U.S. industrial market has been going to a smaller number of firms is very clear. We have already cited data showing that the percentage of all assets in the industrial sector controlled by the largest 100 corporations grew from 39.8 percent in 1950 to 54.9 percent in 1976. Data from the Federal Trade Commission indicate that the 100 largest manufacturing corporations in 1968 held a larger share of manufacturing assets than the 200 largest in 1950, and that the 200 largest in 1968 controlled a share of manufacturing assets equal to that held by the 1,000 largest in 1941 (Fusfield, 1982, p. 355). With respect to increased industry concentration, Fusfield concludes: "The predominance of big business is due more to mergers than to internal growth of firms. Compare, for example, the 200 largest manufacturing firms in 1947 and in 1968. Their share of all manufacturing assets rose from 42.4 percent to 60.9 percent. The total increase between the two dates was 18.5 percent, while the effect of industry growth was only 5.2 percent" (p. 350).[2] Other data also indicate the importance of mergers in explaining the growth of oligopoly, not only in the industrial sector, but in finance, transportation, communications, and utilities as well.

Mergers are classified under three types: *horizontal* (firms producing similar products); *vertical* (firms merging with suppliers, called "backward" vertical integration; or with those farther down the chain, such as producers of particular products, or sellers of the product, called "forward" vertical integration); and *conglomerates* (firms that have little to do with each other). There have been three major periods of merger activity in the United States; the 1890s, a period of great horizontal mergers when many of the large industrial empires in railroads, steel, and oil were founded; the 1920s, a period of intense horizontal and vertical mergers; and the 1960s, a period marked by a new kind of firm, the conglomerate. It appears, also, that the 1980s may also be a period of large and rapid merger activity, including the three largest in United States history: Du Pont's $7.8-billion merger with Conoco in 1981, U.S. Steel's $6.2-billion acquisition of Marathon Oil in 1982, the Occidental Oil's take-over of Cities Service Oil in 1982.

Table 3–7 provides data on type of mergers for selected years between 1948 and 1972. Notice that as a percentage of all mergers, conglomerate mergers rose from 37.5 percent in 1948, to 62.9 percent in 1960–63, to 88.5 percent in 1968, then receded somewhat to 76.4 percent in 1971, and to 62.4 percent in 1972.

Table 3–8 provides data on the number of mergers in the industrial sector between 1948 and 1972, the assets acquired, the number of mergers that involved the 200 largest firms, the amount of assets acquired, and the percentage of the total number and percentage of total assets in which the largest 200 firms were involved. Notice that the largest 200 firms were involved in 42.3 percent of all mergers, involving 58.4 percent of all assets acquired.

[2]From *Economics: Principles of Political Economy* by Daniel R. Fusfeld. Copyright © 1982 Scott, Foresman and Company. Reprinted by permission.

**TABLE 3–7    Types of Mergers, 1948–1972**

| TYPE OF LARGE MERGER | PERCENT OF ASSETS | | | | |
|---|---|---|---|---|---|
| | 1948 | 1960–1963 | 1968 | 1971 | 1972 |
| Horizontal | 38.8% | 16.9% | 4.0% | 23.2% | 30.0% |
| Vertical | 23.8% | 20.2% | 7.0% | 0.4% | 7.6% |
| Conglomerate | | | | | |
|   Market-extension[a] | | 8.0% | 5.9% | 2.2% | 0 |
|   Product-extension | 37.5% | 37.8% | 39.0% | 30.8% | 44.5% |
|   Other conglomerate | | 17.1% | 43.6% | 43.4% | 17.9% |
| | 100.0% | 100.0% | 100.0% | 100.0% | 100.0% |

[a]One may question whether market-extension mergers may properly be regarded as "conglomerate" acquisitions.

SOURCE: Blumberg, 1975. p. 74.

## Investment Sources

We might now ask, where does the money come from for these mergers to take place? To answer this question we need to return once again to the question of profits.

Americans are accustomed to thinking that investment is the result of individual hard work and savings, that particularly clever entrepreneurs are responsible for the large capital formation of the country. The data belie this belief. Of the total amount of investment in any given year, 75 to 80 percent comes from the corporations themselves, another 15 to 20 percent comes from large commercial banks and other financial institutions, and less than 5 percent may be attributed to individuals. *Retained earnings* is that portion of profits that is not distributed to stockholders, but instead is retained by the corporation itself to use as it decides. A major use of these profits has been to acquire other companies.

To get some idea of the amount of money available for investment, total industrial net income in 1973 (after taxes) was $49 billion. Of this total, $38.7 billion, or 79 percent, was earned by the 500 largest corporations in the industrial sector. This represents, obviously, a sizable amount of money and is for the industrial sector only. Similar profits are earned, on a percentage basis, in the other business sector. And these figures are for but a single year. Sufficient funds are thus available for many corporations to increase their share of the market, thereby increasing their oligopolistic position, their control over prices, and their profits for the next year's round. This concentration of profits encourages merger activity and promotes a further increase in the concentration of market shares and assets in the hands of a small number of firms over the years.

The question we must now ask ourselves is: What are the consequences of this extremely high concentration of business wealth in the hands of a relatively few corporations? Here, we shall consider only the economic consequences. The

**TABLE 3–8   Large Acquisitions in Manufacturing and Mining by Firms Ranked among the 200 Largest Manufacturing firms in 1971, by Year, 1948–1972**

| YEAR | TOTAL LARGE ACQUISITIONS[a] | | LARGE ACQUISITIONS BY 200 LARGEST FIRMS[b] | | PERCENTAGE OF TOTAL LARGE ACQUISITIONS BY 200 LARGEST FIRMS | |
|---|---|---|---|---|---|---|
| | NUMBER | ASSETS (MILLIONS) | NUMBER | ASSETS (MILLIONS) | NUMBER | ASSETS |
| 1948 | 4 | $      63.2 | 4 | $      63.2 | 100.0 | 100.0 |
| 1949 | 6 | 89.0 | 4 | 45.3 | 66.7 | 50.9 |
| 1950 | 5 | 186.3 | 1 | 20.0 | 20.0 | 10.7 |
| 1951 | 9 | 201.5 | 4 | 114.4 | 44.4 | 56.8 |
| 1952 | 16 | 373.8 | 6 | 174.7 | 37.5 | 46.7 |
| 1953 | 23 | 779.1 | 12 | 397.4 | 52.2 | 51.0 |
| 1954 | 37 | 1,444.5 | 15 | 930.2 | 40.5 | 64.4 |
| 1955 | 67 | 2,168.9 | 32 | 1,199.5 | 47.8 | 55.3 |
| 1956 | 53 | 1,882.0 | 28 | 1,260.8 | 52.8 | 67.0 |
| 1957 | 47 | 1,202.3 | 20 | 703.7 | 42.6 | 58.5 |
| 1958 | 42 | 1,070.6 | 20 | 721.1 | 47.6 | 67.4 |
| 1959 | 49 | 1,432.0 | 20 | 806.2 | 40.8 | 56.3 |
| 1960 | 51 | 1,535.1 | 23 | 871.1 | 45.1 | 56.7 |
| 1961 | 46 | 2,003.0 | 22 | 1,499.7 | 47.8 | 74.9 |
| 1962 | 65 | 2,241.9 | 25 | 1,052.5 | 38.5 | 46.9 |
| 1963 | 54 | 2,535.8 | 33 | 1,876.3 | 61.1 | 73.6 |
| 1964 | 73 | 2,302.9 | 31 | 1,055.7 | 42.5 | 45.8 |
| 1965 | 62 | 3,232.3 | 24 | 1,845.4 | 38.7 | 57.1 |
| 1966 | 75 | 3,310.7 | 29 | 1,953.6 | 38.7 | 59.0 |
| 1967 | 138 | 8,258.5 | 59 | 5,751.5 | 42.8 | 69.6 |
| 1968 | 173 | 12,554.2 | 83 | 8,225.7 | 48.0 | 65.5 |
| 1969 | 136 | 10,966.2 | 49 | 5,963.8 | 36.0 | 54.4 |
| 1970 | 90 | 5,876.0 | 29 | 2,670.0 | 32.2 | 45.4 |
| 1971 | 58 | 2,443.4 | 17 | 960.6 | 29.3 | 39.3 |
| 1972[c] | 56 | 1,748.8 | 17 | 646.8 | 30.4 | 37.0 |
| Total | 1,435 | 69,902.0 | 607 | 40,800.4 | 42.3 | 58.4 |

[a]Acquired firms with assets of $10 million or more.
[b]Ranked by 1971 total assets.
[c]Figures for 1972 are preliminary.

NOTE: Not included in above tabulation are companies for which data were not publicly available. There were 311 such companies with assets of $7,080.1 million for period 1948–1972, of which 109 companies with assets of $2,653.5 million were acquisitions by the 200 largest firms.

SOURCE: Blumberg, 1975, p. 48.

political consequences—that is, how this concentration of business wealth affects the political process in the United States—we shall save for later chapters.

First, control over such a large proportion of business wealth by a relatively few corporations confers enormous power: the power to determine prices, investment, and the quantity and quality of goods and services. It also confers power to buy other economic assets, fostering further concentration.

Second, there has been a steady redistribution of business wealth in the United States from small business to big business. Small business, in general, means a market system more nearly compatible with the economic model of competition. Big business produces oligopoly, and all of the redistributions of wealth and power that this implies.

Third, there has been a steady redistribution of wealth from consumers to producers. To the extent that oligopolies charge higher prices and make higher profits than under a more competitive system, consumers overpay for what they buy, thus leaving them with less money with which to buy other things.

Fourth, for slightly more complicated economic reasons that we shall not go into here, firms in oligopolistic markets tend to underproduce relative to their most efficient point of production. In markets with only a few giant sellers, the highest rate of profit appears at a point before full capacity is reached. Oligopolistic firms can do this because of their control over the supply of the goods they produce. (In economic terms, marginal costs and marginal revenues are equal before the point of lowest average costs is reached.) Hence we have an economy in which many sectors and industries are chronically producing below full capacity, and such underutilization is purposeful.

Fifth, in situations of higher-than-normal profits and underutilization of capacity, there will be what economists call an inefficient allocation of resources within the total economy. Oligopolistic sectors are using up resources that could otherwise be more efficiently employed elsewhere.

Sixth, as a consequence of all of these factors, there will also be a problem of chronic unemployment. Higher-than-normal profits to business take money away from consumers; lower-than-normal production underutilizes physical plant. Work is harder to find, and high unemployment helps keep wages low.

Seventh, when prices rise as a consequence of price setting rather than market forces (through the interplay of supply and demand), inflation is a very likely result. Inflation hurts most those who cannot control the prices of what they sell, whether this be goods or services (labor). Hence, although the situation is complicated, inflation is a period of redistribution of wealth from *pricetakers* (i.e., those who cannot control the price of their goods or labor) to *pricesetters* (i.e., those who can control prices).

Since politics is about property, and government's first order of business is to protect property, all the consequences of economic concentration will spill over into the political and governmental spheres. We shall have a good deal to say about these ''spill-overs'' in later chapters. For the moment, however, let us now turn to an investigation of the distribution of wealth and property in the individual sector.

# CHAPTER FOUR
# INDIVIDUAL WEALTH
# AND INCOME

Individuals in American society own about 40 percent of Gross National Wealth. In this chapter we shall explore how this property is distributed among the general population, and what effects this has on the economy, the society, and the government. In a later chapter we shall discuss the individual political system that has developed, and how it organizes—or attempts to organize—the political activities of individual persons.

## THE DISTRIBUTION OF WEALTH
## IN THE UNITED STATES

There have been two major studies of the distribution of individual wealth in the United States: one was compiled by the Federal Reserve Board in 1962; the other, *The Share of Top Wealth-Holders in National Wealth,* was done by Robert Lampman, also in 1962. Although each study followed somewhat different methods, the conclusions they reached were very similar. Like everyone else who discusses the distribution of personal wealth in this country, we shall rely heavily on these two sources and on the many studies that have used their data in subsequent years. Perhaps the most complete description of this information may

**TABLE 4-1   Distribution of Wealth in the United States, by Percentage**

| PERCENTAGE OF POPULATION | PERCENTAGE OF WEALTH |
|---|---|
| Lowest 25% | 0.0 |
| Next     32% | 6.6 |
| Next     24% | 17.2 |
| Next     18.5% | 50.4 |
| Top      0.5% | 25.8 |

Source: Heilbroner and Thurow, 1982, p. 41. Reprinted by permission of Prentice-Hall, Inc.

be found in Jonathan H. Turner and Charles E. Staines, *Inequality: Privilege and Poverty in America* (1976). The findings will be surprising to most Americans, but it should be noted that almost everyone agrees that these data, for a number of technical reasons, actually *underestimate* rather than overestimate the amount of inequality in the United States. Table 4-1 summarizes the basic information.

The lowest 25 percent of the population has no net wealth (what little assets they have are counterbalanced by the debts they owe). The next 32 percent of the population has 6.6 percent of the wealth. If we add these two figures together, we see that 57 percent of the population owns 6.6 percent of the wealth.

The next 24 percent of the population owns 17.2% of the wealth. Adding this figure to those in the above paragraph, we see that 81 percent of the population has 23.8 percent of the wealth.

The next 18.5 percent of the population owns 50.4 percent of the wealth, and the top 0.5 percent of the population owns 25.8 percent of the wealth. The top 19 percent of the population then owns 76.2 percent of the wealth, and the bottom 81 percent of the population owns 23.8 percent, with the top 0.5 percent owning *more* than the bottom 81 percent.

What is also interesting to note in these figures is the dollar value that these percentages represent. At today's prices, the net worth of the lowest 57 percent of the population ranges from a negative figure for the bottom 8 percent to $25,000 for the top group. The net worth of the top group in the 81 percent of the population owning 24 percent of the wealth is $60,000. It is only when we reach the top 5 percent of the population that the figure goes over the $100,000 range, and only with the 0.5 percent of the population that owns 25 percent of the wealth that we hit the magic $1-million figure. In other words, the amount of net worth of most Americans is very small, although 75 percent have *some* assets that exceed their liabilities. It is in the top 19 percent of the population, whose net worth exceeds $60,000, that most of the wealth lies (76.2 percent), and in the top 0.5 percent of the population, with net worth exceeding $1,000,000, that slightly more than one-quarter of the wealth may be found.

## Kinds of Assets

When we look at the kinds of assets held by various sectors in the population, we find that the principal ones for the lowest third of the population are some equity in an automobile and some liquid assets (cash, savings accounts, and checking accounts). For the next 50 percent, one can add equity in a home. It is not until one arrives at the next 15 percent that equity in a directly managed business or profession (a small business of some kind) becomes important, and only with the top 5 percent that other assets such as stocks and bonds, other real estate, and assets such as trusts begin to show up as significant percentages. In other words, what the lowest 81 percent with 23.8 percent of the wealth tend to own (or at least partially own) is first a car and then equity in a home, with some savings. Equity in a business is reserved for those in the top 19 percent, with most of the other forms of asset holding (that is, capital that is not directly used by the owner) being found almost exclusively in the top 5 percent and especially in the top 0.5 percent of the population, who own 25.8% of the wealth (Turner and Staines, 1976, p. 34).

## Two Roads to Wealth

Contrary to general myth, one does not become wealthy through saving. Although it is true that those with relatively high incomes are able to save, and that these savings can add up to small "nest eggs" at the end of a lifetime, the road to real wealth, of the sort possessed by the top 19 percent of the population, and certainly by the top 0.5 percent, is altogether different.

*Capital investment.*    There are two major ways to become wealthy. One is through capital investment. Let us assume that someone invents a new type of camera and method of film processing (such as Land did when he founded the Polaroid Company), or that someone takes over a floundering restaurant or other business enterprise. First, this person will need some capital. He or she may already have some money, or have friends who do, or be able to borrow from a bank. Let us assume that the inventor or person going into business is able to amass $1 million in financing. The person is then ready to start his or her business. Let us also assume (although the chances of this occurring are practically nil—that is, most new business enterprises fail) that the profits for the first year of operation (or the third year, or the fifth year, it makes no difference) are $500,000. Let us also assume that the interest rates prevailing at this particular time are 10 percent. How much money would one have to invest at interest rates of 10 percent in order to earn $500,000? The answer is $5 million. The original investment was $1 million. The enterprise is now worth $5 million. The founder may now sell his or her business for $5 million, pay off the debt of $1 million, and realize a capital gain of $4 million. This, in simplified form, is how wealth is created: through the appreciation in the value of investment by showing a large profit relative to the original amount invested. And how does one do this? The answer is what economists call a "random walk" (another way of saying "luck"). No one knows which new enterprises are going to do well. Had they known, everyone would have invested in Polaroid or IBM or McDonald's. One doesn't know until after. Those who invest in an enterprise that becomes really successful are, in simple language, lucky. And they can become very wealthy indeed.

*Inheritance.*    But there is another way to become wealthy, a way that is much easier and entails no risk: through inheritance. In fact, 50 percent of the very wealthy have inherited their wealth. Most economists agree that inherited wealth serves *no* economic function. That is, inheritances are very good for those who inherit them, but they are neither necessary nor even good for the economy. They simply pile up money in the hands of very few people, are sometimes squandered, but more frequently are safely invested in financial instruments that entail no risk (Mrs. Dodge, the widow of the founder of Dodge Motor Company, earned over $1 million per year in tax-free interest by investing in municipal bonds).

If inheritances serve no useful purposes in the economy other than making a very few people very comfortable, why are they permitted? The answer to this question is not very complicated, but it does take some elaboration. This is especially so since American ideology advocates gaining money through hard work and individual initiative, which is hardly the case with respect to inheritances.

The answer lies first in the political power of the wealth holders. If, as Madison has told us, it is the first principle of government to protect private property, there is no reason why this dictum of American politics would not apply to passing on whatever one has amassed in one's lifetime (or, in turn, has been given by one's parents). The political power that the wealthy exercise must be very strong indeed if it can prevail in the face of the myth of rugged individualism and reward through merit.

But there is a second part to the answer, and it is equally as important. As we have seen, 75 percent of the population has *some* wealth. Even though 19 percent of the population has over 75 percent of the wealth, that still leaves 25 percent for the middle 56 percent. Almost *no one* among this middle 56 percent supports inheritance taxes. Theoretically, in a democracy, this middle 56 percent could by itself, or in combination with the bottom 25 percent, who have no wealth, redistribute the wealth of the top 19 percent to itself. (This is, indeed, what Madison considered to be an "improper or wicked project.") And why does it not do so? Why does not the middle group, what we might roughly call the "middle class," see what is in its own economic interests?

Part of the answer lies in the fact that the middle class does not know that 19 percent of the population has over 75 percent of the wealth. And part of the answer is that even if they did, they would not favor inheritance taxes. They wish to keep what they have—even if this means letting the very wealthy keep what they have, even if this means being worse off than if they favored inheritance taxes. Why? The answer is, in part, because they have *something;* and secondly this something is what keeps them apart from the bottom 25 percent, who have nothing. It is indeed an interesting situation. The vast majority of the American population would be better off with inheritance taxes; yet this same vast majority is opposed to inheritance taxes. The power of the very wealthy, ignorance about one's own self-interest, and the important role that ideology plays in justifying not tampering with property rights in any form must all be very strong indeed.

And let there by no confusion about it: the United States, for all practical purposes, has no inheritance taxes. Lester Thurow, who is not a radical economist but who is interested, among other things, in the economic consequences of inheritances has stated: "If one examines the very rich, about 50 percent of the great fortunes are gotten through inheritances. Despite what we often hear about so-called confiscatory inheritance taxes, U.S. gift and inheritance taxes amount to a tax of only 0.2 percent on net worth [written before the Reagan Administration vastly decreased what little tax there was]. For all practical purposes, the current estate and gift tax system has no impact on the distribution of wealth. If you are very rich and want to hand it on to your children, nothing stops you from doing so" (Thurow, 1980, p. 172).[1]

## THE DISTRIBUTION OF INCOME

One's standard of living depends not only upon the amount of wealth one has, but also on what one can earn (although the two, as we shall see, are obviously closely related). The distribution of income shows a similar skewed pyramidal pattern, though not quite as severe as that of wealth. Table 4–2 shows the distribution of wage and salary earnings for individuals in 1977 by income fifths, from lowest to highest.

The data in Table 4–2 show that the lowest 20 percent of wage and salary earners in the United States received 1.7 percent of the total, the bottom 40 percent earned 9.5 percent, the bottom 60 percent earned 25.5 percent, and the top 40 percent received 74.5 percent, with nearly half (48.1 percent) going to the top 20 percent of the population. The top 20 percent received over 28 times as much earned income as the bottom 20 percent.

### Redistribution from Bottom to Top

Historical information with respect to earned income indicates two general patterns:

[1]Reprinted by permission of Basic Books, Inc.

**TABLE 4–2   Percentage of Individual Wage Earnings, 1977**

| INCOME FIFTH | PERCENTAGE OF EARNINGS |
|---|---|
| Lowest income fifth | 1.7% |
| Next highest fifth | 7.7 |
| Middle fifth | 16.1 |
| Next highest fifth | 26.4 |
| Highest fifth | 48.1 |

SOURCE: U.S. Bureau of the Census, *Current Population Reports, Consumer Income 1977*, Series P-60, no. 118 (March 1979), pp. 226, 227. Reprinted in Thurow, 1980, p. 157.

1. The percentages of earned income going to the middle and highest income fifths have remained about constant over the past 75 years;
2. The percentage earned by the lowest 20 percent has been cut by more than half, and the percentage received by the next lowest 20 percent has been cut by over one-third (Turner and Staines, 1976, p. 50).

In other words, there has been a steady redistribution of earned income from the bottom 40 percent to the 60-to-80 percent group. The top 20 percent has always received nearly half of all earned income, but the upper middle class has grown in income at the expense of the poor and the lower income groups.

What has occurred, mostly since the Great Depression of the 1930s and World War II, is that lower-income wage earners have been earning steadily less, and upper-income wage earners have been earning steadily more. In order to make up for their income losses, two things have happened: women have entered the labor force in increasing numbers until, at the present time, half of all wives work; and second, the government has increased the level of transfer payments (Social Security, unemployment insurance, and welfare). What has been taken away from the bottom 40 percent (and especially from the bottom 20 percent) has been replaced by a second salary from working wives and from government transfer payments. Table 4–3 provides data on earned income for households (rather than individuals), and includes all sources of earned income for the household (more than one working member of the household, plus transfer payments).

Comparing Table 4–2 (individual wage earners) with Table 4–3 (which includes the wages and salaries of all members of a household, plus government transfer payments), we see that the only group that remains about the same is the middle group. The income percentage of the bottom 40 percent increases, and the percentage of the top 40 percent decreases. The redistribution of income produced by a decrease in the wages and salaries of the lower income group in favor of the higher income groups has been at least partially offset by working wives and transfer payments.

These findings are important for a number of reasons. First, lower income

**TABLE 4–3    Earned Income among Households, 1977**

| INCOME FIFTH | PERCENTGE OF INCOME |
| --- | --- |
| Lowest income fifth | 4.3% |
| Next highest fifth | 10.3 |
| Middle fifth | 16.9 |
| Next highest fifth | 24.7 |
| Highest fifth | 43.8 |

SOURCE: U.S. Bureau of the Census, *Current Population Reports, Consumer Income 1977,* Series P-60, no. 117 (Dec. 1978), p. 19. Reprinted in Thurow, 1980, p. 51.

groups are receiving less earned income from wages and salaries in the U.S. economy than at earlier times. The data indicate, for example, that before the Great Depression of the 1930s, individuals in the lowest fifth received over 5 percent of earned income. During the Depression, when the average unemployment rate was over 18 percent (and actually reached as high as 25 percent), the share of the bottom 20 percent fell precipitously. They were aided, however, by various government programs. During World War II, their share slowly increased, due to the plentiful jobs available, including a large influx of women into the labor market. Since the end of World War II, however, the upper income groups have slowly taken over the percentage of earnings from wages and salaries that had traditionally gone to the lower 20 percent, and the percentage of earned income from wages and salaries for the lower 20 percent has fallen from well over 5 percent before the Depression to 1.7 percent in 1977. To make up for this difference, an increasingly higher percentage of wives have gone to work, and government has increased its transfer payments. If government transfer payments are now cut, without providing lower income groups with better incomes, then the poor will indeed be less well off than ever before.

The culprit in all of this, however, is not welfare, but the redistribution of earned income from wages and salaries from lower income groups to higher income groups. The poor have essentially been deprived of *working* income. Upper income groups have benefited, to the disadvantage of the general taxpayer (who pays the costs of the welfare payments that help take up the slack), and with the aid of women who now work to bring in a second income. Cutting welfare without giving the poor an opportunity to earn higher wages is simply to perpetuate the historic trend of taking wages and salaries away from the poor, and *then* taking away what was replacing them. Eliminating *both* leaves them with nothing at all.

## The Lowest 20 Percent

Now that we have an idea of the percentage distribution of income among population fifths, it will be useful to see how much this actually means in terms of money income. In 1980 there were 87 million households in the United States, including, of course, households in which there was more than one wage earner. The bottom 20 percent, representing 17,400,000 households, had incomes of $0 to $10,000. These are the truly destitute households in American society. Almost one-half of all heads of households in this group have only a grade-school education, and 63 percent have not finished high school. One-third of all black families fall into this category. Forty percent of this group are unemployed, with 60 percent having at least one wage earner (Heilbroner and Thurow, 1981).

It is easy to understand how the unemployed in this group could be in poverty, but it is not obvious how those households with at least one wage earner could earn so little. One of the best ways of understanding this is to calculate the level of income that one can earn from the minimum wage (which is the *maximum* wage paid to most of those in this group). The minimum hourly wage in 1982 was $3.35. Let us assume that the head of a household works an eight-hour day, five days a week, for fifty weeks out of the year. Let us also give this head of household a wife and two children (the typical family of four). This works out to be $26.80 per day, or $134.00 per week, or $6,700 per year. Now let us assume that this family pays $250.00 per month for rent, or $3,000 a year, leaving $3,700. Let us assume further that this family of four eats on $8 per day. This works out to be $2,920 a year, leaving $780 for clothing, transportation, recreation, and entertainment (a television set is now owned by over 99 percent of all households in America). (Had we given this family $10 per day on which to eat instead of $8, their entire budget would have been taken up by rent and food.) A car, of course, is out of the question, even at $8 per day for food.

It is perfectly clear, then, how a family can be in poverty even with a full-time wage earner. A salary of $6,700 is simply not sufficient to live on. Given the high unemployment level in the United States (10.8 percent according to government figures in 1982, or 13.8 percent if those who have given up looking for jobs are counted), there is no pressure to increase the minimum wage. In fact, the pressures are in the opposite direction. We have already seen that the bottom 20 percent has no wealth, and that its share of income earned from wages and salaries has dropped considerably since the Depression of the 1930s. Working wives and welfare have been the response to the alternative of permitting full-time working people to earn enough to be self-sufficient.

Pursuing the reasons for the economic difficulties of the bottom 20 percent of wage earners even further, we find that *poverty is related more to low wages than it is to unemployment*. In the first place, unemployment can strike at any level, although it is higher for wage earners in the under-$10,000-per-year category than for others. Even so, as we have seen, 60 percent of those living in poverty work. Second, unemployment benefits reach only about 50 percent of the total work force, mainly in those categories that receive salaries and wages considerably above the minimum wage. Third, the unemployed in this group are, in large part, the chronically unemployed, those who find it difficult to find work even under the most favorable of circumstances, but who, when they find work, are paid wages that do not get them out of poverty.

Recent data from a national study conducted by a blue-ribbon panel of government and economic experts found that fully 34.4 million persons, *representing a whopping 29 percent of the U.S. work force,* were paid *less* than the minimum wage on a per hour basis for whatever number of hours they worked, full-time or part-time (*Los Angeles Times,* January 17, 1983). Even when work is available, then, the pay is so low as to leave them clearly below the poverty level. As we have seen, $3.35 per hour for a full-time worker produces an annual income of $6,700. The poverty level for a family of four is slightly above $9,000. So a family of four could have a wage earner working full-time or even two members working full-time and nearly half-time, and still not only fall below the poverty line but also be on welfare. In fact, one-quarter of those households on welfare have a wage earner working full-time! And this study covers only those working *below* the minimum wage. It tells us nothing of those working *at* or slightly above $3.35 per hour.

The next 40 percent of the population, representing 34,800,000 households, made between $10,000 and $25,000 per year. This is sufficient to keep them from relying on welfare, although during periods of high unemployment many of them may collect some unemployment insurance. But, given the general price level, coupled with inflation, even this level of earnings is barely sufficient, especially at the lower end of this salary range. In 1980 the median income of households was approximately $19,000, meaning *half* of all American households made less than this amount.

The next 35 percent of households, bringing our total so far to 95 percent (20 percent making less than $10,000, 40 percent making between $10,000 and $25,000), earns between $25,000 and $54,000. This group, comprising the bulk of what we might call the middle class, is obviously doing well compared to the rest of the population. Most of those reading this book probably fall in this category, or live in families whose parents make between $25,000 and $54,000.

Four and one-half percent of all households, 3,915,000 of them, earn between $54,000 and $100,000 per year. These are our upper-middle-class families. The last 0.5 percent of all households (435,000) earn over $100,000 per year, those that we might call the rich.

## Earned and Unearned Income

There are two general myths which that data contradict. First, it is generally believed that there are very few poor in the United States. In fact, 20 percent of all households live in poverty or near it. Second, it is believed that most Americans are reasonably well off, perhaps even what we call middle class. In fact, 60 percent of the population earns less than $25,000 per year, and 95 percent makes less than $54,000. Incomes above $54,000 are reserved for a scant 5 percent of the population, and incomes over $100,000 are made by one-half of one percent of the population.

These data are in terms of what is called *earned income,* and it is important to explain what this term includes and does not include. Earned income, for example, does not just mean salaries and wages. It also includes almost all forms of welfare (except food stamps, which is income in kind rather than in money). Hence, when we speak (or rather, when the government speaks) of the bottom 20 percent of the population earning incomes of $10,000 or less, this figure *includes* welfare payments. This group's income from wages and salaries is therefore a good deal less than the total. In fact, over 50 percent of its income comes from welfare, and if one adds food stamps (which would increase its total income), the percentage is even higher. Why the government calls welfare payments "earned" income readers may decide for themselves; providing figures on the distribution of income in such a fashion obviously underemphasizes the amount of inequality in income earned from wages and salaries.

But the fact that earned income means, for the poor, more welfare than wages is not the only anomaly in the concept of earned income. It also turns out that *unearned income,* for the wealthy, represents an additional amount of income that is *not* included in government figures describing income distributions and therefore underrepresents the amount of inequality in total income. For the top 1 percent of the population, for example, unearned income is more than double earned income; and this income is not included in the tables and figures that we have used in this chapter. For the top 0.1 percent of the population, unearned income is more than six times larger than earned income. The major source of unearned income for the wealthy is capital gains, a concept we will discuss in the following paragraphs. It is sufficient to note here that in order to have capital gains one must have capital, and as we have seen, over 75 percent of all capital held by individuals is in the hands of the top 19 percent of the population.

## Capital Gains

There are a number of assets one can hold that provide both wealth (and increases in wealth) and income. Real estate, corporate stock, bonds of various kinds, and other financial holdings are examples of these. One can own an apartment or office building, for example, that has value as property, appreciates in value over time, provides income to the owner, and can also be used as a form of income "sheltering," given the large number of deductions that may be taken by owners for tax purposes. We shall discuss taxes and how they affect the distribution of wealth and property in a later chapter. What interests us here is how these asset holdings are distributed among the population.

If we look at individual share holding in corporations, for example, the result is our usual pyramid. There are over 30 million individuals who own shares of corporate stock, but this seemingly wide distribution of stock holding does not tell us very much. The top 20 percent of the population owns 97 percent of all corporate stock, the top 10 percent owns 90 percent, the top 5 percent owns 86 percent, the top 1 percent owns 62 percent, and the top 0.5 percent owns 43 percent (Thurow, 1980; Turner and Staines 1976, p. 118). Another way to look at this is that of the approximately $685 billion in corporate stock owned by individuals, the top 1 percent of the population owns $425 billion of it, and the top 5 percent of the population owns $590 billion.

Not only is there dividend income from the ownership of stock (which, after a small deduction, is taxable as earned income), but there is also the possibility of what are called *capital gains*. The most common form of capital gains for the approximately two-thirds of all Americans who have some equity in a home is the appreciation in the value of the home from the time they buy it to the time they sell it, if they sell it. But any asset can appreciate (or depreciate) in value. For example, the value of corporate stock, in constant dollars (that is, controlling for inflation), has actually gone down during the past ten years. Those who have held on to the same stock over this period of time have, on the average, experienced a net reduction in terms of real dollar value (although measured in current dollars, the value is, on the average, approximately the same as it was ten years ago). Many individual investors, however, trade stock reasonably frequently in the hopes of selling at prices higher than those at which they bought it. Earnings from the sale of stock, or from the sale of any other asset, are considered capital gains, and are not included in earned income. Capital gains, and other unearned income, are also taxed at a much lower rate than is earned income.

## CORPORATE AND INDIVIDUAL WEALTH: THE FIRST LINK

Although there are many ways of becoming a millionaire (there are about 435,000 millionaires in the United States), among them being sports, entertainment, book authorship, real estate, gambling, and crime, certainly one of the most common is participating in a business enterprise of some sort, especially a corporate enterprise. To become a centimillionaire or billionaire, ownership and control of a corporation is essential. Indeed, *all* of the great fortunes in United States since the Industrial Revolution have been made through corporate structures (e.g., those of the Rockefellers, Mellons, Carnegies, Duponts, Fords, Gettys, and so on).

We have already seen how concentrated corporate wealth is in the United States. A similar pyramidal pattern characterizes the distribution of personal wealth and income. It is but a short step, then, to observe that among the giant corporations in the United States, which control most of the assets and sales within business, those who head these corporations are among the richest Americans in terms of personal wealth and income. That is, the two pyramids significantly overlap. To illustrate this point, let us look at the income in 1981 of the chief executive officers of the 798 largest corporations in the United States.

Every year *Forbes* magazine publishes the salaries, bonuses, benefits, contingent remuneration, and exercised stock options of the chief executive officers of the major corporations in America. Of the 798 who headed companies that made one of the *Forbes* leading 500 lists, the average total compensation was $651,629 per chief executive officer, an amount that easily places them—and for that matter, all of the other officers and board members of the company—among the top income earners in the population. This average, however, masks a wide variation in compensation among corporation executives, due mostly to whether or not the chief executive officer exercised stock options for that particular year.

## Stock Options

The largest United States corporations provide their major officers (not just the chief executive officer) the option to buy a certain amount of stock in the company at the price when the option to buy was first offered. This works as follows: Assume that you have just been hired as an officer by a major corporation. You would negotiate your salary, your bonuses and contingent remuneration (extra income under various incentive plans), your benefits (life insurance, club dues, use of company cars and airplanes, size of expense account). You would also be offered, periodically, the option to buy a certain amount of stock (to be negotiated) at current prices. You may, at any later time, exercise the option to buy this stock at the price it was offered you. Let us assume that you were offered 10,000 shares, and the current price is $100 per share. The option to buy would cost $1,000,000. Let us assume, after five years, that the price went up to $250 per share, for a total of $2,500,000. You now exercise your option to buy the 10,000 shares of stock at $100 per share, and thereby clear a profit of $1,500,000.

If we look at the total compensation of the leader in 1981 on the *Forbes* list, Steven J. Ross of Warner Communications, a communications conglomerate, one of whose subsidiaries is Atari, we find that his salary and bonus was $1,954,136, his benefits were $72,835, his contingent remuneration was $1,106,296, and his stock options amounted to a whopping $19,421,143, for a total of $22,554,410 in 1981. Lest one think that taxes would eat up at least half of this sum, the over $19 million in stock options is not taxed as income, but as a capital gain. The tax law with respect to capital gains is that the first 60 percent of a capital gain is tax free. Hence, $11,652,686 is not taxed. The other 40 percent is taxed at a maximum rate of 50 percent, or $3,884,228. Hence, on a capital gain of $19,421,143, Mr. Ross would be left with a minimum of $15,536,915 after taxes, plus of course, his other $3,133,267 in income, at least $1,954,136 (salary and bonus) of which would be taxed at the normal rate. Even if we assume that all of the $3,133,267 is taxed at the maximum of 50 percent, out of his total 1981 income of $22,554,410, Mr. Ross would receive $17,103,548 after taxes, which is an overall tax rate of 24 percent (the same percentage as those making about $25,000 per year). And this, of course, represents only the amount of income that Mr. Ross received from his corporation. We know nothing of the other sources of income that he may have. Nor do these figures include any deductions, which could further reduce his taxable income considerably.

All of those in the top echelons of the corporate world fall into the highest income group in the nation. It should be remembered, also, that those in the highest group collect more than double their earned income in unearned income (such as capital gains). In fact, of the approximately 2.5 percent of total national income that is derived from capital gains (over $50 billion), over one-half goes to the top *0.2 percent* of the population.

## Family Incomes

By contrast, let us look at the average income of the typical American family, and at the number of families who are below the official poverty level (a figure that underrepresents the amount of poverty since it reports income figures for families only, rather than for individuals).

A family's standard of living is determined by two factors: how much money it makes, and the prices it pays for the goods it buys. In 1982, the average American family's standard of living was the same as it was in 1967, That is, over the past fifteen years, the purchasing power of families has not increased, given the amount of dollars they earn and the prices they pay for what they buy. Although, on the average, families make over 60 percent more than they did in 1967, the prices they pay for goods and services have risen an equivalent amount. In fact, after a modest increase in the standard of living through 1979, there was a drop of 5.5 percent in 1980 and a further decrease of 3.5 percent in 1981, bringing the average family back to the 1967 level.

Median family income in 1981 was $22,390. The official poverty level was $9,287. Thirty-one million, eight hundred thousand Americans (14 percent or 1 out of every 7) lived below the poverty line. Nearly half of all families living in poverty were headed by women (1 out of every 5 American families was headed by a single parent). Twenty-one million, six hundred thousand of those below the poverty line were white, 9.2 million were black, and 3.7 million were Latino, although a much higher proportion of blacks and Latinos were living in poverty than were whites. This had to do with the considerably inferior incomes of blacks and Latinos. Median family income for whites was $23,520, $16,400 for Latinos, and $13,270 for blacks. Hence, although blacks constituted about 13 percent of the population, more than one-third of all blacks lived below the poverty level.

## SOURCES OF PERSONAL WEALTH

Less than 0.5 percent of all business enterprises controls well over two-thirds of all business wealth, and less than 7 percent of all individuals has more than 50 percent of all personal wealth in the country. In terms of corporate stocks and bonds, this same 7 percent owns nearly 90 percent. Income from salaries, benefits, and capital gains makes the managers of corporations the highest paid category of persons in America.

This concentration of wealth in corporations, and the high percentage of personal wealth and income derived by individuals in the corporate sector, is the most significant fact one can know about the American economy, American society, *and* American government and politics. Those who control and derive a disproportionate share of the benefits of this highly concentrated wealth are our most powerful citizens, and the organizations they control our most powerful institutions.

As an example of just how large and wealthy our largest corporations are, International Telephone and Telegraph had a larger dollar value in sales in 1980 than the entire Gross National Product of Israel, General Electric sold more than the GNP of Egypt, IBM more than that of Colombia, Standard Oil of California more than Norway, Texaco more than Denmark, General Motors more than Argentina, and Mobil more than Austria. Exxon, our largest industrial corporation, had a larger sales figure ($103 billion in 1980) than the Gross National Product of either the Netherlands or Sweden. In fact, there are only thirteen countries in the world, excluding the United States, with larger Gross National Products than the dollar value in sales of Exxon (Australia, Brazil, Canada, China, France, India, Italy, Japan, Mexico, Spain, the United Kingdom, the USSR, and West Germany).

To get some idea of where great personal wealth comes from, *Forbes* magazine published a list of the 441 wealthiest individuals and families in 1982. These were people who could be called centimillionaires; some fortunes rose as high as several billion dollars, and all possessed personal wealth exceeding 100 million dollars. Four hundred of these 441 were individuals or single families; 41 were extended families, some of them very large.

Of these 441 individuals and families, 152, or 34.5 percent, inherited their wealth, and 65.5 percent represent first-generation wealth. (This is only a very small subset of the previously reported 50 percent of the wealthy who inherit their wealth.) Table 4–4 gives the breakdown of the source of wealth for those who inherited it, for those who earned it themselves, and for the total.

Fully one-fifth (21%) of the total 441 individuals and families were involved in oil. The next highest category was light industry (16%), followed by communications (newspapers, publishing, and television—16%), then real estate (13%), investments and finance (11%), heavy industry (10%), service (such things as entertainment, gambling casinos, sports, and hotels—6%), commodi-

**TABLE 4–4   Source of Great Personal Wealth, by Percentage**

|  | INHERITED (152) | 1ST GENERATION (289) | TOTAL (441) |
|---|---|---|---|
| Oil | 34% | 15% | 21% |
| Light industry | 9 | 20 | 16 |
| Communications | 11 | 16 | 14 |
| Real estate | 3 | 19 | 13 |
| Investments, finance | 13 | 10 | 11 |
| Heavy industry | 24 | 2 | 10 |
| Service | 1 | 8 | 6 |
| Commodities | 2 | 4 | 3 |
| Retail trade | 1 | 3 | 3 |
| Engineering-construction | 0 | 2 | 1 |
| Transportation | 1 | 1 | 1 |

SOURCE: Calculated from "The Forbes Four Hundred," *Forbes* Magazine, September 13, 1982, pp. 99–172.

ties (citrus fruit, ranching, lumber—3%), retail trade (3%), engineering and construction (1%), and transportation (1%). In terms of the Industrial Sector (oil, heavy industry, light industry, and engineering-construction), 51 percent of the total fell within this area, with 49 percent accounted for by nonindustrial activities.

Perhaps even more interesting than the total figures, however, are the differences that appeared between those who inherited their wealth and those who had recently established their fortunes. As Table 4–4 indicates, inherited wealth was highly related to oil and to heavy industry (34% vs. 15%, and 24% vs. only 2% for current wealth makers). By contrast, first-generation wealth depended much more upon light industry (20% vs. 9%), real estate (19% vs. 3%), service activities (8% vs. 1%), and to a lesser extent communications (16% vs. 11%). Indeed, oil and heavy industry together made up 58 percent of the sources of inherited wealth, as opposed to only 17 percent for the new generation. Light industry, real estate, service, and communications, on the other hand, comprised 63 percent of the sources of wealth for first-generation wealth holders, contrasted with only 24 percent for those with inherited wealth. These figures, of course, reveal the influences and emphases of the Industrial Revolution during the late nineteenth and early twentieth centuries, during which much of the inherited wealth was made; the figures also reveal the trend away from heavy manufacturing and the emphases on such things as computers, home building, television, and service industries during the Post Industrial Revolution following World War II.

This, then, completes our survey of personal wealth and our examination of the close relationship between personal wealth and the corporate structure.

Nearly 40 percent of the total wealth of the United States resides in the business sector, and most of this wealth is located in a relatively few giant corporations. In addition, most personal wealth, comprising slightly over 40 percent of the total wealth of the country, is in the hands of a very small percentage of the population, most of whom have close connections, either as owners or as managers, of the corporate sector. What we need to explore now are the questions of how America's largest corporations are governed, how decisions are made concerning the distribution of these vast resources, how priorities are set, and how this control and these priorities are translated into political power. The next chapter will provide data on these questions.

# CHAPTER FIVE
# THE CORPORATE
# ECONOMIC SYSTEM

Everyone is interested in how well the United States economy is doing. Domestically, the standard of living of all Americans is directly affected by the size of the Gross National Product (which measures the total national ouput of goods and services), how fast the GNP is growing or declining, the amount of wages earned, the general level of prices, the percentage of unemployment, the rate of inflation, the level of interest rates, the amount of money available for investment and where and how it is invested, and the quantity and quality of goods and services. And, since the United States produces 25 percent of the *world's* Gross National Product, and since the value of the dollar has a sharp impact on world prices and world economic conditions, what we do at home has major consequences for world markets, world financial conditions, and the economic well-being of millions, if not billions, of other human beings. How our economy is structured, then, and who makes decisions regarding prices, wages, and investments, and how such decisions affect our growth rate, employment, inflation, and our interest rates are of central importance to the lives of nearly everyone on this planet.

In Chapters 3 and 4 we explored in some detail the structure of the U.S. economy and the relationships between this structure and the distribution of personal wealth and income. Approximately 200 corporations control 50 percent of all business assets; approximately 500 corporations control 67 percent; and 1,000 corporations control 75 percent. One-third of the labor force is employed by the largest 200 corporations, and their sales represent three-quarters of the dollar value of all sales in the nation. Further, the enormous economic advantages that go to a small percentage of all Americans is very closely linked to the corporate sector. No one could deny that how well these corporations do determines to a significant extent how well we all do. At the minimum we would expect that those who control these corporations and who derive so much personal wealth and income from them would show an extra amount of interest in the general health of the corporate sector and in their own particular industries, organizations, institutions, and companies. That is, after all, what they are paid so well to do.

We have also seen that the most salient feature of the American economy is the high degree of oligopoly (few sellers sharing a large percentage of the market) that exists, especially in the all-important industrial, transportation, utilities, communications, finance, and, to an increasing extent, wholesale and retail sectors. It is through oligopolistic (and monopolistic) markets that large firms are able to exercise great power over supply, demand (through advertising), rates of profit, retained earnings for discretionary investment (including mergers and investment abroad), employment, wages, and other economic factors that are central to the U.S. economy (as they are, for that matter, to any economy).

## THE INFLUENCE OF THE CORPORATE SECTOR

But just how important is the corporate sector of our economy as opposed to the individual and governmental sectors? Is the power of 200, or 500, or 1,000 corporations really that great? Can they transform their uncontestably large economic power into political power?

Let us assume for the moment that we have three contenders for power. One small group controls almost 40 percent of the total economic resources of the country—those that are primarily responsible for the economic well-being of the nation. Another small group controls almost 40 percent of the wealth and income in its sector. Furthermore, these two groups, who together control 80 percent of the economic resources of the nation, are closely linked and tend to be the same group of people. The third contender is also controlled by a small group, although it has the power to represent everyone. But it has only 20 percent of the resources. In the event of a conflict, which group will win?

First, one might expect at least a loose coalition between the two groups that represent 80 percent of the resources, since they are essentially the same people anyway. Clearly, we would expect this combined group to prevail over the 20 percent if occasion demanded it. But, secondly, wouldn't we also expect the small groups who control the 80 percent to try to control the small group who runs the 20 percent? In other words, might there not be a general coalition among the three small groups who control 100 percent? Might not, in fact, the groups who control the 80 percent determine to a large extent who those in the 20 percent are likely to be, and to have a great deal of influence over them? Wouldn't all the members of these small controlling groups be better off under these conditions?

Now, substitute a small number of corporations for the first group, the small percentage of major wealth holders for the second group, and government for the third group. In any conflict, we would expect the coalition of business and personal wealth to prevail over government. But we would also foresee efforts to reduce conflict between business and personal wealth on the one hand, and government power on the other. We would anticipate, in general, that the three would work together. Any other model of how such a system would function would require quite extraordinary assumptions about human nature and the exercise of power. Indeed, given the cardinal importance of the economic sector to the nation as a whole and its vast concentrated wealth, combined with the wealth and power of a small group of individuals, many of whom are directly associated with the economic sector and whose combined wealth accounts for almost 80 percent of the total wealth of the country, it is not surprising to find that the corporate sector exercises extensive power over the governmental sector.

This is not to say, however, that conflict never occurs within, between, and among the three contenders. It is simply to say that any conflict that does occur will be within a general context of wide agreement over the issues. In general the conflicts will revolve around who is to benefit the most in the general distribution of wealth and income ("property," as Madison would say).

The weakest party among the three will be government, of course, not business and not those who control large personal wealth. Given the overwhelming importance of the corporate giants to the economic well-being of the country, and their vast wealth, it would be naive indeed to suppose that government was an independent, hostile force working primarily for the interests of someone else against those institutions and persons who are most successful in our economy and in our society. In fact, our system of government was *designed* to be porous, to be open to influence from the outside.

## The Democratic Model and the Ideal of Equality

The democratic model—the one taught in all civics classes in grammar schools and high schools, the model that forms the basis of American ideology and thought about democratic government—has it that government is supposed to represent the "will of the people." But, as we have already learned, there are two kinds of persons in the United States: individual persons and corporate persons. And among individual persons, there are the 19 percent who control over 75 percent of the nation's personal wealth, and the 0.5 percent who control over 25 percent of it — and then there are the others.

Although, in the ideology, "all men [*sic*] are created equal," it is perfectly clear that the ideal of equality is not an economic one, nor a social one, nor even a political one. It is, at best, a kind of legal ideal or fiction—not a bad ideal by any means, but not a reality either. Once again, it would take a good deal of torturous reasoning to conclude, for example, that all persons in the United States have equal access to government. If David Rockefeller, chairman of the board of the Chase Manhattan Bank, a centimillionaire who inherited his fortune from his grandfather (who founded the great Standard Oil [Exxon] fortune), and member of the board of directors of several other major companies, was outside your door, and a fuller Brush salesperson, or even 100 Fuller Brush salespersons, were also there, it is not difficult to predict that the person you would admit first into your office would be David Rockefeller. You would probably also listen to what David Rockefeller had to say with some attention. (Everyone has a sense of what is important and who is important.) We shall reserve for the next chapter a more detailed discussion of the democratic model and the individual political process. Our major concern here is with the corporate sector and its influence. In this context, then, it is not irrelevant to point out the overriding importance of the economy in general to the lives of all Americans, and hence to the overriding importance of those who are in control of it.

## The Relationships between Government and Business

Contrary to popular belief (which is "popular" because it is the one which is taught to all of us), the business community is not at the mercy of government regarding the management of its own internal affairs. Although there is a minimum wage level of $3.35 an hour for many job categories, there is no government control over wages in general. Business units decide for themselves, sometimes in bargaining with labor unions, in most cases not, what will be paid to employees, including top management. Except in time of war or other serious crises, there is no government control over most pricing practices, although with natural monopolies within the public utilities sector (electric power, telephone, and water systems, for example), there is a form of "public" approval of such pricing. Businesses are quite free to decide on the quantity of goods they produce, although the quality is loosely inspected by government agencies from time to time. Investment decisions are entirely in the hands of business units, with the possible exception of decisions involving mergers, which may, if the units are large enough, be subject to scrutiny by the Department of Justice or the Federal Trade Commission.

However, the relationship between government and business over wages, prices, quality of goods, and investment in the form of mergers is far from being an adversary one, as indeed the data in all of the fields of government "regulation" indicate that it is not. As industry, finance, and communications have become more and more oligopolistic in structure (in spite of the antitrust legislation in force since 1890), the ability of corporations to influence both supply and demand—and hence prices, wages, employment, and profits—has not diminished. In fact, it has increased, especially given the fact that when companies in oligopolistic markets face increased costs they are able to pass them on to consumers in the form of higher prices. What we are dealing with in the corporate sector is a form of administered pricing, a mutual agreement to limit price competition, profit levels that can be set by influencing not only prices but supply and demand as well, and a general level of control over government and those elected and appointed to it that makes the overall agreement between the corporate sector and government very high indeed.

## The Ills of the United States Economy

It is very common to blame the ills of the U.S. economy on factors other than the corporations themselves. Primarily this is because those who tell us what is wrong are either corporate executives or government spokespersons who, as we should now be aware, are likely to be highly supportive of the corporate structure. Thus we hear that our difficulties are due to foreign competition, or high domestic wages, or insufficient funds in the hands of corporations and the wealthy for investment, or the price of energy (most notably oil), or an inflationary spiral due to an excess amount of money in the economy (necessitating higher interest rates), or the unwillingness of poor Americans to work, or overregulation of corporations by government, and on and on. The "culprit" is always elsewhere. Almost never do we hear through normal channels of information that oligopolistic economic structures misallocate resources, that control over supply by a few firms in each industry produces higher than normal profits, that our industrial capacity is underutilized, that high unemployment is simply due to a lack of jobs, that inflation is due to the corporations' ability to absorb costs and turn them into higher prices, that plants have become obsolete (as, for example, in the steel industry) because the corporations have not made capital investments in new methods but instead have diverted their retained earnings into mergers or foreign investment.

Instead, we are likely to hear nothing but praise for the corporate sector. This, by itself, should make us suspicious. Individuals and groups of individuals are being blamed (the unemployed for example); foreign countries are being blamed; the money supply is being blamed; government spending is being blamed; regulation is being blamed. Since nothing in this world is perfect, shouldn't we hear, if only occasionally, that at least *some* corporations are doing a bad job? But the fact that some individual corporations may make mistakes, as do all human organizations, is not even the issue. That there may be something inefficient and wasteful in the whole corporate structure—that, for example, extra-normal profits and the ability to set prices are *characteristic* of oligopolistic structures—is not even mentioned. Since our economic structure has produced the highest Gross National Product in the world (though no longer the highest in terms of Gross National Product per capita), it tends to be immune from criticism. And the major reason why we do not hear even the slightest criticism is because those who control the mass media and those in government who are able to capture the attention of a national audience (such as presidents, members of Congress, and department secretaries), are primarily obliged to the corporate sector for their positions in the first place.

We do not mean to categorically indict the American corporate structure; we simply do not like seeing so many American citizens having their legs pulled. If improvements are to be made, we at least have to know what the problems are. It is useless to think about improving the American economy if we are neither informed about its structure, nor find it legitimate to talk about the most important component of the economic system itself: the corporations.

But the problem, in any case, does not lie with individual corporations. There are forces built into the corporate structure itself that produce, over the long run, oligopolistic firms; and it is these oligopolistic market structures that permit individual corporations to earn excess profits through the control of supply and the consequent ability to control price. Let us explore in more detail how this works.

## THE CONSEQUENCES
## OF OLIGOPOLISTIC MARKET STRUCTURES

We are all aware that the goal of business is to make a profit. In competitive markets there are many firms, none of which controls a significant portion of the total supply of goods and services produced. Each firm is subject to the whims of the marketplace: each is influenced by how much is produced by the total number of producers (supply); and by how much of the goods or services consumers want to buy (demand). If too much is produced, prices will fall, profits will drop, and some firms will be forced to leave the market (either the least efficient, or those who do not have access to other sources of funds). If too little is produced, prices will rise, existing firms will have an incentive to produce more, and new firms will be encouraged to enter the market. Similar effects occur with fluctuations in demand (simply substitute "an increase in demand" for "too little is produced," and "a decrease in demand" for "too much is produced"). In a competitive system, no one has control over the market, and individual sellers are at its mercy. Such a market structure may be very good for consumers, for whom prices reflect a competitive market situation at normal profit levels; but it is very hard on producers who never know from one year to the next what their profits are likely to be. It is, in other words, a high-risk system.

The conditions of a competitive market, however, are met in only a very small percentage of American business; and this is especially true in the corporate sector. Competition between multiple sellers, none of whom controls a significant portion of the market, is much more prevalent among *proprietorships* (what are called "mom and pop" stores) and *partnerships*. These businesses are characterized by small assets, small sales, and small profits. That is, it is among the relatively poor businesses, those that can least afford a bad year, that risk is highest, which accounts for the fact that most bankruptcies occur in this sector. It also helps to explain why small business is considerably more "conservative" in its political philosophy than is big business. Small businesses are the ones who must cope with real competitive markets and for whom labor costs, interest rates, taxes, and inflation are frequently a matter of survival.

One of the major sectors of the economy where competitive conditions are partly met is agriculture (although, as you recall, this sector accounts for only 3 percent of GNP). The high-risk component of competitive markets is present here, with overproduction being the major problem. In order to prevent incomes from falling and producers being forced off their farms, agriculture has become a major recipient of government subsidies that are designed to keep the price of their products high and assure them of income and work. At the present time, for example, the federal government is spending over $2 billion each year for the purchase of surplus milk, butter, and cheese, and spends an additional quarter of a billion dollars to store it. This is one of the ways in which the government protects business units from the hazards of the market; but as we shall see, in most corporate sectors of the economy, firms have devised other means to shelter themselves from risk.

## The Goals of Business

The optimum market situation for any firm is that of being the sole supplier of a good or service. To have no competitors means that one can charge what one wants to for what one sells. Monopolies, although not uncommon (especially in the utility sector), are difficult to establish and maintain, since, if the entry into the market is not overly costly, other firms, seeing the profits to be made, will be tempted to enter. Monopolies, by the way, need not always be large firms. One can have the only shoe repair store in a given area or be the only chimney sweep (demand for this latter service, however, is not likely to be high).

The next best market situation is where only a small number of sellers control a large share of the market (oligopoly). As we have seen in Chapter 3, it is irrational for firms in oligopolistic markets to compete with each other over price, since all firms are likely to lose in such a competition. Having significant control over supply, then, and being in a position to affect demand (through advertising), oligopolistic firms are in the comfortable position of avoiding most of the risks of competition and can count on a much more stable market situation. Indeed, this is one of the major goals of business firms: *stability*. Avoiding market fluctuations allows them to make long-range plans, to know that they will continue to be in business in the future, and to decide on what their next steps will be. Control over supply allows them to determine price and hence to count on a certain level of profit—to be used, as we shall see, for various purposes. It also, incidently, makes them less concerned with costs, since these can be passed on to their customers in the form of higher prices.

There is another goal of firms which, like stability, is quite compatible with the profit motive. This goal is *growth*. Firms want to increase their levels of profit, both in terms of percentage increases (20% instead of 10% for example), but also in terms of absolute amount ($500,000 instead of $200,000). Growth is also compatible with the goal of stability and the effort to control supply. (Stability, in business terms, does not mean standing still. It means doing at least as well as in the past.)

## Economies of Scale

In addition, there are some economic advantages of growth for the entire economy—what are called *economies of scale*. Larger firms are better able than smaller firms to cut certain costs—by buying raw materials in bulk, for example; they are able to utilize expensive capital equipment that small firms can not afford; and they can employ labor practices such as assembly-line production methods, which require firms of a certain size. These economies of scale, in reducing costs, are good for consumers in that they permit lower prices— assuming, of course, that the firms are not yet large enough to constitute an oligopoly. Unfortunately, this latter situation is the one usually reached; and given the costs of entry into some businesses (such as automobiles, defense equipment, and steel production), there are usually a few large firms within any given industry, and they generally constitute an oligopoly. Further, the costs of entry into these markets by potential new firms are normally so high that few of them ever try to challenge the large firms.

There is also, however, a limit to economies of scale, and business firms pursuing growth run into a point of diminishing returns as they increase in size. They eventually confront what are called *diseconomies of scale*. These are increasing costs due to inefficiencies of size, such as multiple plant operations, for example, and problems of organization and control.

There seems to be an optimum level of firm size in any given industry, but the attractiveness of increased profit, growth, and protection from downward fluctuations which oligopolistic market positions offer will encourage individual firms to go beyond the optimum level. It would, after all, be quite fortuitous if the ideal market structure and the goals of individual firms happened to coincide. (It is, indeed, more or less a law in social science, documented in every field, that the interests of individual members of a community and the interests of the totality rarely are identical.)

There is a natural tendency in business toward oligopoly and monopoly, given the goals of profit, stability, and growth of individual firms. Managers of large corporations are, after all, charged with making a good profit and increasing the wealth of the firm, goals that are more likely than not to be incompatible with ideal market structures and the interests of the economy as a whole. It is in this sense that our present-day economic ills are not the "fault" of individual firms. Corporations are simply doing what comes naturally. The goals of control over supply, price, and profit level encourage them to continue to expand. And besides, in an interesting sense, they must do something with their profits. If there is a culprit in all of this, it is, rather, the resulting oligopolistic and monopolistic market structures that are the consequence of these natural forces toward large size and control over supply.

## The Investment of Earnings

Individual firms, then, will use their *retained earnings* in further investment to achieve increased profits, stability, and growth. (Retained earnings are that part of profits not given out to stockholders and constitute the source of more than 75 percent of all corporate investment.) Although large sums are borrowed from banks and financial institutions, the availability of internal funds means that big corporations have almost guaranteed access to a lot of money that they are relatively free to invest as they choose.

How corporations decide to invest is of considerable importance to the economy as a whole, and "the economy" has no say in the matter. The number of options are plentiful. They can reinvest in their own corporations (modernization and growth); they can merge with other firms that produce the same or similar products (horizontal mergers); they can buy firms that supply them with raw materials (backward vertical integration) or that use the products they produce to fashion other products or that market the original products (forward vertical integration); or they can acquire firms in businesses unrelated to what they produce (conglomerate mergers). They also have a choice of domestic vs. foreign investment.

Which of these alternatives a firm chooses has significant consequences for the national economy. The steel industry, for example, has a strong, well-established oligopolistic market structure and is noted for its outmoded methods of production. U.S. Steel, the leading firm in the industry, decided to buy an oil company (Marathon Oil) with its considerable retained earnings, constituting the largest merger in American history, rather than to modernize its own plant. Because the steel industry is decaying and is unable to compete with foreign producers, those who run U.S. Steel have apparently decided to search elsewhere for their profits.

If we cannot fault individual corporations for the present-day plight of the American economy, we may wish to take a closer look at the economic, political, and social consequences of oligopolistic market structures. We may even no longer feel like blaming the government, although government practices are certainly an essential reason for the existence, maintenance, and continued growth of oligopolies, as we shall see.

Oligopolistic market structures have had a number of major consequences on the U.S. economy. Due to the extra-normal profits that are given to some businesses, profits that could have been better used elsewhere in the economy, a great deal of the nation's wealth and resources has been misallocated. There has also been much inefficiency because oligopolistic firms have been under little pressure to reduce costs, and many have grown beyond their optimum size. Because such firms have total control over the amount of goods produced and because the maximum rate of profit is reached before full capacity is attained, many plants are underutilized. And because resources have been misallocated and plants underutilized, unemployment has reached a high rate. Other effects of oligopolies include a high rate of inflation (due to the ability to raise prices at will), increased economic concentration (through the use of retained earnings for mergers), and—what is perhaps of most interest—an enormous and increasing amount of political power.

## HOW CORPORATIONS ARE GOVERNED

Before discussing in detail the external relationships between corporations and government, it will be useful to examine how these large business enterprises are governed internally. This will give us a better idea not only of how business firms are managed but how much discretion and power are available to a surprisingly small number of people.

There are three components to corporate organizational structure: stockholders (owners), boards of directors, and officers of the corporation (the chief executive officer being far and away the most important). In principle, the stockholders elect the board of directors, and the board of directors appoints the executive officers. The actual operation of the organization, however, is not as simple as this organizational flow chart would have us believe. In summary, we can say that the average stockholder has nothing to do with the operation of the corporation, and that the chief executive officer is much more likely to be the person appointing members of the board than vice versa. How and why this occurs, however, is a subject that requires more elaboration.

### Characteristics of Stock Ownership

Two major factors tend to give executive officers of corporations (and in particular, chief executive officers) nearly total control of their organizations. The first is the large number of total shares of stock in each corporation and the consequent *relatively* large number of stockholders. Over 30 million persons own some stock in corporations. For example, 92.5 percent of the 200 largest nonfinancial corporations have between 20,000 and 500,000 shareholders (Herman, 1981, p. 71). American Telephone and Telegraph (AT&T) has the largest number of stockholders: over 3 million. On the other hand, the concentration of ownership of this stock in the hands of a relatively few individuals and institutions is very high.

The second factor accounting for the high degree of corporate-officer (management) control is the high dollar value of all shares of stock in any of our largest corporations and the consequent inability of any individual or institution to own a large proportion of shares, even in one company. (This does occur, however, during mergers, when one corporation buys a majority interest in another firm.) The value of corporate stock in 1978 was slightly more than 1 trillion dollars. Of this total, 65.6 percent ($683 billion) was owned by individual shareholders, and 34.4 percent ($358 billion) was owned by institutions (banks, pension funds, insurance companies, investment firms, and state and local government retirement funds being the most important).

We saw in Chapter 4 that the concentration of individual holdings by a relatively small proportion of the 30 million individual stockholders is very high: the top 20 percent own 97 percent of all individually held stock; the top 10 percent own 90 percent, the top 5 percent own 86 percent, the top 1 percent own 62 percent, and the top 0.5 percent own 43 percent. Further, each of those in this 0.5 percent have holdings of over $1 million (not necessarily, however, in one company). At the institutional level (with one-third of all stock holdings), 99 financial institutions, each with more than $1 billion in stock, accounted for over two-thirds of all institutional holdings. These 99 firms consisted of 43 banks, 31 investment companies, 10 insurance companies, 6 government pension funds, 6 private pension funds, 1 foundation, 1 university, and 1 private trust company (Herman, 1981, p. 139).

In general, then, given the multibillion dollar assets of the major corporations and the large number of shares involved, it is rare that any single individual stockholder would own even as much as 5 percent of the stock. On the other hand, it is perfectly clear that *if* our largest corporations were controlled by owners, they would be controlled by a relatively few large individual and institutional stockholders (the number of votes one has is determined by the number of shares one owns). And, indeed, a small percentage of them are. The estimates vary, but most seem to put the percentage of large corporations controlled by some combination of owners at about 15 percent. This leaves approximately 85 percent that are considered management controlled (Blumberg, 1975, p. 88). Herman concludes, for example, "that virtually all the major corporate decisions are shared in or finally decided upon by a small group of high-level leaders of the organization, whereas outsiders with influence usually exercise it in a much narrower sphere'' (1981, p. 23).[1] Dye estimates that 3,562 corporate leaders in industry, utilities, communications, transportation, banking, and insurance (which include all of the members of the boards of directors, an inclusion that considerably over-estimates the number of those with real influence) control over half of the assets of these corporate sectors (1979, p. 14).

Whatever the number, whether it be 500 (a conservative estimate), 1,000, or even 5,000 (undoubtedly the upper limit), a very small number of people controls the economic decision making of the largest corporations in America, a group of giant firms that accounts for over 50 percent of all assets and sales in the business sector, and one-third of all employment in the United States. The leaders of these 200 corporations essentially control the supply of goods and services produced, prices, employment, investment, mergers, and even, to some extent, demand. Nearly all of the corporations they head are oligopolies, having market structures in which cooperation and common action are the most rational and profitable policies; and competition, to the extent that it exists at all, is conducted via brand names. Occasionally there are squabbles among these giant firms; in 1982, for example, Bendix and Marietta, two aerospace and industrial firms, attempted to take each other over in an unprecedented kind of merger. At one point, each firm had bought up a controlling stock interest in the other firm! But outside of these ''family feuds,'' the normal course of affairs dictates a policy of noncompetition and even of significant cooperation in the major lines of policy regarding supply, prices and profits.

### Characteristics of Corporate Leaders

This small group of corporate leaders who control our largest business enterprises is also, as might be expected, a *select* group; and they have a number of characteristics in common. Of those who occupy the top 3,562 positions in Dye's study, 99.7 percent were men (1979, p. 154). Nineteen percent attended private high schools, and a remarkable 11 percent attended the same 33 prestigious private high schools. Two-thirds attended private colleges and universities, and perhaps most remarkable of all, *55 percent* attended the 12 most prestigious universities and colleges in the nation: Harvard, Yale, Princeton, Columbia, Cornell, Pennsylvania, Dartmouth (all Ivy League schools), Stanford, Chicago, M.I.T., Northwestern, and Johns Hopkins.

### Corporate Interlocks

Not only do these corporate leaders have extraordinarily similar backgrounds, but, once in position, they tend to work together rather closely. Although the Clayton Antitrust Act of 1914 prohibits direct interlocks between firms that are considered competitors (*interlocks* occur when officers or members

---

[1]Reprinted by permission of Cambridge University Press.

of the board of directors of one firm are also officers or members of the board of directors of the other firm), it does not prohibit interlocking directorates of firms that are not considered to be competitive, nor does it prohibit *indirect interlocks* (members of competing firms on the same board of directors of a noncompeting firm). Of the top 3,562 positions that Dye identified in the corporate sector, 1,560, or 44 percent, were held by people holding more than one of the top positions (1979, p. 134). Herman found that of the total 3,060 directors of the 200 leading nonfinancial corporations, and the 50 leading financial corporations, 1,298 (42.4%) were members of more than one of the 250 (1981, p. 201).

Herman went on to study more intensively the nature and number of the interlocks among America's 250 largest financial and nonfinancial corporations. He discovered that only 16 (6.4%) of the 250 had no interlocks with the others. Fully 234 of the 250 (93.6%) had officers or members of the board serving on the board of directors of at least 1 of the other companies. One hundred seventy-three, or 70 percent, had 5 or more interlocks with the other 250. One-third of the nonfinancial corporations had 10 or more interlocks, and 1, AT&T, was directly linked with 76. Twenty-nine of the 50 financial institutions (58%) had 10 or more interlocks, and one-third had 15 or more. One financial institution had 42 direct interlocks with the other 250 corporations.

The number of indirect interlocks (both with competitors and others) is even greater than the number of direct interlocks. Herman, for example, cites a 1978 Senate study which documented that the 13 largest U.S. corporations not only had 249 direct interlocks, but an incredible 5,547 indirect interlocks (members of at least 2 of the 13 firms meeting on the boards of other firms) (1981, p. 202). The web of contact and cooperation can be quite close and very widespread at the same time.

### Joint Ventures

Interlocking directorates, whether direct or indirect, involving the officers and board members of our 200 to 500 largest corporations (which, in turn, using the 500 figure, represent well over half of all business assets, two-thirds of sales, and one-third of total U.S. employment), are not the only way in which these corporations are closely linked. Contact and cooperation can be—and is—quite informal. Most of these people either know or are aware of each other, and they share in social as well as economic activities. But contact and cooperation can also involve other, more formal business activities that bring them together for mutual profit.

One such activity is called a *joint venture*. In a joint venture, two or more companies pool resources, share contracts, engage in joint research or exploration, share management, or otherwise engage in collective and cooperative economic behavior; many joint ventures involve companies that are direct competitors. They are quite common between and among firms in oil, natural gas, iron, steel, mining, and chemicals, to name but a few of the most important.

To give an example from a more popular field, professional football, the owners in the National Football League (NFL) share equally in the $2.13 billion television revenues they receive (over 5 years), and split—60 percent for the home team, 40 percent for the visiting team—gate proceeds. The football strike in 1982, in fact, was over the desire of the players to split the television revenues with the owners, from which they would then pay their own salaries and bonuses. In other words, the players wanted to be a part of the joint venture with the owners, the latter providing money capital and the players providing human capital. This is actually a quite revolutionary idea, owners and "labor" sharing the proceeds in a joint venture. This proposal by the players was refused outright by the owners and was not a part of the eventual settlement.

As for joint venture in the industrial sector, a study in 1975 found over 2,700 joint ventures among the 20 major oil companies (Herman, 1981, p. 208). This study also gave data on other ways in which the 20 oil firms had occasions to meet, cooperate, and establish common points of contact. Out of a possible 190 pair combinations of the 20 firms, there were 106 *major* joint ventures (those involving over $10 million), and 176 *minor* joint ventures. Other points of contact included 27 in the use of a common auditor, 42 in a common investment bank, 190 (complete) in common representation on federal advisory boards, 135 in common major club memberships (an example of social ties), and 112 in representation on nongovernment advisory or research boards. The data would be even more striking had only the seven major oil companies (the "seven sisters" as they are called), which by themselves control most of the oil revenues in the country, been used as a comparison.

In addition to joint ventures, there are also a number of ways in which companies are linked with each other in terms of joint ownership. Figure 5–1 shows the ownership relationship (an example of vertical integration) in the coal, iron ore, and steel links between the M.A. Hanna Co. and its related firms. This complicated chart is a good example of the extensive cooperative mergers in the industrial sector.

## Trade Associations
## and Government Advisory Boards

There are also approximately 2,800 *trade associations* (groups of companies in the same or related product lines) which represent the industry in a number of activities, including lobbying (which we shall discuss in the next chapter). These associations also serve as a common source of contact and activity for the sharing of information and the development of a sense of unity within a particular industry. Besides trade associations are what could be called super corporate groups, representing the cream of the corporate elite, about which we will have a good deal to say in the next chapter. Government advisory boards, as we have already seen in the oil industry, are also a source of cooperation and contact, and, of course, serve as a direct link to government. The membership of

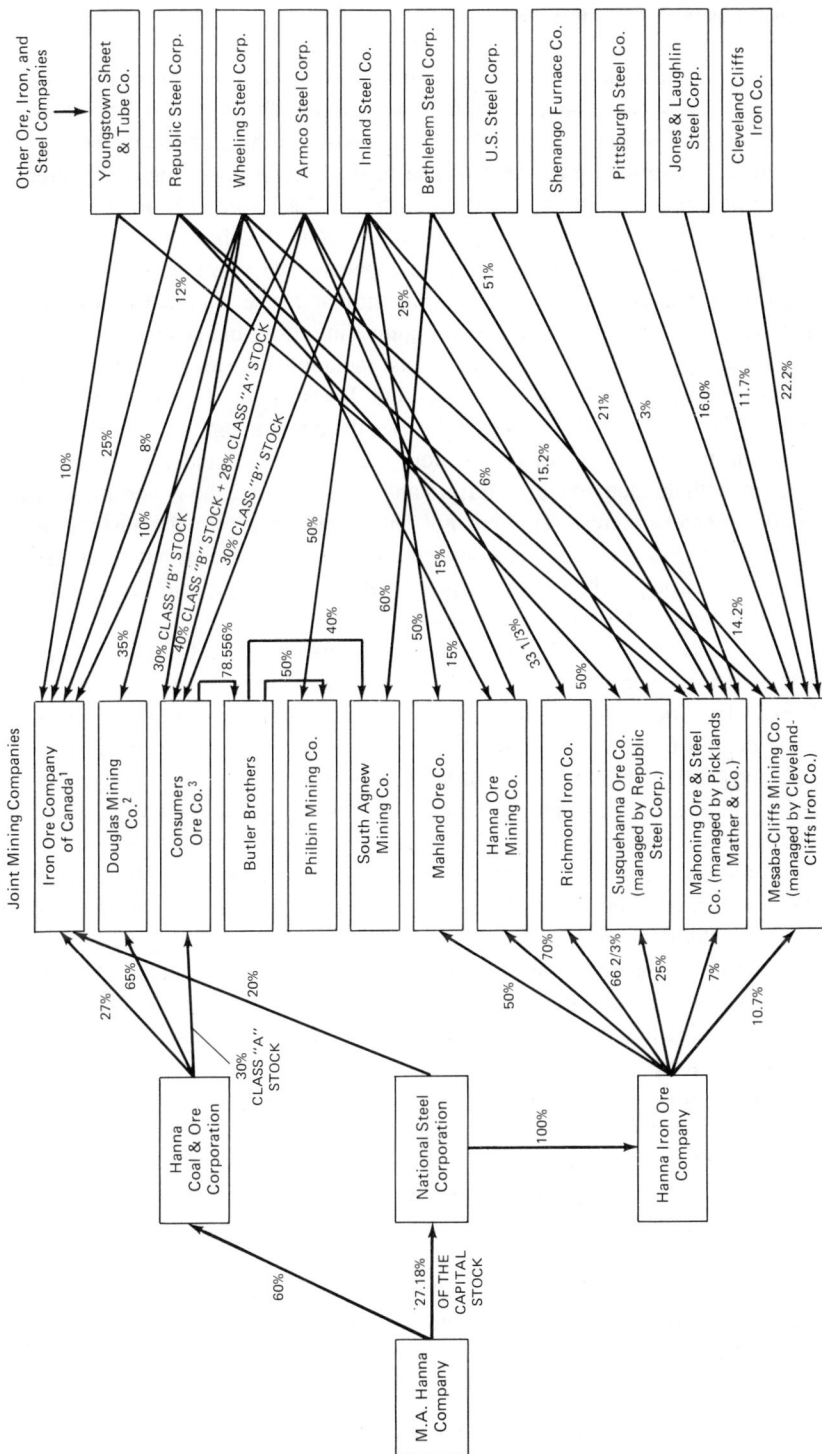

**FIGURE 5–1  Joint ownerships ties of the M. A. Hanna Company.**

Source: Federal Trade Commission, Control of Iron Ore, report published by the House Judiciary Committee, December 1952. Reprinted in Herman, 1981, p. 210. Reproduced by permission of Cambridge University Press.

these boards includes both leaders of industry and government officials, who meet to talk about common problems. For example, the National Petroleum Council is an advisory board established "to advise, inform, and make recommendations as requested by the Department of the Interior regarding any matter relating to petroleum or the petroleum industry." There were 126 members in 1974, 33 of whom came from the largest corporations, and included "virtually all the large oil, natural gas, and pipeline companies" (Herman, 1981, p. 215). There are now 820 advisory boards that are similar to the National Petroleum Council; these bring together members of competing firms and government officials from almost all government departments, including the Departments of Agriculture, Commerce, Defense, Energy, and Interior. As Herman suggests (1981, p. 216): "In literally scores of industries the government advisory body is a vehicle through which major competitors meet regularly, under government imprimatur, with de facto exemption from antitrust, to advise the government on matters of common interest. This has not only been a real plus for business in getting its view across and gaining a desired access to government, but it has also been a vehicle through which businesspeople of the same trade can get together on a regular basis, with the public excluded."[2]

A relatively small group of corporate managers (and, in a few cases, large owners) exercises enormous power in our economic system. Most of these corporate executives occupy more than one top position, and as a consequence there is a great deal of overlap, communication, and coordination among them. Further, the corporations that these executive leaders head are themselves linked together in a number of ways (joint ventures; trade associations; vertical, horizontal, and conglomerate integration; government advisory boards; and private advisory boards are but several examples). Functioning in essentially oligopolistic markets, they control to a large extent supply, price, and profit; and through the use of retained earnings they control investment, merger activity, and the increased concentration of economic power. The consequences for the economy as a whole are very large indeed, including such factors as prices, standard of living, unemployment, inflation, foreign vs. domestic investment, and quality of goods and services.

We have already had a glimpse into how this economic power translates into political power through the device of government advisory boards. We have also explored the overall power potential of what happens when business wealth and personal wealth, comprising 80 percent of the national wealth, are pitted against government. It would be surprising if we did not find this coalition of corporate and personal wealth prevailing in the vast majority of confrontations with government. In fact, it would not be at all surprising to find most government officials primarily beholden in numerous ways to the corporate sector. It is to a detailed analysis of the relationship between corporate power and political power that we now turn.

[2]Reprinted by permission of Cambridge University Press.

# CHAPTER SIX
# THE DIFFICULTIES
# OF DEMONSTRATING
# WHAT IS INHERENTLY
# IMPOSSIBLE TO PROVE

The most important concept in political science that is used to explain political events and policy outcomes is the concept of *power*. Such matters as why the United States is giving large amounts of military assistance to El Salvador; or why we need to spend $1.6 trillion on a defense buildup over five years; or why Senator Dole of Iowa, chairman of the Senate Finance Committee, is fighting the American Bankers Association's demand for a repeal of withholding on dividend and interest income; and anything else that has to do with winning and losing whatever people hold dear, are usually related in one way or another to the concept of power. The concept of power is the glue that holds political theories together and allows political scientists and others to explain and understand the flow of political events and activities. Political *outcomes* are viewed as the play of power relationships within the society or within any group that is being studied.

## THE PROBLEMS OF INFERENCE
## AND MEASUREMENT

The usual way power is defined is in terms of, at one level, a quite simplistic set of symbols: A gets B to do what A wants and which B would not have done otherwise. Stated in this manner, power is a *relationship* of dominance between A and B.

The most important point to notice about this definition of power as a relationship between people is that a relationship is not a physical object—that is, it is not something that one can see directly. A relationship is, rather, something that exists *between* and *among* people. Although we say people *have* relationships, this is not the same thing as saying that people *have* arms, or legs, or $1 million worth of stock, or what have you.

Why this is important to point out is obvious: in order to talk about relationships we shall have to *infer* them from something else—from behavior, for example, or from what we hear people say to each other, or from the resources they have at their disposal, or from other data or combinations of data.

Not only, then, is there an *inherent problem of inference* with respect to power, that we have to look at other things in order to establish its existence, but there is also a problem of *measurement:* what "other things" are relevant to be examined, and how available are the data that we want to look at.

A second difficulty in establishing and measuring power relationships is knowing what both A and B want. "Wants" and "interests," as psychological or imputed desires, are also not physical objects that we can directly see. This state of desire or interest is also very difficult to ascertain and measure and *must also be inferred.*

The apparent definitional simplicity of power, then, masks a number of very real difficulties faced by a researcher who even attempts to *demonstrate,* let alone to *prove,* that A dominated B, or that A exercised power or influence over B. For example, in any particular matter, was A directly involved? Could B *anticipate* what A wanted? In this case, A was not even a visible party in a direct communication with B. (Students often do this, for example, when they write term papers or examinations in ways slanted to agree with what they perceive to be the opinions of the professor.) How would one prove that power was exerted? Would B tell us that this was what he or she was doing? Would it even be possible that B did whatever he or she did "unconsciously," without specifically thinking about it? And how would we know *that?*

Second, how do we prove that A dominated B if we do not know what B would have done without A's intervention, assuming A does intervene? We can, in fact, *never* know this, since it is contrary to fact. A did intervene, and we cannot run the entire scenario over again. All we can do is infer that the reason B did what he or she did was because of A's intervention.

Third, there is the possibility that B's attitude toward what A wants (or is presumed to want) may be similar to A's anyway. Hence, what B did she would have done on her own with or without A's intervention—maybe even *in spite of* A's intervention.

Fourth, B's entire *attitude* might have already been influenced by A, but in a way that is not detectable. We have already seen that a society develops an ideology in order to get people to comply voluntarily to what those who establish the ideology want. This is obviously "power"—indeed, this might be the most important form of power there is. Certainly it is the most effective. But how do we *prove* this general societal influence?

Fifth, B might already have been beholden to A. In other matters that preceded the event, A might have done something for B (that we may or may not know about), and B was simply carrying out an obligation.

Sixth, A's communication to B could have been hidden from us. In this case we either have to infer it or attribute what B did to the influence of some other factor or person.

There are other difficulties as well, but you undoubtedly get the point. All but the most blatant forms of power—forcing someone to submit to torture in the presence of witnesses, for example—are inferred; and even with the blatant ones we can never be sure that someone else didn't tell A to torture B.

It would be unrealistic, then, to expect anyone to prove that A has power over B. One infers power from a whole host of circumstances, including authority relationships (between parents and children, presidents and staff, owners and workers, and so on), resources available, knowledge of the communications between the parties, inferences about their wants and desires, and other matters. In courts of law such inferences are made constantly, centering around the concepts of opportunity, motive, and means. Did the accused, A, have the opportunity to murder the victim, B, the motive to do so, and the means to carry it out? It is in such inferences regarding power that all ideas about who influences or dominates whom revolve.

Proving power relationships is therefore impossible. The causal connections in human activities are too complicated to unravel—especially if we include such factors as societal influences, what is going on in people's heads, what they would have done anyway, and so on.

In the absence of proof, one makes inferences. This generalization applies to all of political science, not just to the questions of property and corporate power that are being examined here. Those who study international relations, or roll-call votes in Congress, or actions of the president, or political campaigns, or what have you, must infer relationships of power to be able to say that A "caused" B. Those who study elections, for example, or public opinion, *assume* that the relationship between the "will of the people" and policy outcomes is important. In doing their research they further assume that the statistical relationships they find are also *causal* relationships (if they talk about power). While statistical relationships are important and significant findings from which to *infer* causal relationships, we should not assume that they prove causality.

## IDEOLOGICAL BLINDERS

I am making the argument in this book that those with property, and especially those who control corporate property, dominate the American political process. They transform their economic resources into political power, and at all levels: in the creation and teaching of ideology in the society itself; in the determination of what issues are important (agenda setting); in the selection of candidates; in the election process; in what goes on at the legislative level; in the bureaucracy and regulatory agencies; and in the interpretation and enforcement of public policy. This is, obviously, a large order. But it is no larger than proving that the democratic process, through elections, determines public policy. One cannot prove either one. One can simply look at the data and make inferences. One can only attempt to demonstrate, through data and argument, that what one says makes sense.

There is also another problem. What I am suggesting here is *contrary* to the democratic ideology that we all learned as we grew up. Not only have we been taught that the system actually works according to democratic ideology, we have also learned that this is how it *ought* to work. Hence our impulse is to apply much more stringent standards of demonstration on someone who is suggesting power relationships contrary to those that are already assumed, believed in, and even revered. We might even demand the impossible, that the person *prove* it. Our only "solution" to the problem of inference and the difficulty of demonstration is to present, in as coherent a fashion as possible, the available data.

One of the functions of an ideology, however, is to encourage people to believe something without looking very closely at the data, as though it were *already* demonstrated that what the ideology says is true, and perhaps as though it were already proven or somehow unnecessary to prove. Hence those who provide an interpretation which is different from the ideology might be called upon to provide incontrovertable proof of their argument and that the ideology generally believed in would be permitted to exist with less substantial evidence.

Powerful forces of "good and "bad" are operating here. As we have already seen, ideologies are not only statements about what goes on, they are also *valued* statements. Data and arguments that go against what is thought of as good may be seen as untrue simply because they do not conform to the valued parts of the ideology. The truth of something, however, has nothing to do with its goodness. Indeed, part of the reason we have for wanting to change things is that what we see does not conform to our ideals. On the other hand, if what we see—or what we think we see because we are reluctant to look or are encouraged not to look—already conforms to our ideals, then we have less trouble in looking at what is out there. And if we do look, what we are likely to search for and find is what we already have been taught to believe is there. And not only that, we are also likely to conclude that data and arguments that controvert what we believe is "there" are not only wrong but "bad." Thus the status quo is likely to remain intact—which, of course, is exactly what those who support the ideology want to happen. (This argument about what one is likely to "see," by the way, is as true of those who write about politics as it is about those who read about it.)

## PROBLEMS IN STUDYING POWER RELATIONSHIPS

Let us look, then, more closely at some of the particular problems of studying power relationships in the United States. Politics is concerned with who gets what and how. Almost everyone agrees with that. There are winners and losers. We have already gone a long way in describing the who and the what. Property, as Madison has told us, is the most important component of what there is to win or lose. Property, as the data have told us, is very unequally distributed in the United States, not only among individual persons but among corporate "persons" as well. The next chapters will be concerned with the how. Put in courtroom terms, we have already discussed motive and opportunity—we shall now concentrate on means.

It should be clear, however, that we can only *suggest* the general lines of influence and communication between the corporate sector and government. We shall not be able to show *exactly* what goes on in terms of conversations, agreements reached, money and favors changing hands, informal understandings, what "really" caused someone to act in such and such a way, and so on. However, we shall be able to give a number of examples of how the general process works. We can then infer from these examples that such communications and influence are probable in other cases—and even, in the examples we have given, that they *have* taken place.

We are made aware of these examples daily through the work of some very persistent and hard-working journalists and researchers who collect bits and pieces of information from which demonstrations of power can be constructed. Sometimes this all comes together neatly, as in Watergate, for example, or in other case studies of particular political interests and activities. Indeed, the literature is filled with just such *examples*. But while examples, like statistics, help demonstrate the plausibility of a general thesis, they do not prove it. It is difficult to demonstrate what is inherently impossible to prove, primarily because what we really want is proof, not simply interesting or plausible interpretations. In addition, the impossibility of providing absolute proof permits a multitude of different, and even competing, interpretations. For every demonstration, no matter how cogently argued, and no matter how much data are offered as evidence, there are likely to be other interpretations and other data. The impossibility of proving something presents us with a dilemma: which of several interpretations shall we believe?

There is no simple answer to this question. In part the answer will be determined by what we believe already and how satisfied or dissatisfied we are with how well our current beliefs square with the constant flow of new information that inundates us daily. The answer is partly affected by how much data are brought to bear on the argument and how convincing the data are. The answer also depends upon how well the author argues his or her position. Ultimately, we will decide which interpretation makes the most sense. Or we may decide not to decide at all, that the problems and work involved in making such a decision require too big an effort.

There *are* competing interpretations of American politics. One is the prevailing ideology: the belief that public policy decisions represent ''the will of the people'' as expressed primarily through elections, that justice and equality exist at some reasonable level, that no single set of people dominates the political scene, and that politics concerns majority rule and to some extent minority rights as embodied in the first ten amendments to the Constitution. Certainly nothing in our ideology emphasizes the importance of the gross concentration of wealth and income in the hands of individuals and corporations. Rather, if inequalities are ever mentioned, they are seen as merited, as part of the individualistic tradition of America, and are treated as a consequence of our freedoms, not, as Madison forthrightly suggested, as touching the very foundation of our government. The ideology of capitalism, which stresses property rights, is kept fairly separate from the democratic creed and is usually treated as derivative of, though congruent with, our political freedoms and individual liberty. (However, the capitalist creed, which stresses free competitive markets, is just as strongly belied by the data as is the democratic creed, which stresses individual participation and competition within the electorate. But more of that in the following chapters.)

The premises of the argument I am making, as an *explanation* of how politics works, not as a justification for it, are expressed in Chapters 1 and 2, and suggest that property is in fact what politics is all about, and that societies, all societies, develop ideologies, and institutions which propogate them, for the purpose of justifying property relations, relations that are rarely stated explicitly, at least not in the democratic creed (Madison's Federalist No. 10 being a significant exception in this regard). To understand American politics it is necessary to understand, not the capitalist *creed,* but the economic practices which actually describe the economy and the consequences of these practices on the distribution of wealth and income within the population and within corporations. This argument has already been developed in Chapters 3, 4 and 5.

In deciding which interpretation is correct one might compare the ideology with other interpretations (the one in this book is certainly not the only alternative), using the criteria mentioned above: (l) Is the argument congruent with what you already know? (2) Is there a good deal of data, and is it convincing? (3) Is the author's position well argued? Three Yes's will undoubtedly buy you into a position; two or one will leave you less convinced. Notice, however, that one of the questions asks you to check the interpretation with how satisfied you are with what you already know. If you agree with the prevailing ideology of American politics concerning how governmental decisions are made and the crucial role that elections are said to play, then you will probably be less demanding about the answers to questions two and three. In other words, the prevailing ideology has a head start on all the others. One arguing a contrary position will have to be particularly persuasive.

The process of demonstrating power relationships, then, and providing interpretations of them, is a twofold task. It is the responsibility of the researcher to provide the best data and argument he or she can. But it is also the responsibility of the reader to sift through, with as open a mind as possible, what he or she has read and to assess how well the thesis has been demonstrated. This is obviously not a trivial task, since what we believe and do not believe is at stake. It is also not an easy one and is sometimes even frustrating, since what we really want in arguments is something we cannot have: absolute proof. Just remember, however, that this problem exists for any interpretation that you believe, and that you are also highly likely to believe in something. (Of course, whatever you do believe about power in America can never be proved either.)

## PRIVATE COMMUNICATIONS AND COVER-UPS

There are several very important reasons why it is so difficult to demonstrate that those who control property dominate the American political system (indeed, constitute a somewhat separate political system of their own). These reasons are related both to *how* these communications and understandings are accomplished, and how politics in general is usually studied.

The major problem is a lack of access to what are obviously private, hidden, and even secret communications. Let me give two examples: one in which, twelve years later, the data were finally made available; and one in which the data were still in the process of being collected.

The first example concerns a secret meeting between President Nixon and the two top executives of the Ford Motor Company, including Henry Ford II himself. It is an excellent example of secret corporate-government communications, in this case even bypassing the secretary of transportation under whose jurisdiction the matter lay. The relevant White House tape, eventually released by Nixon in order not to have to testify at a trial, contains the exact words of the parties involved, a rare research finding for those interested in establishing that these communications actually take place and what exactly is said. The following story was reported by Allan Parachini in the *Los Angeles Times*.[1]

### Tape Reveals Nixon Move
### to Suppress Air-Bag Rules

The two top executives of Ford Motor Co. met secretly with then-President Richard M. Nixon in 1971 in an apparently successful effort to quash federal regulations that would have put air bags in every new car sold in the United States, a long-sought White House tape discloses.

And auto safety experts say, the actions taken as a result of that decade-old secret meeting have been a key factor in keeping the safety devices out of automobiles sold in this country.

"That conference and what apparently flowed from it have made a very important contribution to the fact that, still today, Americans cannot buy

[1]Allan Parachini, *Los Angeles Times* (November 29, 1982), pp. 1, 12. Reprinted by permission of the *Los Angeles Times*.

air-bag protection at any cost, in any car," said Ben Kelley, senior vice president of the Insurance Institute for Highway Safety.

Although there have been rumors in auto industry circles for more than a decade that such a meeting took place, its existence was never verified—or even officially acknowledged—until a transcript of a White House tape recording of the meeting surfaced recently.

The meeting, on April 27, 1971, was attended by Nixon, John D. Ehrlichman, his domestic affairs adviser, and Henry Ford II and Lee A. Iacocca, then the two top executives of Ford Motor Co.

Years later, according to Kelley, Ehrlichman boasted to him that he had put a stop to the air-bag rules.

At the beginning of the Oval Office meeting, Nixon pointedly told Ford and Iacocca that the conversation would be kept in the strictest confidence. Later, he told the two auto executives that Ehrlichman was their White House contact in the confidential air-bag matter.

Attempts to obtain reaction from the present management of Ford Motor Co. were unsuccessful. Henry Ford stepped down from his post two years ago and Iacocca now heads the Chrysler Corp.

Although a chronology of events assembled from National Highway Traffic Safety Administration documents confirms that Erhrlichman subsequently intervened in the air-bag rule-making process—not even John A. Volpe, Nixon's secretary of transportation, was told of the secret meeting between the President and the Ford executives.

Volpe told The Times that he had heard rumors about such a conference but had never been able to get White House officials to confirm it.

"The suspicion has to enter your mind that if they (Ford and Iacocca) go directly to the White House, that they must have had something in mind," Volpe said. "Why did they have to do this? I can imagine that they didn't get the answer from me that they wanted."

WANTED REGULATION KILLED

What the Ford executives wanted, the tape transcript shows, was for Nixon to quash a then-pending federal regulation that would have required air bags on every new car, starting with the 1973 model year. The rule was subsequently rescinded by the Department of Transportation.

Although the House investigations subcommittee had twice—in 1975 and 1980—attempted to obtain transcripts of White House tapes of any such meeting, neither attempt was successful.

Attorneys for the House Commerce subcommittee said the panel suspected that the secret conference, if it occurred, may have constituted "improper, back-door" influence by Ford Motor Co. A 1976 report by the subcommittee concluded that Ehrlichman, in a confidential memo, had ordered the Transportation Department to delay imposition of the air bags regulation.

Now, a transcript of a tape recording of the meeting has been disclosed in a Pennsylvania wrongful death suit filed against Ford Motor Co. by the parents of a teen-age girl killed in the crash of one of the company's cars. The transcript confirms that the meeting occurred and that Nixon ordered Ehrlichman to intervene in the air-bag matter. An out-of-court settlement terminated the Pennsylvania suit.

The transcript shows also that:

—Although Ford Motor Co. was officially urging at the time that an interlock device to force auto passengers to use their seat belts was an acceptable substitute for air bags, even Henry Ford recognized that the interlock—which emitted a loud buzzing noise if belts were not fastened—would be unacceptable to the public.

Ford, in fact, volunteered to Nixon, the transcript shows, that, although it would be illegal for new car dealers to disconnect the interlocks, customers would simply take their cars to independent garages to have the devices disabled.

—Although Nixon agreed that the interlocks—subsequently required as an air-bag substitute in 1973 through 1975 model cars—were sufficient, the President said he would "never" have one of "these damn gadgets" on his own car.

## PROFITS AFFECTED BY SAFETY

—Although Ford Motor Co. was publicly saying it was concerned with designing safety features into its cars, Iacocca, in his comments to Nixon, ridiculed two key safety devices. "The shoulder harnesses (meaning seat belts that fasten over the shoulder) and the head rests are complete wastes of money," he flatly told the President.

—Although Ford Motor Co. recognized that federal safety standards save lives, Ford and Iacocca repeatedly stressed that their firm's profits would be affected by the standards, leading to their pleas for relief.

—Nixon dismissed the environmental, auto safety and consumer movements as "a group of people that aren't one really damn bit interested in safety or clean air. What they're interested in is destroying the system."

The President added, "The safety thing is the kick, because (consumer advocate Ralph) Nader's running around, squealing about this and that and the other thing. We can't have a completely safe society or safe highways or safe cars."

Even at the time of the 1971 meeting, Ford and Iacocca concluded that Ford Motor Co. was an "inefficient" firm that would be hard put to compete on an even footing with foreign car makers, whom Nixon referred to as "the Japs."

Although the investigations subcommittee of the House Commerce Committee tried twice to get transcripts of the White House tape of the 35-minute-meeting, investigators were unsuccessful because the tape was one of hundreds whose release is controlled by Nixon.

"We were checking into this," said former U.S. Rep. Bob Eckhardt (D-Tex.), chairman of the investigations subcommittee in 1980, "because we were fighting what was apparently a rather underhanded way of avoiding the law." Eckhardt presided over the most recent congressional attempt to obtain release of the tape transcript.

Washington attorney Michael Lemov, chief counsel to the committee at the time of the 1975 investigation, said, "There is no question about it" that the newly released transcript establishes that apparently improper influence was exerted on the air-bag regulation process as a result of the secret White House conference.

Air bags have been delayed, in one way or another, continuously ever since. The Reagan Administration, which has tried to kill the air-bag standard entirely, is now being challenged on that decision in the U.S. Supreme Court by a coalition of insurance companies and consumer groups.

The release provisions for the tape in question were established when, after Nixon resigned in the wake of the Watergate scandal in 1973, his White House tapes were taken over by the Archives of the United States.

Except for tapes bearing directly on Watergate-related matters, however, release of information from them is still under Nixon's control.

The former President finally agreed to release of the Ford Motor Co. tape as part of a settlement that quashed a subpoena that had been issued for him to testify in the Pennsylvania accident case.

On Nov. 18, an obscure lawyers' newsletter published the transcript as it had been accepted in evidence in the Pennsylvania court.

This story involves a conversation and agreement that was denied ever to have taken place and for which the facts did not emerge until twelve years later. The second example involves the continuing attempts to find out what exactly transpired in the Environmental Protection Agency (EPA), a regulatory agency of the U.S. government, during the tenure of Anne M. Burford, its chief administrative officer.[2]

A $1.6-billion "superfund" had been established by Congress to clean up toxic waste dumps. Anne M. Burford was cited for contempt of Congress on December 16, 1982, for refusing to hand over documents requested by a congressional committee looking into a number of charges, including:

1. "sweetheart deals" with the industries involved;
2. the 1982 congressional campaign manipulation of funds for political purposes;
3. shredding of documents;
4. destroying appointment calendars;
5. conflict of interest in negotiations with industry.

The following story, reported by Eleanor Randolph in the *Los Angeles Times,* presents what was known to that point.[3] Congress, the Justice Department, and the FBI are still investigating.

### Burford Problems Reflect
### Reagan Ecology Approach

WASHINGTON—Two years ago, when Anne McGill Burford took command of the Environmental Protection Agency, she was a woman with a mandate direct from the President himself: to turn around what the new Administration saw as a rebellious outpost of liberal zealots whose anti-business attitudes were unfairly stifling business.

[2]Formerly Anne M. Gorsuch (she was married while still in office). Mrs. Burford resigned on March 9, 1983.

[3]Eleanor Randolph, *Los Angeles Times* (March 10, 1983), p. 1, 12, 13. Reprinted by permission of the *Los Angeles Times.*

Now, after almost three months of conflict with Congress and a widening inquiry by the Justice Department, Burford has stepped down amid charges that the agency she presided over had become too cozy with the polluters it was supposed to control.

The former Colorado legislator, known for her tough, conservative-political views, had little experience with the complex technical problems posed by environmental hazards. Nor was she experienced in managing a sizable government agency. As a result, she was a tempting target for congressional Democrats.

In a larger sense, however, Burford's problems were not personal. Rather, they were symptomatic of problems with the basic approach of the Reagan Administration to a serious and emotion-charged national dilemma: how to clean up toxic chemical dump sites all across the country that threaten the lives and health of millions of Americans.

As several senior White House aides have acknowledged in recent interviews, the controversy swirling around Burford runs far deeper than a handful of EPA officials having too many lunches with polluters or of paper shredders that mysteriously appeared in offices where there were key EPA documents being requested by congressional committees.

Although the EPA had been created during the administration of former President Richard M. Nixon and nurtured during former President Gerald R. Ford's years, the Reagan team came to office declaring that "balance" must be restored to enforcement of the nation's pollution laws after the "do-gooder" excesses of President Jimmy Carter's appointees.

What may have started out as an effort to hear industry's side of the story, however, began to look like an effort to circumvent the federal government's relatively new "superfund" program, created by Congress to clean up toxic waste dumps.

And, beneath the undoubted political grandstanding of some in Congress, the controversy was fueled by the fear among increasing numbers of Americans about the witches' brew of toxic chemicals that are in their air, their water, their food and perhaps their bodies.

It was that fear that created a political explosion when congressional investigators charged that the $1.6-billion superfund set up by Congress in 1980 was being misused or manipulated politically. The fund, a national trust account built up with money from the chemical industry, was designed to clean up the worst toxic dumps, like Love Canal in New York.

For the White House, the political disaster came when a cast of characters at EPA appeared before congressional committees to explain why they were spending most of their time listening to representatives of the industries whose names are on the drums and tank cars in hundreds of hazardous waste dumps around the country. They were charged with making "sweetheart deals" with the companies they were supposed to be regulating.

Among the key players are the following:

—Rita M. Lavelle, a former public information official with Aerojet Rocket Liquid Corp. in Sacramento and a longtime friend of presidential counselor Edwin Meese III, was fired by President Reagan Feb. 7 after being accused by Burford and others within the agency of promoting the concerns of business too vigorously in settlement cases involving cleanup of toxic dumps.

Lavelle's personal calendar shows that she was wined and dined by representatives of chemical companies at some of Washington's most expensive restaurants, an apparent violation of agency ethics regulations. Lavelle—a bouncy Reagan loyalist who worked for then-Gov. Reagan as a press researcher after she was graduated from college—has insisted that she was doing the job required by the President and Burford when she spent most of her time working as a "salesman" trying to talk industry into negotiating cleanup deals with the agency.

—James W. Sanderson, a Denver lawyer whose private clients have included Adolph Coors Co. and the Denver Water Board, is being investigated by the Justice Department to determine whether he used his inside knowledge at EPA to help his private clients or clients of his law firm that might be affected by the agency's regulations.

## LIFTING OF BAN ON DUMPING

The most serious charge being looked into by the FBI is that Sanderson participated in agency discussions about whether a ban on allowing dumping of liquids in landfills should be lifted for several months. One of his law firm's clients is Chemical Waste Management, which owns a dump near Denver and which dumped 1,500 barrels of liquids within a few days after Burford lifted the ban on Feb. 18, 1982.

The "window" on dumping of liquid chemicals in ordinary landfills was closed shortly afterward because of intense public criticism.

Burford originally wanted Sanderson to fill the No. 3 post in her agency but the White House, which had been pushing for months to get her to fire Sanderson, refused, and Sanderson backed out of the job.

—Robert Perry, chief counsel for EPA, was an attorney at Exxon for 12 years before joining the agency. Perry is the latest counsel in charge of enforcing environmental laws after Burford reorganized the enforcement operation three times—provoking criticism that she was trying to defang the agency's legal branch.

The first appointee to the position was Frank Shepherd, a Miami attorney who helped in President Reagan's 1980 campaign in Florida but was forced to resign about three months after Burford appointed him. Perry, who was constantly at odds with Lavelle before her resignation, is being investigated by the House Commerce Committee oversight subcommittee on charges that he lied about whether he kept "green books" or personnel files on key employees Burford wanted to fire.

—John A. Todhunter, assistant EPA administrator for pesticides and toxic substances, is being investigated by the agency's inspector general, Charles Dempsey, on charges that he erased and destroyed his personal calendars, which have been requested by House subcommittees investigating the EPA.

Todhunter has said through spokesmen that recent erasures were caused by changes in his schedule, but he has acknowledged that he destroyed calendars on a month-to-month basis after an attorney told him last year that such items are misleading and could be harmful in potential lawsuits.

He is also being questioned about a noncompetitive contract awarded last year to a company that paid him for services in 1981 and about whether he softened agency rules on formaldehyde use after sessions with industry representatives.

## RESIGNED UNDER PRESSURE

—John Horton, former assistant administrator for administration, is a New Jersey businessman who also worked in Reagan's 1980 campaign. Horton resigned under pressure from the White House after it was disclosed that he was being investigated for alleged use of government staff, phones and equipment for private business.

—Matthew Novick, inspector general at the agency, also resigned at the White House's request after it was reported that he was being investigated for using his secretary to do private business work. The White House moved in replacements for Novick, Lavelle and Horton on Feb. 24 as part of an effort to give Burford a "fresh start" with a new management team.

At issue finally, however, was what the EPA team accomplished and whether its approach to the regulated industry, favoring conciliation and negotiation rather than long court battles, has eroded environmental laws enacted over the last decade.

Burford, who is considered a bright lawyer who came to the job with no managerial experience, said that she achieved "a great amount of progress" in her term of office. She told congressional committees over the last few weeks that she was "proud" of changes at the agency that made it more efficient and responsive to the primary goal of cleaning up the environment.

However, Burford, a soft-spoken woman who never raised her voice during bouts with congressional critics and was known to lose her temper only in private, came under increasingly intense criticism from Republicans as well as Democrats for her changes at the agency.

Among the most controversial were the following:

—Budget cuts, which have pared the agency's spending from $1.25 billion to $826 million since Burford took office. The cuts, which Burford repeatedly has said are not harmful to the agency's purpose, are even more dramatic because the agency has been receiving superfund money.

—Morale, which has been low among some more action-oriented EPA officials since Burford took over, has plummeted in the last few months. As a result, talented EPA employees have slowly found other jobs. At the same time, the number of persons working at the agency has dropped from 14,000 in January, 1981, to about 11,000 at present.

—Authority is steadily being shifted from EPA in Washington to state governments, a much publicized goal of the agency. However, at the same time, federal grants to the states by EPA are diminishing, leaving the states with less money and more authority.

## BLOCKAGE OF GRANT ALLEGED

Against that general backdrop of change at EPA have come specific charges. One of the most common allegations from House Democrats is that the agency has used the superfund for political reasons, in some cases speeding up announcements of grants—which is not particularly unusual for any Administration. On a more serious note, the Congress and the Justice Department are investigating charges that Burford blocked a $6.1-million grant to clean up one of California's worst dump sites, Stringfellow Acid Pits, near Riverside.

The Times reported last week that White House officials have been told that at least two Administration officials heard Burford say on Aug. 4 during a luncheon aboard the former presidential yacht Sequoia that she had held up the grant because it might give a political boost to then-Gov. Edmund G. Brown Jr. in his campaign for the Senate. She assumed, it is said, that Brown would take credit for cleaning up Stringfellow.

In addition, congressional investigators believe that they have evidence that Burford and Lavelle, who ran the superfund program, held up another grant for the Reilly Tar and Chemical Co. outside Minneapolis in an effort to provide political cover for the Stringfellow delay.

Rep. Gerry Sikorski (D-Minn.) argued recently that the EPA has "acted with either incompetence or outright wrongdoing" in handling the $1.9-million superfund grant for the Minnesota site. The grant was announced with great fanfare last August but then was delayed for four months while, Lavelle said, the EPA was deciding whether more state money should be contributed to the cleanup. Similarly, EPA officials said that the delay at Stringfellow happened in large part because the EPA had decided that California should chip in more state money to help with the site work.

Minnesota officials have argued that the delay until December, when EPA decided the state did not need to contribute the additional funds after all, means that now the site will not be cleared for another six months to a year because of the difficulty of working in the harsh winter.

However, the key to Burford's ouster undoubtedly comes from the thousands of Americans like Susan Wirsch, 35, whose family home in Hamilton, Ohio, sits across the street from thousands of rusting chemical drums, their deadly contents seeping into the ground and vaporizing into the air of her neighborhood.

## "SOMEBODY IS ALWAYS COMING"

"They keep telling us somebody's coming. Somebody is always coming to clean it up," she said, shrugging her shoulders about the Chem-Dyne Corp. dump, which was abandoned three years ago and named one of the nation's worst chemical burial grounds.

"But all we get is red tape and government b.s.," Wirsch said. "It'll be 10 years before anybody moves that junk, mark my words."

For people like the Wirsch family, who must drive their children across town when the wind blows its acrid pharmaceutical odor their way, the controversy over the EPA in recent months uncovers what they have seen and smelled first-hand for years.

"Nobody cares about us," said Wirsch, a Reagan supporter in the 1980 election. "Especially not in Washington."

Indeed, the White House, preparing for the 1984 presidential election campaign, will have to convince Americans who are frustrated and afraid of what is happening to their air and water that this Administration has not given some of the companies that put pollutants there the final control over who cleans them up.

These two examples illustrate not only the types of negotiations that take place between government and corporations, and the efforts to cover up what is taking place, but also the excellent investigative reporting that can be done by journalists who attempt to penetrate behind the wall of secrecy, and denial of information which makes it so extremely difficult for the American public, let alone diligent researchers, to discover what is really going on.

## THE EXCLUSION OF ECONOMICS
## FROM POLITICAL SCIENCE

Besides the difficulty of access to information, there is a second major factor related to the study of corporate power that merits further discussion. We touched upon this matter earlier in the chapter. It is a sensitive issue, since it has to do with what is considered to be legitimate in the context of American ideology.

Most political scientists, though by no means all, who study American politics do so within the democratic model that we have already discussed. They generally avoid economic matters and hence lose the possibility of considering corporate power both in the economy and in government. One can understand very little about American politics—its policies *and* its processes—without knowing something about economics. A familiarity with the field of economics, however, is not a requirement of political science, neither for undergraduate political science majors, nor for those who receive their doctorates and who eventually teach, do research, and write. Hence an important source of data and understanding is systematically *excluded*. Although political scientists do interest themselves in other disciplines, these tend to be the fields of sociology and psychology, not economics.

In part this exclusion has to do with the belief that economics is too difficult. (Economists, in their emphasis on sophisticated mathematical techniques, have done nothing to discourage this perception.) But the whole answer does not lie there, since sophisticated mathematical techniques are frequently employed in a number of areas by political scientists, especially in studies of voting and political participation.

In part the reason also has to do with the fact that many feel that economics is irrelevant to an understanding of politics. And in fact, for all practical purposes, it is—that is, economics *is* all but irrelevant to the way in which politics in the United States is *actually* studied. That the *idea* of its irrelevance may have some basis in ideological considerations will be considered shortly.

There is little information on the connections between economics and politics, then, because very few scholars know very much, or even care about, the economic component of the relationship between the two. For example, that there are 820 government advisory boards (discussed in Chapter 5) to facilitate continuous discussions between corporate leaders and government officials is something I learned in a book on economics (Herman, 1981) and have never seen discussed in a book on political science. Data are relevant only if the area in which they lie is seen as relevant. While economics is excluded from political science, economic data are obviously relevant to the question of how public policy is made.

The study of economics, like that of politics, also has its ideology: capitalism. One must look past this ideology, as one must look past democratic ideology, to discover the facts about the economic system and how it functions. A good deal of economic data *does* show direct linkages between the economic sector—particularly the concentrated corporate sector—and government. One cannot include this data in an explanation of American politics if one does not read it.

In addition to the problem of the divorce between politics and economics (it may even be one of the factors that is responsible for it) is another consideration that is inevitably raised when economic data are used in conjunction with the democratic creed. Since U.S. political ideology emphasizes democratic decision-making, equality and justice, and political participation, mainly through elections, *actual* economic and political data on how both systems in fact function together are likely to belie what is exposed in the democratic and economic creeds themselves. That is, the use of actual economic data concerning the distribution of wealth and economic power within the corporate sector, and the manner in which government assists in this concentration of wealth is *inherently critical. The data simply do not square with either ideology and are all the more damaging when they are combined.*

In some sense, of course, we should expect this. After all, the ideology represents, at least in part, an *ideal,* and ideals are never reached. But while this is true, it is also true that the ideology is taught and learned as though it were in fact *real,* not just ideal. People don't just believe that the United States *should be* a democracy—they believe the United States *is* a democracy. Indeed, many readers may already be shocked, even to the point of disbelief, by the data that we have already presented.

## CRITICIZING INEQUALITY

All societies will devise means to protect themselves and their ideologies from criticism. One of the reasons why the press is constantly in conflict with presidents, for example, is that journalists look for actual facts that go beyond what presidents and their spokespersons tell them. But journalists, after all, are just looking for "news." They are not so much interested in being critical as they are in "getting the scoop," writing a good story, and collecting facts on their own that may or may not support what they are being told from official sources. The problem of being "critical" is even more serious for those who use economic data to analyze American politics, for indeed the data do produce the picture we have drawn in the first five chapters of this book.

This leads us, inevitably, into an explosive issue, because we run right smack into another, and very *powerful,* component of American ideology. Those who use economic data that put the American democratic and economic creeds in a bad light are often labeled with a term that is anathema to both creeds: *"left-ist."* This word has a variety of meanings (socialist, communist, even liberal); but regardless of the disagreements about what positions constitute "leftist" politics, it is certainly easy to agree that the word itself is a term of opprobrium. People who are called "leftists" are rarely being complimented.

All of us are aware of how important economic well-being is to our lives, especially since we live in a country that stresses material comfort. Indeed, most of us are proud of this country's economic prosperity. On the other hand, if it is pointed out how material wealth is in fact distributed, or if it is suggested that economic matters are at the very core of our political system, that is somehow crossing the boundary—at least for many people—between what is permissible and what is impermissible to say. Defenses against the incontrovertable data on the grossly unequal distribution of wealth and income, for both individuals and within the corporate sector, are likely to range widely. By and large, the major defense is that we are a land of opportunity, and if one works hard enough one can succeed. That is, the rich deserve what they have because they have earned it.

However, this justification for inequality itself holds some difficulties, especially with respect to the question of wages (remember that 29 percent of the work force earns *less* than the minimum wage), and with respect to inheritances. We shall have more to say about these matters in the chapters that follow. But another way to protect oneself against these data is to charge that those who use them to explain political events are speaking in a manner which puts them beyond the pale as far as legitimate American politics is concerned.

There are historical reasons for this, having to do, of course, with the very large presence of Karl Marx as one of the first, and certainly the major, interpreter of the role of economics in society and politics. There is also the conflict in the world between the USSR and the United States, the former the chief proponent of communism, the latter the major proponent of capitalism. Hence, according to many people—and this is a response that is encouraged extensively in the polity, in society, and in the economy—if one uses economic data that are critical of the ideology, one is "leftist," perhaps even "Marxist." I would like to say a few tough words about this.

If one is what is called leftist, one is likely to be critical of American politics. But it is an elementary logical fallacy, and in some noteworthy cases a monumental moral error, to assume that if one is critical one is leftist. There are many reasons for being critical other than those having to do with political beliefs.

I don't happen to be a leftist. What prompts me to use economic data is the realization that, as Madison told us, ownership and control of property are what politics is all about. In reading in sociology and in writing on some nonpolitical subjects, I also came to certain conclusions about the role of ideology in a society: how it is used as a means of social, political, and economic control, and how important it is in giving us our first outlook on what our country is all about. Politics made a lot more sense when I combined my knowledge of it with economics. And when I combined what I knew about politics with certain notions about society and ideology, it made even more sense.

If, in drawing conclusions from the data, I wind up being critical, then so be it. If the data do not fit the ideology, I can't be expected to reject the data. If one notices that the emperor has no clothes when in fact the emperor has no clothes, is that the fault of the observer or the emperor? I would not at all mind if my interpretation of how politics, economics, and society fit together were wrong. To the contrary, I would be delighted. I would mind a great deal, however, if people dismissed my argument because they imputed to me some political position that I don't have.

In the following chapters we shall explore in close detail the relationships between politics, economics, and society. Of course, any discussion of power will be incomplete because absolute proof is not possible. There is simply too much involved in the concept of power to arrive at an air-tight case.

I do invite the reader, however, to read carefully. Holes in the data and in the suggested connections between economic power and political power will be evident. The question is, can we, in the future, fill in these gaps? If we can, then the argument I am making will increase in strength. If we cannot, if the data we collect do not fit, then I would be the first to suggest that we change the argument.

# CHAPTER SEVEN
# THE CORPORATE
# POLITICAL SYSTEM

Given the fact that much of what takes place in politics is not public, it is often difficult to find out not only what is happening but who is making it happen as well. It is, as a consequence, much easier to believe what one is told—about politics or anything else—than it is to find information for oneself. This is especially true if what one is being told is generally believed by everyone else— since one will have little incentive to search—and if the information one finds runs counter to prevailing beliefs. It is far easier to see a tree as a beautiful provider of fruit than as a complex natural system, with sap flowing up and down the trunk and through the branches, nutrients being exchanged through the root system, and photosynthetic processes taking place in the leaves. If we do not probe behind a tree's external beauty, we learn very little about how it functions and what is required to keep it alive.

## LEARNING THE TRUTH ABOUT POLITICS

Most of us learn the broad outlines of the democratic creed in grammar and high school and from our parents. We learn about the Founding Fathers (although not necessarily in sufficient depth to find out what James Madison was talking about in Federalist No. 10), about the struggles of our republic to establish its independence, about the importance of elections and the free enterprise system, and about freedom of speech and religion. We are taught that, in a democracy, government is responsive to the will of the people, and that we live in a democracy.

Because of our early training in the ideology of American government and politics, we know very little indeed, and what we do know is stated in idealized form. A society must have strong support for its government, and all societies attempt to indoctrinate their citizens.

If we wish to learn how government actually works, however, we must push considerably beyond the level of grammar and high-school civics courses. But this enterprise entails considerable risk. If we watch our cat out by the birdfeeder we may, on occasion, see her leap high in the air and catch a bird, kill it, perhaps make a meal of it. If we explore the past of our friends or parents, we may learn things that do not match the image of them we would like to have, or have been taught to have. If we explore the debates and writings concerning the Constitutional Convention in 1787, we learn that protection of personal property was as important a consideration in the founding of this country and its constitution as were the ideas of freedom of speech, press, and religion (indeed, these latter ideas were not even a part of the original constitution but adopted later and written in as amendments).

The purpose of this book is to teach you something about American politics, something more than you have learned in civics classes and from spokespersons within the system itself. It is not an attempt to persuade you to change the American political system, nor to "criticize" it in the sense of disparaging it. Rather, the purpose of this book is *inherently* critical in that it goes considerably beyond the ideology itself and explores the ideology as a fundamental and integral part of the system. What you read, then, is likely to be disappointing—at least in the sense that is does not fulfill the ideological dream of American politics. This, I submit, is not my fault. It is not your fault either. It is simply a part of our education, yours and mind. This book is an explanation of how the American political system functions—not a justification of it nor a polemic against it. It is not my role to tell you what you should do. It is my job, however, to tell you how the system actually functions. If all you know is what you have learned in high school, then you have had your leg pulled. And having your leg pulled continually is a silly way to go through life. All you can do then is to repeat inanities.

The purpose of education, however, is not to propagandize or indoctrinate, at least not beyond high school. A great deal of information is available, although it is not readily accessible to the general public; it has been collected and analyzed by scholars and journalists. We have, for example, drawn upon books, articles, and research reports to provide the information found in this book. Almost none of this information has been discussed by government spokespersons, although some of it, especially the economic data, was collected by government agencies and university professors. Little of this data would be considered ''flattering'' to the American political system.

It is well and good for citizens to be proud of their country. But it is also well and good for them to be so for the right reasons and to possess the right information. It is never wrong to know the truth. One basic truth is that property is important to people. That politics is about the control of property does not make it wrong. It is simply what politics is all about. It is perhaps more comfortable to live in a dream, where right and wrong are clearly discernable and separate, but it has no intellectual merit, and it does not help you to understand. The world is an interesting place, and there is a lot to know about it. To bury one's head in the sand, to cling to one's cherished beliefs, because they are good, is to confuse what is good with what is correct or true. There are a great many young Americans who never came back from Vietnam, a war which almost everyone now repudiates. You can have more than your leg pulled.

The goals of anyone in politics are threefold: (1) to control the general policy-making process; (2) to control the details of specific policies that are of benefit to you in particular; and (3) to control the personnel who will be making, interpreting, and enforcing the policies. The corporate political system is well structured to perform each of these three activities. The number of people involved is reasonably small, they are similar in background, and interest, they meet frequently, they have the same broad goals, and they govern most of what there is to govern in the economic sphere. They also have what can only be called a fabulous treasure chest of funds to underwrite their activities; for all practical purposes they control an unlimited source of money that, in the case of corporate leaders, does not even belong to them. We shall discuss, in turn, each of these three major political activities.

## CORPORATE CONTROL OF GENERAL LINES
## OF PUBLIC POLICY

In order to control the general lines of public policy in this, or any other country, the first thing one might think of doing would be to get rid of, or prevent the formation of, an opposition. In some countries, when an opposition does appear that is funadmentally opposed to the way in which the political or economic system operates, it is severely suppressed. This tactic is not unknown in the United States, and instances of the use of force abound. Indeed, our own revolution in which we fought to escape from British rule is an example. But once our country was established it became necessary, from time to time, to suppress—sometimes through bloodshed—those who desired some fundamental change, or who resisted some fundamental change, in social, political, or economic policy. Although we cannot give a general historical account of the suppression of political, social, and economic groups in the United States, we can mention some of the most important.

## Suppressions of Freedom in the United States

We have already discussed one of the most celebrated, Shays's Rebellion, which took place in 1786 and concerned a revolt by a large group of farmers in Massachusetts who were in peril of losing their farms due to high taxes levied by the state of Massachusetts to help pay off the Revolutionary War debt. There were numerous clashes, and the rebellion was finally quashed by federal troops sent in by the secretary of war under the Articles of Confederation, Henry Knox. A similar farmer's revolt over taxes, the Whiskey Rebellion, occurred in 1794 and was put down by federal troops sent by President Washington.

The Alien and Sedition Acts, under the presidency of John Adams, were legislative efforts by the Federalist party to suppress criticism of the government then being conducted by the defeated presidential candidate Thomas Jefferson and his Republican party, and a number of Jeffersonian newspapers were put out of business.

Our most serious case of political, economic, and social conflict was, of course, the Civil War. At this time the South was producing *seven-eighths* of the world's cotton, using slave labor. Being a large exporter, the South wanted low tariffs on imported goods, not only to be able to purchase whatever it wanted from abroad more cheaply, but also to encourage foreign countries to keep their tariffs on cotton low. The North, on the other hand, was at the start of the Industrial Revolution and wanted its beginning manufacturing interests protected by high tariffs on imported goods. The stage was set, and the resulting war was one of the bloodiest in history.

With the advent of the Industrial Revolution came many disputes, some of them very violent, between labor and the managers of corporations. The two most famous, and costly in terms of human lives, were the Homestead Strike (1892) and the Pullman Strike (1894) in which federal troops were used in both cases on the side of the corporations.

The Palmer raids (Palmer was the U.S. attorney general under President Woodrow Wilson) occurred during this country's first "red scare" (the Bolshevik Revolution had just taken place in Russia), and is a classic example of the suppression of political freedoms (as are the activities of Senator McCarthy during the Eisenhower Administration, and the suppression of the Chicago marchers who protested the Vietnam War during the 1968 Democratic Convention).

The Great Depression during the 1930s witnessed a number of clashes between the unemployed and the corporate-governmental sector, but perhaps the most famous incident during this period was the Bonus Army. Thousands of World War I veterans and their families seeking early payment of a promised veteran's bonus went to Washington, D.C., and camped in tents between the

Capitol building and the George Washington monument. Led by General Douglas MacArthur and his aides, Dwight D. Eisenhower and George S. Patton, the camp was raided, tear gas was used, and the families were forced to flee.

The incidents cited here are examples of conflicts in points of view between one segment of society and another that resulted in the violent suppression of political, economic, and social freedoms and activities. There have also been thousands of instances of racial violence throughout our history, beginning with the slaughter and displacement of the Indians, the treatment of blacks (first as slaves, then—and still—as citizens subject to multiple abuses, not the least of which are economic in nature), and the displacement of thousands of American citizens of Japanese descent who were shuttled off to camps in Utah and Nevada during World War II.

There is, however, a much preferred alternative to the use of force against those who do not accept the prevailing doctrines and patterns of behavior. Instead of forced compliance, societies prefer *voluntary* compliance. This is achieved, as we have already seen, primarily through indoctrination, socialization, and instruction into the prevailing ideology. To exist, societies must have order—and order is achieved either through acceptance of things as they are, or through forced compliance.

All societies have their economic values, and private property and free enterprise are the American ones. In terms of the distribution of property and the control of wealth in this country, those who benefit most from our ideology are those who either possess great wealth or control it. Our major ideological pronouncements thus come from the business and corporate sector and from most public educators.

The business sector works closely with the government; in fact, it is the guiding arm of government. This relationship can be termed the *corporate political process*. Government is thus another major source of the ideology that prevails in this country. In fact, it is the major enforcer of this ideology, and it works very cooperatively and effectively with business in the establishment and enforcement of public policy. And, as we shall see, to a very large extent government officials, at all levels, are beholden to the business community for their positions.

## POLICY-PLANNING GROUPS

Most governmental policy in this country is developed by *policy-planning groups*; these include large interest groups (trade associations) and certain research organizations that are funded primarily by corporations, foundations (whose money comes from corporations), and government. These groups have extensive contacts throughout the government, with each other, and with important segments of the political, economic, social, and cultural structures of this country. Policy-planning groups are composed of a mixture of major corporate leaders (the preponderant group), government officials, and, to a lesser extent, foundation officers and university professors and researchers. Because of their concern with the initial agenda of politics, their relationships are mainly with the executive branch, and more particularly the president's office, since it is the president who controls the major items on the political agenda in this country (budget, taxes, defense, foreign policy, and domestic legislation).

Policy-planning groups are responsible for the major lines of governmental policy. They make proposals with respect to the great issues of taxes and expenditures, foreign policy, the structure of government, energy, law, commerce, transportation, communications, inflation, crime, and economic regulation; and they have the clout to see them through. These groups (with the exception of interest groups) have received little attention by political scientists and economists for several reasons. One reason is that their meetings and considerations are closed to the public (although their conclusions and studies are sometimes published). Another reason is that their power over public policy in this country violates the democratic, electoral process. A final reason is that political scientists and economists have paid relatively little attention to the *agenda-setting process* of politics, clearly the most important function of any political system. Let me give some examples of the major policy-planning groups and interest groups in this country. Much of this data comes from Manheim (1982), Dye (1979), and Dolbeare and Edelman (1981).

*The Business Roundtable.*    One of the most powerful policy-planning groups is the *Business Roundtable,* about which very little is yet known. Founded in 1972, its membership consists of 192 chief executive officers of America's largest corporations. Its major areas of interest are in antitrust, corporate organization, environment, government regulation, employment, and taxes. Given the fact that its members head corporations that represent 50 percent of the nation's business assets, its ability to meet and consult with government officials at the highest level is unquestioned.

*The Committee for Economic Development.*    The *Committee for Economic Development* (CED) is a group of about 200 corporation heads, university presidents, and others, with very close links to other policy-planning groups (the Council on Foreign Relations, the Business Roundtable, the Conference Board, the American Enterprise Institute, and the Brookings Institution). Formed in 1942, the CED has a budget of about $3 million, financed from corporate and foundation contributions. It also has affiliates in Australia, France, Great Britain, Japan, Spain, Sweden, and West Germany. The CED has been instrumental in a number of important public policies, including the Employment Act of 1946 (which, among other things, created the Council of Economic Advisors). It was very important as a policy-planning group under President Carter, especially in the fields of energy, urban problems and unemployment, monetary policy, welfare, and international trade. Its recommendations provide an important contribution to governmental agenda setting. "Recently the committee has focused its attention on general and specific policy recommendations to fight inflation, promote innovation, improve relations between multinational corporations and lesser developed countries, reverse the decline in productivity, stabilize the Social Security System and individual savings patterns, and revitalize urban areas" (Manheim, 1982 p. 121).[1]

*The Conference Board.*   *The Conference Board* is a somewhat larger and broader-based organization with approximately 4,000 corporate, university, and individual members. It is concerned with both domestic and international corporate and financial problems, and has members in forty nations. The main purpose of the Conference Board is to analyze general business trends and to provide data and reports that will be helpful for general policy making. "In recent years the group has increased its emphasis on urban problems, government regulation, and antitrust issues" (Manheim, 1982, p. 122).

In addition to the Business Roundtable, Committee for Economic Development, and the Conference Board, whose interests reside in the broad lines of domestic policy, there are two major policy-planning groups funded and run by the corporate sector that, for all practical purposes, determine our foreign policy. The list of secretaries of state, national security advisers to the president, and others who determine our foreign policy and are members of one or both of these organizations is very long indeed (for example, it includes John Foster Dulles, Dean Acheson, Averell Harriman, Dean Rusk, Henry Kissinger, Cyrus Vance, Zbigniew Brzezinski, Walter Mondale, Harold Brown, Jimmy Carter, and many others).

*The Council on Foreign Relations.*   The more important of these two groups is the Council on Foreign Relations, with approximately 2,000 members, 1,500 of whom come from the corporate, banking, and legal sectors. The major sources of funding for this group are corporate contributions, dues and subscriptions, foundation grants, and its own endowment. The Council on Foreign Relations has been active in all major policy initiatives, including U.S.-USSR relations, the Vietnam War, and nuclear armament and defense; it is also interested in the structure of the world economy, oil, international finance, and other economic questions that obviously have a great impact on political policy.

*The Trilateral Commission.*   The second of the two foreign-policy-planning groups is the Trilateral Commission, established in 1972 by the head of the

---

[1] This and the citations on preceding pages are from *American Politics Yearbook 1982–83* by Jarol B. Manheim. Copyright © 1982 by Longman Inc. Reprinted by permission of Longman Inc., New York.

Council on Foreign Relations, David Rockefeller. The Trilateral Commission is composed of a small (about 260) number of corporation heads and government officials from the United States, Japan, and Western Europe. Its purpose is to coordinate policy among these industrialized nations and the multinational corporations, which control most of the economic relations both within the Western countries, and between them and the nations of the Third World.

There are a number of general points to be made about these five policy-planning groups and their dominance in both domestic and foreign policy. First, and foremost, is that these are *supracorporate groups,* the majority of whose members are the heads of our largest corporations. Second, their interest tends to be in policy matters that affect the economy (and the world) as a whole. That is, they represent a wide range of corporate interests (industry, banking, foreign trade, communications, transportation, and utilities) and serve as forums for cooperation among these large commercial, financial, and industrial sectors. Third, there is a good deal of overlap of personnel and of cooperation among these policy-planning groups. Fourth, the members who are not directly part of the large corporate sector are associated with foundations, universities, the mass media, and government, and serve as important links between the corporate and other sectors of the society. Fifth, these organizations also have important ties with similar leaders in foreign countries. And sixth, the heavy concentration of corporate and economic interests within these groups makes it clear that the major concerns of public policy in this country, and between this country and other countries, are *economic.* That is, political policy is formulated, proposed, and directed by those who have a clear economic stake in those policies. Property— once again, as we have already learned from Madison—is the basis of politics, and corporate property is the major form of wealth in the twentieth century.

## Research Organizations

There are also a number of ''auxiliary'' policy-planning groups that are funded and directed by corporate leaders. Their resources come overwhelmingly from foundations and corporations, and their boards of directors are dominated by those in the corporate sector. These policy-planning groups conduct extensive research on the major areas of public policy, the findings of which are then used as the basis of individual foreign and domestic policies. There are five important research organizations of this type, and they are directly linked to corporations, to the five major policy-planning groups, and to foundations, universities, and government.

*The Brookings Institution.*   Perhaps the most important of these auxiliary policy-planning groups is the Brookings Institution, whose board of directors is closely tied to corporations, foundations, and universities, and whose research centers on the major areas of economic policy (taxation, the budget,

Social Security, regulation, inflation, productivity and growth), governmental processes, and foreign policy. The Brookings Institution has been very instrumental in the areas of poverty and welfare, health care, tax policy, and government organization. Its 1980 budget was $9.2 million. It has its own endowment of $42 million, and also receives contributions from corporations, foundations, and government grants.

*The American Enterprise Institute.*   A second major research organization, which has become especially active during the Reagan Administration (Jeane Kirkpatrick, ambassador to the United Nations, and Murray Weidenbaum, chairman of the Council of Economic Advisers, are both members) is the American Enterprise Institute for Public Policy Research. The AEI had a budget of $10 million in 1980 for studies in economic policy, political and social processes, regulatory policy, legal policy, foreign and defense policy, health policy, and American system studies. In contrast to the Brookings Institution, which has a reputation of being a more liberal body, the American Enterprise Institute is quite conservative in its philosophy and in its policy recommendations. Members of Congress and other members of government serve directly on several advisory committees. "At present AEI is supporting studies of defense (personnel, the role of navies, nuclear targeting doctrine, military readiness, financing increased defense spending), the economy (minimum wage, inflation, immigration, food policy, Social Security), energy (price regulation, supply problems), foreign policy (identifying U.S. national interests, investment opportunities in Latin America), government regulation, tax policy, and other issues" (Manheim, 1982, p. 120).

*Resources for the Future.*   Resources for the Future is an auxiliary policy-planning group that conducts extensive research on a number of policy issues concerning the use of natural resources, energy policy, economic growth, and environmental issues. Its 1980 budget was $4.6 million. It receives its funding from a variety of large corporations, foundations, and government agencies. "Recent projects have examined energy in developing countries, energy in the People's Republic of China, energy and national security, politics of radioactive waste, energy taxation, macroeconomic effects of environmental policy, impact of environmental regulation on the economy, alternatives to direct regulation of the environment, agriculture and water quality, implementing the Toxic Substances Control Act, and western water issues" (Manheim, 1982, p. 125).

*The Rand Corporation.*   There are several auxiliary policy-planning groups whose major interests lie in national defense and foreign affairs. The largest of these is the Rand Corporation, with a staff of over 1,000 and about 500 consultants. Its budget was $46.5 million in 1980, of which 89% came from the U.S. government, and 10% from foundations. It is a major source of data, research, and analysis for the Defense Department, the U.S. Army, Navy, and Air Force, and a large number of other governmental agencies. Much of its research is classified. Its board of trustees includes such corporate officers as the chairman of Coca-Cola, the vice president and chief scientist of IBM, the chairman of the Wells Fargo Bank, and the chairman of Citicorp. "Its research divisions include Project Air Force (national security strategies, force deployment, technology applications, resource management), national security (applied science and technology, strategic assessment, international security policy, manpower and mobilization, readiness, information processing systems, security and subnational conflict), domestic (criminal justice, education and human resources, energy policy, health sciences, housing and urban policy, labor and population, regulatory policy and institutions), and an Institute for Civil Justice" (Manheim, 1982, p. 124).

*The Hoover Institution on War, Revolution, and Peace.*    A second auxiliary policy-planning group concerned mainly with foreign affairs, national security, and defense, is the Hoover Institution on War, Revolution, and Peace. Its 1980 budget was $6.6 million, of which 18 percent came from an endowment, 29 percent from Stanford University, 44 percent from individual, foundation, and corporate grants, and 2 percent from the government. Its two most celebrated associates are Philip Habib, President Reagan's Middle East negotiator, and conservative economist Milton Friedman. "Recent Hoover interests include the political implications of Russian nationalism, Eastern European regimes, the Chinese economy, trade unionism and government in Great Britain, Latin America (a comprehensive study is in progress), the draft, health and medical economics, perceptions of U.S. institutions, monetary policy, government regulation of corporate structure, U.S. energy options, and U.S. naval power" (Manheim, 1982, p. 123).

To get some idea of the extent to which the corporate world is represented in these planning groups, and the extent to which personnel flow from the corporate sector to government positions and back again, *each* of the 25 board members of the Council on Foreign Relations averaged 3.7 corporate directorships, and 4.6 government positions during their careers. The figures for the 22 directors on the board of the Committee for Economic Development are an average of 3.8 corporate directorships and 2.8 government positions for each member. The totals for the 20 trustees of the Brookings Institution are very similar: an average of 4.6 corporate directorships and 3.0 government offices held (Dye, 1979, p. 223). Clearly the ties between the corporate sector, government positions, and the boards of directors of policy-planning groups are very close.

The five major supracorporate policy-planning groups (Business Roundtable, Committee for Economic Development, Conference Board, Council on Foreign Relations, and Trilateral Commission), and the five major auxiliary policy-planning groups (Brookings Institution, American Enterprise Institute, Resources for the Future, Rand Corporation, and the Hoover Institution) constitute the heart of corporate control of the major lines of United States domestic and foreign policies. *All* of the major areas of public policy are included: taxes, budget, economic regulation, defense, foreign policy, national security, nuclear weapons and other weapon systems, urban development, highways and transportation, criminal and civil justice, welfare and Social Security, energy policies, housing, natural resources, education, employment, agriculture, immigration, inflation, minimum wage, health, domestic and international finance, monetary policy, multinational corporations, and international trade.

From these groups emerge the major directions of government expenditures and programs. However, they are not only the source of government programs and policies, they are also a major source of government personnel; and, taking the corporations and their officers by themselves, *the* most important source of campaign contributions to political candidates. (We shall return to this subject at the end of the chapter.)

Since it is the president and the executive office, and not the Congress that initiates most domestic and foreign policies, the activities of these groups are centered in the executive branch of the government. This is where public policies are designed and sent on to Congress. A clear distinction should be made, then, between the *policy formation* process, which concerns the vital interests of the corporate sector *taken as a whole,* and in which these major and auxiliary policy-planning groups are dominant, and the *lobbying* process, which is most often associated with the narrower interests of specific corporations, industries, and activities. It is, then, to this latter process, that we now turn.

## CORPORATE CONTROL OF SPECIFIC LINES OF PUBLIC POLICY

Not only do corporate interests control the major lines of public policy through policy-planning groups, and control the content of American ideological thinking about property and free enterprise, but they are also organized and well funded to dominate the policy-making process in detail through what is known as the *interest group,* or *lobbying,* process. In this case, however, the particular corporate interests break up into individual industries, and even individual corporate concerns. There are general interest groups for the major sectors of the economy (agriculture, banking, retail trade, wholesale trade, industry, insurance, transportation, and utilities), and within these large sectors there are trade associations for tobacco, peanuts, cotton, steel, automobiles, mining, oil, natural gas, savings and loan associations, commercial banks, life insurance, and so on. The number of corporate interest groups in this country is very large, and they represent every conceivable type of activity, including individual companies. (Recall that many U.S. corporations are larger in dollar sales than the Gross National

Products of most nations in the world.) The following is a very selected list of the major corporate interest groups and a short sketch of their activities (Manheim, 1982).

*The American Bankers Association.*    The American Bankers Association has a membership of 13,200 banks, a staff of 415, and an annual budget of over $40 million. It works for the specific interests of the banking community (variable rate mortgages, for example), and frequently opposes the interests of the savings and loan associations (against interstate branching, for example). But it has also worked together with savings and loans against the drain of funds away from banks and savings and loan associations into money market funds. In 1982, for example, Congress passed a bill granting banks the right to sell insured money market certificates, and to severely restrict the ability of a home buyer to take over an existing, low-interest-rate mortgage. The legislation also eliminated the difference in interest rates that banks and savings and loans pay for passbook accounts.

*The American Bar Association.*    The American Bar Association has a membership of 550, and a budget of $37 million. This is the major organization representing the legal profession and its interests. One role that it plays in most administrations is that of consultant on Supreme Court nominees by the president. In recent years it has opposed "no-fault" insurance, since such legislation would obviously cut into the workload of many lawyers.

*The American Farm Bureau Federation.*    The AFBF is the largest of the agricultural groups, representing well over three million farmers. It takes positions in favor of governmental programs aiding the farmer (such as direct subsidies and soil banks), and opposes federal spending on welfare and the implementation of the Occupational Safety and Health Act as it applies to agriculture. It is strongly against the unionization of agricultural workers and in favor of the importation of foreign agricultural workers.

*The American Medical Association.*    The American Medical Association has a membership of nearly 250,000 physicians, a staff of nearly 1,000, and a budget of over $62 million, a little over half of which comes from dues, and most of the rest is income from securities and real estate holdings. The AMA resists any attempt to regulate the medical profession and favors increased federal aid for medical education. Interestingly enough, although the medical profession as a whole is against abortion except under certain circumstances, the AMA has supported federal spending for abortion.

*The American Petroleum Institute.*    The American Petroleum Institute, perhaps the most powerful interest group and lobby in the country, given the wealth it represents and the obvious importance of oil, has a membership of 320 corporations, a staff of 460, and a budget of $40 million. It has shown a remarkable ability to win favorable legislation (for example, tax cuts, oil depletion allowances, private development of public lands, and government participation in oil investment guarantees). The API works very closely with various agencies within the government to plan and execute public policy with respect to oil. In many ways it could be considered its own policy-planning group.

*The Edison Electric Institute.*    The Edison Electric Institute represents the investor-owned electric utility companies, whose member corporations provide 77 percent of the nation's electricity. Policy is made by a 45-member board of directors, who represent the association's largest companies. "The group has recently opposed the Department of Energy establishment of energy performance standards for buildings, and favored limiting the Clean Air Act and decentralizing its enforcement, further study (as opposed to legislation) on acid rain, limiting the Clean Water Act, accelerated recovery of capital costs, easing rights-of-way for coal slurry pipelines, coal conversion of power plants with certain safeguards for the industry, and continued nuclear licensing and the separation of licensing from waste disposal considerations" (Manheim, 1982, p.154).

*The National Association of Home Builders.*    Given the recent slump in the housing industry, the National Association of Home Builders has been particularly active in seeking federal legislation to aid their industry. "It seeks a mix of fiscal, tax, regulatory, and monetary policy to reduce interest rates, reduce unemployment, and increase economic growth; a more consistent monetary policy to reduce and stabilize interest rates; emergency housing legislation triggered by a significant decline in housing production; tax incentives for rental apartment construction; revision of the Consumer Price Index to reflect housing costs more accurately; production of government assisted and insured rental units for the poor and elderly at a steady rate; federal discouragement of rent control, discriminatory zoning, and restrictive land use ordinances; developing a strong national energy policy with increased production; creation of tax-exempt housing savings certificates with proceeds to go into mortgages (in effect, an interest-rate subsidy); tax-exempt savings accounts to be applied to a first home purchase; development of a strong secondary market for a variety of uniform mortgages including graduated payment, variable rate, and adjustable; and elimination of the competitive advantage of money market mutual funds over savings and loans" (Manheim, 1982, p. 163).

*The National Association of Manufacturers.*    Representing about 12,000 companies, the National Association of Manufacturers is the major organization representing smaller corporations. It has a staff of 200 and a budget of $10 million. The NAM favors strict control of government spending (mainly in the welfare sector), increased tax advantages for businesses and corporations, reduction of federal regulation of business, and a limiting of federal environmental protection legislation.

*The National Federation of Independent Business.*   The National Federation of Independent Business is the largest of the business associations in terms of numbers, with a membership of over 600,000 businesses, all of them small and most of them unincorporated (that is proprietorships and partnerships). The NFIB does much to promote the idea of free enterprise and to restrict government regulation. Since the executive branch is concerned mostly with the welfare of large business corporations, the NFIB works mainly through Congress and favors strong congressional control over the executive departments, and especially over the independent regulatory agencies. "The group favors cuts in and limits on federal spending, balancing the federal budget, reducing Social Security taxes and separating the retirement fund from other Social Security programs, accelerated depreciation, congressional veto over agency regulations, a sunset law, redirecting the Occupational Safety and Health Administration to a more cooperative role, reducing the minimum wage in small businesses, reorganizing the Small Business Administration, and eliminating estate taxes for small family-owned farms and businesses. Its most recent legislative scorecard includes votes for repealing portions of the Davis-Bacon Act that set prevailing wage requirements, limiting the Occupational Safety and Health Administration's inspections, prohibiting federal energy conservation plans from restricting hours of business, setting a cap on Social Security benefits, a block grant approach to social programs, congressional veto of Federal Trade Commission regulations, continued nuclear power construction, self-insurance cooperatives on product liability, and trucking deregulation" (Manheim, 1982, pp. 169–70).

These are but a few of the literally thousands of interest groups at the federal, state, and local levels that work actively, and spend many hundreds of millions of dollars to promote legislation and government programs in their own interests. Several generalizations can be made about this process.

First, these groups are wealthy, have large full-time staffs, and know intimately the ins and outs of executive, congressional, and agency offices.

Second, they have well-formulated *specific* and *detailed* demands. They usually even draft their own legislative proposals (although these proposals may not, of course, be adopted as they write them).

Third, the groups are sometimes in conflict with each other (big business vs. small business, for example, or commercial banks vs. savings and loan associations). They also frequently work in close cooperation, depending upon their own specific interests and the interests of the other groups. Hence, they do not always get everything they want. On the other hand, these interest groups, together with the policy-planning groups discussed earlier, clearly dominate both the executive and the legislative processes—both in the general formulation of public policy and in its specific details. As we shall see, they and their members contribute the vast majority of all campaign funds.

Fourth, our private-property, free-enterprise ideology has it that what business really wants is to be left alone and that the role of government should be minimal, if not nonexistent. As a corollary to this, we are led to believe that any government activity in the business sector is the result of forces outside of the business-corporate sector that restrain business from operating as it would like to. From even a cursory reading of the extensive and intimate activities of policy-planning groups and interest groups in the government sector, however, the demands by those in the business community for government aid and government programs that help them are very large indeed. Not only do many government activities provide various forms of protection for business (tariffs, for example, and various trade agreements, government activities that are as old as our country itself), but business interests also demand positive steps by government to insure their income (various preferential tax policies, various loan agencies, and subsidy programs), to provide them with resources (land and mineral deposit leases), to establish spending programs that help them grow (expenditures for research, buildings, and equipment, for example), to establish agencies that will help control markets (for example, the Interstate Commerce Commission, the Federal Communications Commission, and the Department of Commerce), and to protect foreign investment. The major demands upon government, in fact, clearly come from those who own property and who want help in both protecting it and in insuring and expanding their wealth. We shall explore the role of government in much more detail in a later chapter, but it should be clear by now that most regulatory, spending, and taxing programs benefit some business group in the economy. There may be others who are opposed to whatever becomes public law, but this is a matter of power among the business groups themselves; and we should not confuse conflict and the consequent winners and losers within the business sector with the idea that most of such conflict occurs within the business sector itself.

This is not to say that the *only* function of government is to respond to the overall needs of the business-corporate community and to settle conflicts among the various economic sectors. Government also has other functions, including at least some of those items in the Preamble to the Constitution of the United States: "insure domestic tranquility, provide for the common defense, and promote the general welfare." Domestic tranquility usually means the protection of property against those who have none; and national defense can mean defending the resources, markets, and economic interests controlled by large corporations. But general welfare is also a function of government, and it is here that there is likely to be the greatest division between corporate interests and the general population. In addition to subsidies and programs that benefit business, there are also subsidies and programs that benefit the poor (although the amount of the budget devoted to such expenditures is quite small compared to other government programs). Corporate interests already enjoy a large degree of "welfare," since most of the nation's wealth is located in the corporate sector and with those individuals who share in its ownership. Demands by the poor, however, and programs designed to promote the general welfare (as opposed to particular business interests) may be the very ones that are opposed by most of the business community. And given the *relatively* small number and dollar amounts of these programs compared to those in support of business, they might be said to have "won" in this policy area as well.

Let me give what may seem like a trivial example of the power of corporations and the relationship between this power and one aspect of the general welfare.

At the end of most legislative sessions, in both state legislatures and Congress, there is a flurry of activity to pass hundreds of bills that benefit particular interests and that would have very little chance of passing if legislators knew what was in them. The end of the 1982 congressional session, for example, saw Congress pass 150 bills involving the expenditure of billions of dollars without debate and without recorded vote, including new tax breaks for the tabacco lobby, a new rule allowing trucks on federal highways to be seven inches wider, a 4 percent pay raise for some Senate employees, a Sleeping Bear Dunes national monument in Michigan, and literally hundreds of other expenditures in the military, highway, health, and other areas.

In California, a similar event occurred at the end of the legislative session on August 31, 1982. Hundreds of bills were introduced and passed, involving matters that had either been bottled up in committees or were introduced at the last minute with the cooperation of the leadership. There is no time for debate on these bills; and members, happy to have one or more of their own pet projects included, pay no attention to the projects of their colleagues.

One such bill, a measure that had been buried in committee for over a year, was introduced by the Republican senate leader William Campbell for a friend and constituent, Patrick Moriarity, president of the Anaheim-based Pyrotronics Corporation, the nation's largest producer of fireworks. This bill, which was passed without debate (and without most legislators knowing anything about it) would have made it illegal for cities and counties in California to ban the sale of fireworks. Eighty-two cities, including four of its largest (Los Angeles, San Diego, San Francisco, and Long Beach), have ordinances banning such sales.

This is the general picture then. One legislator, the senate leader, representing one constituent (the president of the nation's largest fireworks company) was able to get a bill passed that took away from 82 cities representing the vast majority of the state's over 20 million population the right to control the sale of fireworks. The power of corporate leaders, even minor ones, is indeed very large. (The end of this story, by the way, is that Governor Brown, who was made aware of the contents of the bill, vetoed it. But then, as one wag had it: "Governor Brown does not live in Anaheim.")


## CONTROL OF GOVERNMENT PERSONNEL

Those who are interested in controlling the political-governmental sector of a society would not only want to control the ideology, the policy formation process, and the enactment, interpretation, and enforcement of specific legislation and programs, they would also want to determine *who* occupies the positions that are empowered by the society to make binding decisions. Hence we find that corporations and those individuals who benefit materially in their ownership and control play a predominant role in decisions that affect who is elected and appointed to public office. Since the process of election and appointment are quite different from each other, we shall consider each separately.


### Corporate Involvement in the Election Process

Although, in theory, any citizen who meets the minimum requirements of age, citizenship, residence, and several other easily fulfilled qualifications, can run for public office simply by announcing his or her candidacy and filing the necessary papers, in fact no one is ever elected who does not succeed in finding considerable financial backing. Since most of the wealth and property in this country are in the hands of a small number of corporations and individuals, it is not surprising that they often use some of this money to insure that candidates favorable to their point of view are nominated and elected. For example, in 1972 it is estimated that political campaigns for all federal, state, and local offices cost over $425 million. One thousand seven hundred and fifty persons (1,750) alone contributed $73 million (17% of *all* political spending for that year). Richard Nixon's campaign cost $63 million. One hundred fifty-three (153) persons contributed $19.8 million of this sum, about one-third of the total Nixon campaign fund (Adamany, 1977, p. 291). In fact, about 90 percent of all campaign contributions come from less than 1 percent of the population (Rodgers and Harrington, 1981, p. 146).

*Political action committees.*   In addition to individual contributors, corporations and trade associations, through political action committees (PAC's), are the second largest source of campaign funds. In 1982, for example, the primaries and general elections of congressional candidates are estimated to have cost $239 million. Of this total, political action committees contributed $55.2

million. Of the 3,149 PAC's, nearly one-half of them are direct arms of individual corporations (1,415), an additional 613 are committees of trade associations, and 127 are related to business cooperatives or nonstock corporations, for a total of over two-thirds of all PAC's which are business related (*National Journal*, 1982, p. 1,368). Labor has 350 PAC's (11% of the total), and 644 (20%) are not directly connected to either business or labor. The business PAC's contributed $37.1 million, or two-thirds of the total $55.2 million contributed by all political action committees.

In most states, the first step in an election is the primary; and it is at this stage that corporations, trade associations, wealthy individuals, political action committees, and other interested parties begin to support the candidates that will best promote their interests. These groups are often instrumental, as well, in choosing candidates to enter the primary and encouraging them (financially and otherwise), to run for office. In other words, it is in the *selection* of the candidates who will finally run in the election that much effort is already expended. At the highest level—that is, the office of the presidency—policy planning groups will be very influential in backing some candidates over others. Many believe that the Council on Foreign Relations and the Trilateral Commission were very instrumental in putting forth the candidacy of Jimmy Carter in 1976.

By the time of the general election, then, the two candidates supported by the major parties have already passed the first hurdle of corporate approval; and few, if any, candidates reach this level without the backing of most of the business community within their electoral districts. Whether the eventual winner is a Democrat or a Republican is affected more by the nature of the constituency represented (that is, whether it is predominately poor or wealthy) than by whether or not the candidate has the support of important business elements within the constituency. Indeed, most large contributors give money to the campaigns of *both* final candidates. The important weeding out of candidates unacceptable to business has already been done at the primary election level. This is probably the major reason why Republicans and Democrats are so much alike, and why, for many people, the final choice is between tweedledum and tweedledee. What distinguishes Democrats from Republicans in most states and electoral districts is the kinds of constituents they represent *in addition to* the business interests located in their constituencies. We shall have more to say about this, however, in the next chapter.

Most elected officials, at the federal, state, and local levels, are therefore winners who believe in protecting private property and promoting the free enterprise system; in fact, the overwhelming majority of elected officials are lawyers and businesspeople, and are already among the top 5 percent of the population in terms of wealth (and more likely in the top 1 percent). Their social, economic, and educational backgrounds dictate a natural affiliation with the business community; and the majority of their financial support comes from the same source. Although differing in the kinds of business interests they represent (e.g., agriculture, defense contractors, steel, financial institutions, and so on), they differ very little in the fact that they represent *some* business interests. These business interests may not be the only ones they represent, especially if they are elected from poor constituencies, but they all share the idea that it is through the business community that public policies must take shape.

One example of the extent to which elected representatives are similar in profile to others in the top 5 percent of the population, and the extent to which they are directly linked to the corporate world, can be found in the *Congressional Quarterly,* which provides data on the financial and corporate interests of members of Congress. For the U.S. Senate in 1978, 36 senators had direct financial investments in banks and financial institutions, 13 in broadcasting and the mass media, 19 in the chemical industry, 36 in the leading defense contractors, 31 in agriculture and timber, 18 in insurance, 11 in minerals, 31 in oil and gas, 11 in pharmaceuticals, 18 in utilities, 47 in real estate, and 12 in transportation industries. In addition, many of those who hold financial interests in particular corporate sectors also sit on the committees that handle legislation affecting those industries. For example, 12 of the 36 senators with direct holdings in the leading defense contractors also sit on the Senate Armed Services Committee or the Defense Subcommittee of the Senate Appropriations Committee; 9 of the 31 senators with interests in agriculture sit on the relevant Senate agriculture committees; 8 of the 31 senators with financial interests in oil and natural gas companies sit on the Senate committees that handle legislation for those industries.

The situation in the House of Representatives is similar: 108 members of the House have direct financial interests in banks and financial institutions, 27 in broadcasting, 23 in the chemical industry, 74 in defense, 74 in agriculture, 44 in insurance, 28 in minerals, 63 in oil and natural gas, 18 in pharmaceuticals, 38 in utilities, 151 in real estate, and 33 in transportation industries. Similarly, 14 members who hold investment interests in banking and financial institutions are members of the relevant House committees that consider legislation affecting banking and finance, and 22 who have interests in agriculture sit on the relevant agriculture committees.

## Corporate Involvement
## in the Appointment Process

Most public officials, however, are not elected, but appointed. They are, of course, appointed by those who are elected. Hence it is even *less* likely that persons hostile to corporate and business interests will be put in positions of power; and if for some reason they should, they, unlike elected officials, can be dismissed. Study after study has indicated that appointees to regulatory commissions are not only likely to be favorable to the interests of the regulated industries, but frequently come from those industries themselves. Most cabinet appointments are given to those who have shown, in the past, a favorable attitude toward the business community, and who have themselves been associated with those interests.

Let me give just one example of the tangled web of association and direct interest that the appointment process can produce. For the past decade, the U.S. government has considered building a nuclear breeder reactor at Clinch River, Tennessee, a reactor that uses uranium and produces plutonium (also a nuclear fuel) as one of its by-products. Originally projected to cost $400 million, over $1 billion has already been spent on this project, although ground is yet to be broken to begin construction. Estimates are now that the total cost will exceed $7 billion and may go as high as $9 billion. Part of the problem in stopping what has been called a "plutonium pork barrel" by Senator Gordon J. Humphrey, Republican from New Hampshire, and a "technological turkey" by others, is that the Clinch River project is located in Senate Majority Leader Howard H. Baker's home state.

The plot, however, now thickens considerably. In order to separate the plutonium from the other by-products, another plant will have to be built, and it is to be located in South Carolina. The major backer of this second project is W. Kenneth Davis, deputy secretary of the Department of Energy (a political appointee). His boss, James B. Edwards, secretary of the Department of Energy, is, as it turns out, a former governor of South Carolina. Davis, the deputy secretary, was for twenty years the head of the nuclear division of the Bechtel Group, the world's largest construction company, which has built nearly one-half of all U.S. nuclear power plants and even more abroad. It should be noted, also, that George P. Schultz was president of Bechtel immediately before becoming President Reagan's secretary of state (Schultz had also been secretary of the treasury in a previous administration), that Secretary of Defense Casper W. Weinberger is also a former Bechtel official, and that Philip Habib, President Reagan's special negotiator in the Middle East, is a Bechtel consultant.

The upshot of the story is that Bechtel is interested in buying and running the plant in South Carolina, and will be negotiating with Davis concerning the entire arrangement, including guarantees that the federal government will buy the plutonium produced. Hence we have a former head of the nuclear division of Bechtel, appointed as deputy secretary of the Department of Energy, negotiating with Bechtel over a plant in South Carolina, the state in which Davis's boss, the secretary of energy, was governor. Given that it is also not unusual for government appointees to return to private business, even to the company from which they originally came, it may turn out that Davis is essentially negotiating with himself.

U.S. government officials, whether elected or appointed, have their roots deep in the business community. They tend to come from the corporate-business world, and when they leave government they return to it. Those who are elected may face, depending upon the constituencies they represent, other pressures in addition to those from business, but those who are appointed do not have this additional worry. We are a nation in which the concerns of business, and especially of big business, are paramount. The state of the economy, and of particular sectors within it, is the dog that wags the tail of government. Given the tremendous resources and power located in the hands of a relatively small percentage of the population, and of the business community, it would indeed be aberrant if this were not the case.

All of this, of course, runs counter to the democratic ideology that we all learn in school and want to believe in. It is now time, then, to explore this ideology and its workings in more detail, what I shall call the individual political system.

# CHAPTER EIGHT
# THE INDIVIDUAL
# POLITICAL SYSTEM

Running parallel to the corporate political system is "the other" political system; for many, it is the only political system they know anything about. This consists of the openly acknowledged political institutions of parties and elections—those organizations and procedures that are considered legitimate by the democratic ideology. This system does in fact exist, and it does in fact operate. But it does not function in the way in which we are led to believe. It is the corporate political system which is the major influence in public policy-making in this country, both domestic and foreign. This corporate political system operates under certain constraints (as do all political systems). Some of these constraints have to do with the American political ideology of democracy and with the formal and informal institutional and organizational structures that have grown up around this ideology. But because some constraints partly determine the *formal* rules of the game, neither are these the only "rules," nor do the formal procedures in fact accomplish what the ideology says they do.

One major constraint on the corporate political system is that, because its operation does not fall within the purview of the democratic ideology, much of what it does must be, and is, kept secret. In addition, a good deal of fraud and corruption take place within the corporate political system and in its interactions with the individual political system, mostly because the *realities* of the politics of property and the democratic creed are quite far apart from each other. The role of policy-planning groups, of interest groups, of government advisory councils, and of the many direct relationships between business and government are hidden from most of us and only surface from time to time when a scandal is particularly obvious (Watergate and the Environmental Protection Agency are examples). Most Americans prefer to believe that the democratic creed is the sole influence in the governmental process, mainly because it is, in principle, obviously more just, more equal, and, at the simplest level, more easily understood.

## LYING TO THE PUBLIC, CORRUPTION, AND FRAUD

Not only are many matters secret and hidden, there is also a good deal of evidence that we are often *lied to* regarding what is going on, and that there is a large amount of corruption and fraud. Let me give five brief examples of how the public is often misled and how outright fraud is often practiced. Each of these examples involves a separate sector of the government and the society: the military, a large steel corporation, the medical profession and related health establishments, the U.S. Congress, and wealthy U.S. citizens.

　　1. A federal trial is currently under way concerning the effects of radioactive fallout (deaths from cancer and other illnesses) as the consequence of 102 aboveground nuclear tests conducted by the federal government in Nevada during the 1950s. A government study, for example, has shown that children growing up in the area have died of leukemia at more than three times the expected rate.

　　Both a subcommittee of the U.S. House of Representatives and the Veterans Administrtion have found the atomic tests to be responsible for the effects on the population; the House subcommittee also found that the federal government "falsely reported" the amount of radiation involved. One federal judge has ruled that the government was "negligent," and another that the U.S. government had committed a "fraud on the court" in a case initiated in 1955 *by suppressing evidence and pressuring witnesses*.

　　2. There is currently a *civil* suit against the Youngstown Steel Corporation and its three chief executive officers for fraud involving a $10-million loan from the Economic Development Administration of the Commerce Department. (This is, incidentally, a minor example of how the federal government aids private corporations. Most of us believe that private enterprise borrows exclusively from private banks, not the U.S. government.) The loan was granted in order to rehabilitate a steel mill. The company failed to use the loan for this purpose. The suit charges that company officials submitted statements they knew to be false or fraudulent. In addition, the company made no interest or principal payments on the loan. No *criminal* action is being brought against the company or its officers.

3. Contrary to what is frequently believed, the Select Committee on Aging of the House of Representatives concluded that Medicaid recipients (a federal program designed to provide medical care for the indigent aging) account for only a "miniscule" amount of fraud, while anywhere from $2.5 to $6.2 billion dollars is fraudulently charged against the program by hospitals, physicians, nursing homes, and pharmacies.

4. Eight members of the Ninety-seventh Congress (1980–1982) were involved in criminal prosecutions and were forced to resign from office:

—Representative Daniel Flood, who pleaded guilty to a charge of conspiracy to solicit illegal campaign contributions
—Representative Charles Diggs, convicted of payroll padding and mail fraud
—Representative Michael O. Myers, convicted in the Abscam bribery scandal
—Representative John Jenrette, convicted of sharing a $50,000 bribe
—Representative Jon Hinson, after being charged with sodomy
—Representative Raymond F. Lederer, involved in the Abscam scandal
—Representative Frederick W. Richmond, who pleaded guilty to charges of income tax evasion, possession of marijuana, and illegal payments to a federal official.

5. A study by the permanent subcommittee on investigations of the Senate Governmental Affairs Committee indicates that as much as $40 billion is being placed in Caribbean banks by what the subcommittee refers to as "otherwise ordinary citizens." These funds are being funneled into a number of illicit tax shelters that are designed to hide earnings by businessmen, lawyers, doctors, and others.

As I think is now already clear from the evidence we have presented in the previous chapters, we are literally led astray by a belief in the democratic process as the only political system functioning in America. For reasons which will be made clear in this chapter, the individual political system is incapable of doing all that it is called upon to do by the democratic creed. Not only that, the distribution of wealth and property in this country, and especially within the corporate system itself, is such that resources in the exercise of political power are simply too out of whack for the individual political system to function as it is said to.

There is also another idea, well-supported in the sociological literature, that would lead us to suspect that the formal democratic system would spawn an informal "under system" in which the real decisions were made. This is the notion that all organizations—the larger they are the more this is true—will develop *informal,* unwritten ways of circumventing formal, legal rules. This informal system will center around those who have the most resources and who are therefore in a position to act more quickly and efficaciously to get what they want. In a related idea, Robert Michels in 1915 propounded what he called *the iron law of oligarchy,* which suggests that any organization, regardless of its formal rules, will be run by a relatively few number of its members.

We need not, of course, in spite of the many ways in which practice deviates from the ideal, abandon the democratic creed. Its ideas are obviously "good" ideas. But its role as a belief system, and its power to explain the operation of American politics, are two different things. To *explain* how the American political system works (as opposed to *justifying* it) we need more than the democractic creed. We also need to know a good deal about the informal system and how decisions are actually made. We may not wish to beieve in, as an ideology, the corporate political system; but in order to understand how public policy is made in this country we certainly need to know something about it and how it functions. Believing that the "will of the people" makes public policy, or that elections automatically produce democracy, is to allow oneself to be not only in a position of not knowing very much, but also subject to being duped and even manipulated. One of the functions of an ideology, after all, is to make people believe that something works the way the ideology says it does. Since the ideology is "good," it makes people feel good about their government and society. It therefore acts as a strong barrier against the exploration of activities which do not fit into the ideology. Hence ignorance, and duplicity.

It is interesting to observe, also, that in spite of what was said in Chapter 6 of the impossibility of proving power relationships and of the consequent difficulty of demonstrating them with utmost certainty, especially in the corporate political system where access to information is difficult to attain, there will be many who will criticize Chapter 7 for not having shown in more detail the relationship between corporate organizations and political outcomes. We are not, however, finished. To this point we have established the existence of the corporate political system, its structure, its impact on the economy, and how it is organized to influence government. In Chapters 9, 10, and 11 we will show how the decisions of government favor the corporate political system. If the corporate political system is as powerful as indicated here, it should be able to control the outcomes it seeks.

In this chapter we will explore the alternative to the corporate political system, how it is structured, and its impact on public policy. But it should also be pointed out that in spite of the tremendous energies and resources poured into the study of elections and public opinion in this country in the past 25 years, and the almost total absence (with a few significant exceptions, many of which are cited in this book) of money and attention spent on the relationship between corporations and government, the connections between citizens and government in the individual political system are far from having been cogently demonstrated. What relationships there are—for example, on party voting in Congress, and the relationship between elected representatives and their constituents—are very weak, and few studies have undertaken the task of showing explicitly just how ordinary citizens express their policy preferences to officeholders. In fact, one of the major findings is that citizens in general lack both information and interest, that very few participate beyond the act of voting, if they even do that.

Hence, if this book is attacked for not showing enough specific detail on the linkages between corporations and government in an area where the data is not only *private* but there is cause to believe that the participants have good reasons for wanting it hidden, I would suggest that those who study elections and political parties, *areas which are much more open and public,* look to their own poor showing for comparison.

To share with you something of a little "sermonette," one of the problems I obviously have in writing this book is that I am telling most of you things you really don't want to know. Few of us can believe (although some of us do—see Dye and Ziegler, for example) that the wealthy and powerful *ought* to rule. To the extent that we learn that they do, then, to that extent we may become cynical about the democratic creed, and being cynical is not something which all of us can handle. It *is* nicer if the democratic creed were not only something to believe in, but something to believe as *true* as well. Then we wouldn't have this terrible problem of being taught that how things ought to work is how they do work and then finding out that they do not in fact work that way. I am the bearer of bad tidings—and I am very conscious of being such. My only excuse is that I place correct understanding above ignorance. You, on your own, will have to wrestle with the problem of beginning to reconcile what you know with what others (and myself, for that matter) want you to believe in as good and just. Understanding that the world isn't necessarily as it ought to be may be part of what it means to live in the world as we find it. It may also be part of what it means to grow up. Fairy tales are for the very young, the very naive, and the very romantic. It is also clear that if you want to have some impact on the world, you must understand not only how it ought to be but how it actually is as well.

We sometimes forget that *ideology* is a system of *values,* and that such things as "equality," "justice," "liberty," "material well-being," "happiness," "free enterprise," "competitive markets," and the like are *goals.* There is a strong tendency for an ideology to play *two* roles: as a system of values, of things which we can all believe in as "good"; and as a *description* of what is actually the case. But goals, by definition, are never a description. They are what we are aiming for—not what is already realized. If they were the latter, they wouldn't be goals any longer, but actuality. To the extent that we think that the goals we believe in actually describe the functioning of the real world, to that extent we confuse values with fact. Heaven on earth is not possible—that's why we have two separate words, heaven *and* earth. Believing in an ideology requires that we be very careful to keep this distinction in mind. The consequences for not doing so are two-fold: we will be little interested in trying to describe how the world actually works; and we will tend to use the ideology to explain, as well as to justify, the world in which we live. A belief in the goodness of the democratic creed (not, I might add, as Madison described it in the Federalist No. 10—he was clearly describing how the democratic creed could be circumvented), need not blind us in our attempts to understand what is really going on, although it is likely to—much as a belief in the idea that the earth is the center of the universe was used to prevent us from understanding how the heavenly bodies actually move.

In this chapter we will explore the democratic creed from three points of view: what it is, how it functions, and why it cannot do what it claims it can do. The democractic creed is not a bad thing to believe in, as a goal. It is simply not adequate to the task of organizing a society politically and of producing public policies all by itself. Not only does the democratic creed not take into account the clear description by Madison of ways to get around it, but as a description of how things work, it leaves out certain essential realities involving wealth, interest, and power—realities that could hardly be incorporated into an ideology that is worth believing in as a goal. Hence, the American political system is, in reality, two political systems: the corporate system, which organizes the centers of wealth and determines public policy; and the individual political system, which among other things teaches us to ignore the corporate system because its functioning is not consistent with the ideology which underlies the individual political system, which tells us that what ought to be is, and which is incapable of existing as the *only* mechanism of politics and governmental decision-making.

## PRIVATE PROPERTY VS. MAJORITY RULE

The individual political system is based on the democratic creed, which essentially goes as follows: all citizens above a certain age are equal; such citizens are likely to differ in what they want; in its decision-making, a society ought to take into account the freely expressed opinions of these diverse citizens, on an equal basis, and translate those opinions into policies that work toward the common good of all.

Stated in this rather stark way, we can say two things about the individual political system right off the bat. One, it sounds like a good idea— wouldn't it be nice if it could really work that way. And second, look at all the loopholes: equal citizens, expressing free opinions, collected together and organized in such a way that what is finally decided is for the benefit of everyone. Few could argue that there is anything wrong with this ideal as an ideal; but the gaps are large enough to drive trucks through. Remember, in this context, that our economic creed has it that private property is sacred, and that people can amass as much of it as they can. Remember, too, that the first principle of government is to protect property. And now what do we have? Individuals pursuing their own private interests in a governmental system that is supposed to represent the "will of the people'' equally. Indeed, a knotty problem, one which is not likely to be solved in favor of the individual political system and the democratic creed. And why not? Because the corporate political system has *content* built into its ideology—property; and the individual political system is only an idealized description of a *process*. The corporate system knows what it wants—and what it wants is real. The individual political system doesn't specify what the content of the decision should be about—only, in a very idealized fashion, in whose general interest decisions should be made, i.e., the common good. What is in the common good will obviously be interpreted to mean what those in power (like Madison) decide that it means. And they have decided that the common good is served by protecting the unequal division of property. Hence, in modern America, a corporate political system dedicated to preserving unequal distribution of property, a system which dominates, in ideology, in policy formation, and in detail, the content of what the process produces and how it goes about its business.

The ways in which this principle of the protection of property was translated into our Constitution are many, all of them having the effect of insuring that the ''common good'' and the principle of ''majority rule'' are not to be considered identical. The barriers against majority rule are legion: separation of powers among the legislative, executive, and judicial branches; various checks and balances; a bicameral legislature, each with different terms of office; indirect election of the president through the Electoral College and of the Senate by state legislatures (changed in 1913 to direct election); and federalism. The major justification for this distinction between the common good and majority rule is stated in the idea that the common good is a *combination* of majority rule *and* minority rights. And, although the notion of minority rights can mean a number of things, *one* of the things it clearly means is the rights of property.

And hence the central ''paradox'' of American democracy: if the ''people'' are going to rule (which is what the democratic creed imples—indeed, it is what the word ''democracy'' means), the only equitable system of decision making is majority rule. Anything less or more allows the minority to rule. Since property is unequally distributed, and since, as Madison feared, the majority may want a fairer distribution of property, protection of minority rights is in great measure a protection of the unequal distribution of property.

## Representative vs. Direct Democracy

But this, of course, is not the only difficulty in the democratic creed, although it is undoubtedly the most serious. We also have the problem of the process itself. Even if we assumed that the protection of property did not specify the *content* of politics (in which case we would have to argue that Madison didn't know what he was talking about), and even if we assumed that all citizens above a certain age *are* equal, we would still have the question of how the opinions of this diverse population would be aggregated into a collective and organized ''common good.''

Part of the answer to this question is that we, in fact, gave up on the principle of democracy from the outset, in the sense that democracy means direct participation of all the citizenry in governmental decisions. That is, we established a *republican* form of government, a system of *representative* democracy, rather than of *direct* democracy. We obviously did this, in part, for very practical reasons, although there was some sentiment among certain sectors of the population for the establishment of a form of "town council" direct democracy. As Madison, and others, clearly argue, if one is going to have a government that covers a vast territory, and a large number of citizens, direct democracy is probably an impossibility. I say "probably," because, in fact, not much thought was given to this alternative. It was also clearly in the interests of those with property to avoid a system of direct democracy in favor of a republican form of government—a form they foresaw as one they could better control.

## The Two-Party Political System

Once a system of representative democracy was chosen, the mechanism of how the "will of the people" was to be expressed developed slowly and with difficulty. What eventually emerged was a two-party political system that grew naturally (that is, it was not planned) from several major cleavages in the population (agricultural vs. manufacturing, slaveholding vs. nonslave holding, North vs. South). To this day, the two-party system attempts to organize the 230 million individual citizens of this country by means of an election process. This is the foundation of the individual political system, and it is essential that we now explore how effective a mechanism it is in determining public policy. That is, is it possible for a two-party system to express the "will of the people"?

In an ideal democracy, each individual citizen would be able to express his or her views on all matters. Each citizen would, in effect, be his or her own representative. In addition, we would expect some people to have like interests, so much alike that they could be adequately represented by a single representative. Just exactly how many such groups there would be, no one knows. But one thing is perfectly clear: the number would certainly be larger than two. Why then, with the exception of a few minor parties whose chances of winning any office are practically nil, do we have only two major parties? Why does such a large and diverse country such as ours have a two-party, instead of a multiparty system?

First, the Constitution says nothing whatever about political parties. Indeed, political parties did not even exist at the time of its adoption. The constitution and the subsequent amendments simply specify an election system and the offices that will be open to election. We could, in theory, just as well have developed a multiparty system as a two-party system, *had we wanted to*. There is nothing "natural" about a two-party system. In fact, given the European system as a point of comparison, a multiparty system is the rule and a two-party system the exception.

While political parties grew "naturally," the party system that eventually developed is clearly related to the rules of the election process, rules that were consciously adopted by all of the states. And, to arrive at the figure of 2 parties, rather than 8, or 70, or 432, we might ask the following question. Does a system of two parties better represent the diverse interests of a large population than does a multiparty system? If there were more than two parties, would not the spectrum of opinion represented be larger? And would not that spectrum be more difficult to control? The answer, in my view, is clearly yes in both cases. A two-party system submerges differences of opinion, moderates political conflict (at least in the election process) by not allowing it to surface, and is more easily controllable by those for whom the first principle of government is to control property. Differences may separate those who control property (e.g., big business vs. small business, banks vs. savings and loan associations, manufacturing vs. agriculture), and these differences may surface at the party level. What these interests have in common, however, may also produce a two-party system that, in general, represents the common interests of property, *together with* other interests that will be muted as a consequence of having to be a part of one of the two parties, both of which reflect the general interests of the business community and the prevailing ideology.

## ELECTION LAWS AND THE TWO-PARTY SYSTEM

Let me illustrate how election laws and the two-party system go hand in hand by describing the election procedures for members of the U.S. House of Representatives. The laws are similar, however, for all state legislatures in the country.

The relevant passage in the Constitution is Article I, Section 4: "The Times, Places and Manner of holding Elections for Senators and Representatives, shall be prescribed in each State by the Legislature thereof; but the Congress may at any time by Law make or alter such Regulations." In other words, state legislatures may determine how members of Congress are to be elected, except that Congress itself may step in if it wants to—something that it has never done with respect to the general election procedures we are discussing.

### Single-Member Districts

The number of House members to which a state is entitled is determined by the total number of members (set by Congress at 435) and the proportionate population of each state. California, for example, the most populous state in the union, had forty-five representatives in 1982; New York, the second most populous state, had thirty-four; and so on. *Each state is free to determine how its share of members are to be elected, and all states have chosen the system of single-member districts.* The states could have chosen other ways of electing members of the House that would have been less favorable to a two-party system, more favorable to the development of a multiparty system, and hence more favorable to the representation of a wider range of interests. For example, if all the members were elected statewide, instead of by districts, with each party receiving the number of representatives as their proportion of the total vote, such a system would have provided for the possibility of numerous parties being assured some representation in Congress. For example, with forty-five representatives being elected statewide, a party in California that received as little as 5 percent of the vote would receive two seats. Instead, however, *all* states chose to divide themselves into districts, with one winner in each district; this system distinctly favors the development and maintenance of two parties and hence considerably blurred representation. There is nothing in the Constitution that requires a system of representation by district. Each state can decide its own method of election.

### Plurality Vote

Along with single-member districts, the second law, adopted by all states, for the election of members of Congress (and state legislatures) that strongly favors a two-party system is the mechanism of *plurality vote*. That is, the winner within each district need not receive an absolute majority (50 percent plus one) in order to win—he or she need receive only the largest percentage. Let us assume that there are five candidates representing five different parties, Party A, B, C, D, and E. Let us also assume that the candidate for Party A receives 25 percent of the vote, Party B 22 percent, Party C 20 percent, Party D 18 percent, and Party E 15 percent. The candidate representing Party A would win the election. Under this system the strongest parties can win elections even without gaining a majority, and strong showings by minor parties leave them with nothing (this is another consequence of single-member district elections).

Our election laws, then, adopted at the discretion of state legislatures, and not tampered with by Congress, are specifically designed to discourage the development of minor parties by providing them with nothing in the way of representation until they become major parties (which has not happened in the last 120 years). Hence, significant groups of people, who may feel they are not adequately represented by one of the major parties, have nowhere to go. This is a major reason why voter turnout in U.S. elections is the lowest of any democratic country in the world. Only about 50 percent of those eligible to vote did so in the 1980 presidential election, and the average for Congressional elections in nonpresidential election years is about 33 percent.

## THE NATURE OF REPRESENTATION
## IN A TWO-PARTY SYSTEM

The consequences of the two-party system in the United States cannot be underestimated. It not only produces a very blurred form of representation and a very low rate of voter participation in elections, but the election laws that maintain the two-party system also have a number of much broader social, political, and economic consequences.

One major consequence is the fact that two, and only two parties, cannot develop consistent party platforms that appeal to the common interests of party members. Indeed, our political parties do not, in any real sense, even have members. One simply votes, if one wants to, for the candidates of either major party for whatever reasons one chooses. The two parties themselves compete with each other for the same voters. (Blacks are the only group that significantly favors one party over the other, and they have the lowest rate of voter participation of all groups.) Both parties, then, aim toward the middle. This produces an even greater blurring of differences between the two parties, such that many people find it very difficult to tell them apart. Appeals to voters tend to be very general, symbolic, and essentially contentless. They will also tend to be very similar. Hence voters either have *no* choice, or a very *unclear* choice. Political parties in the United States are, in reality, simply organizations developed for the purposes of winning office and have very little to do, except perhaps symbolically, with *issues*.

There is also another serious flaw in the argument that elections can be significant determinants of public policy in the United States. In any given election it is reasonable to suppose that the number of important issues is greater than one. Even if the parties did offer clear, alternative policies, and voters voted on the basis of these policy differences, if there is more than one issue, how can we know what issues the voters are supporting? Theoretically it would be possible, even with as few as three issues, that one-third of the population would feel intense enough on issue A to vote for Party X, even though it opposed Party X's stands on the other two issues. Another one-third of the population could vote for Party X because of its stand on issue B, even though opposed on the other two issues. And another one-third of the population could vote for Party X because of its stand on issue C (and be opposed on the others). Party A could capture 100 percent of the vote when in fact two-thirds of the population *opposed* its stands on the three issues. Had each issue been voted on separately, *none* would have won. (This problem is very nicely discussed in Robert A. Dahl, *A Preface to Democratic Theory*.)

The upshot of this is that, if *specific* policies and *specific* laws are to be made, they are going to have to come from elsewhere. And that "elsewhere" is the corporate political system. The lack of policy direction from political parties leaves a void that is filled by the country's most powerful, wealthiest, and best organized group.

Another major consequence of an essentially undifferentiated two-party system concerns the political activity of those groups and individuals who are not a part of the corporate political system and who are among the least advantaged socially and economically in the United States. Having little, if any, representation within the two major parties, they must seek means of expressing their needs and interests *outside* the normal political channels. In the United States this expression has taken the form of public demonstrations, sometimes violent demonstrations, among labor groups, the unemployed, the poor, blacks, and other groups who are not likely to find candidates that represent their interests. We do not, in the United States, have a Labor party, a party for the poor, a black party, and so on. To the extent that their interests are represented, it is in terms of whatever those in power are willing to give them; and frequently what they are willing to give depends upon just these activities that fall outside the scope of what is considered "legitimate" in the American political system. The history of the U.S. labor movement and of blacks, the two most important groups that fall outside of the corporate political system (although on many issues *organized labor* is definitely within the corporate system), is filled with strikes, sit-ins, and violent confrontations. In more recent times those who oppose war and nuclear armament have also found themselves outside of the normal political channels.

Those solely within the individual political system have also made considerable efforts, where possible, to organize into interest groups. This is especially true of blacks and of labor, but considerably less so for the poor, who lack a natural organization and the necessary resources. The American Federation of Labor-Congress of Industrial Organizations (AFL-CIO), the International Brotherhood of Teamsters, Chauffers, Warehousemen, and Helpers of America, the National Association for the Advancement of Colored People (NAACP), the Mexican-American Legal Defense and Education Fund, the United Automobile, Aerospace, and Agricultural Implement Workers of American (UAW), and a number of "civic-minded" groups such as the American Civil Liberties Union (ACLU), Americans for Democratic Action (ADA), and Common Cause, have been instrumental in working for the benefit of those underrepresented by the two-party system.

We should not, however, overemphasize the extent of power held by these groups. Less than 25 percent of the American labor force is unionized, with only a few sectors of the economy representing the major areas of union activity. For example, less than 1 percent of all agricultural workers are unionized, and only 13 percent of service workers (both are heavily weighted by those who earn near the minimum wage). More successful labor union activity is recorded in the large industrial sectors such as steel, automobiles, and transportation. And wages are considerably higher for unionized workers than for the vast majority of those in nonunionized work. In addition, such programs as unemployment benefits go mainly to the unionized and higher wage categories. The economic and social plight of minorities in this country, blacks, Mexican-Americans, and Indians being the most significant, has been well documented. These minorities have the lowest wages, highest rates of unemployment (more than double that of whites), and lowest rates of union representation of all groups in the country. Another significant labor group, women (who now make up almost 50 percent of the labor force), also find themselves in lower-paying, nonunionized jobs with significantly lower wages than their male counterparts (over 40 percent lower).

## ELECTIONS AND THE DEMOCRATIC CREED

Up to this point we have been able to offer a good deal of data, all from the best sources available, much of it from the government itself, for many of our conclusions and interpretations. This section, however, will offer an hypothesis that is unprovable, given the kind of interpretation it is. But we have reached an impasse in this examination of the political system. The democratic creed and its major organizational component, elections, have been shown to be inadequate to *explain* how public policy is made in this country. This, in itself, is not bothersome from the point of view of our knowing what mechanism *does* explain how public policy is made. We have already seen that this function is performed by the corporate political system. Our problem is, rather, the following: if elections and the democratic creed do not explain how public policy is made, then what is their major function? My answer to this question is to be considered tentative and interpretative. (You may wish to develop your own explanation.)

The major clue we will work with involves the nature of ideology. Ideologies frequently serve two functions, as was pointed out earlier; these functions, if put together, will cause nothing but confusion. Ideologies specify *goals*. They indicate what a society values and what it claims to be aiming at. But being goals, they are not yet attained and are probably, as is true of almost all abstract values, unattainable. Often, however, ideologies are used to describe and explain whatever it is we are trying to understand—that is, ideologies are often mistakenly believed to be factual and accurate descriptions of things. And this is exactly what is happening with respect to the democratic creed.

To the extent that we use the democratic creed to explain how public policy is made, to the extent we are taking it to be something factual instead of a system of abstract values. We are trying to explain something that exists—public policy—with something that does not—a set of unrealized goals. Hence, the democratic creed, in describing how the individual political system *ought* to work, cannot explain how in fact it *does* work. The corporate political system, not being a part of our ideology, does not suffer from the same difficulties. We shall have to look elsewhere, then, for an explanation of the role which elections play in American politics.

### Rites, Rituals, and Elections

Let us explore this process a little further. *All* societies develop ideologies, or characteristic ways of looking at what they consider important. Anthropologists have studied this process in so-called "primitive" tribes all over the world. Social anthropologists have also tried to describe these strong cultural values in other types of societies as well. The democratic creed and the election process are major components—along with free enterprise, competition, and the other features of our economic creed—of *American* ideology. These beliefs help to hold us together and provide us with an explanation of something very important to us: how public policy is made and what "moves" government.

Connected with ideologies and cultural values are *rituals* or repetitive activities that are performed in the name of the ideology. Anthropologists and sociologists find rituals in every society they study, including ours. These rituals are designed to invoke the *meaning* of the ideology, to bring to bear on a problem the values and beliefs described by the ideology.

If the democratic creed is the foundation of American ideology, what, then, are the associated rituals? The answer, in my opinion, is elections. Rituals are designed to celebrate the ideology, they are ceremonies in which all members of the society are asked to participate. Indeed, we can go one step further. Rites are rituals that deal with what a society holds *sacred,* and the democratic creed is something that most Americans hold sacred. It is the sine qua non of American society—that is, if it were not present, we would no longer believe we lived in the same society. Further, rites are frequently associated with sacred texts, documents that lay out the fundamental principles of the ideology. We, indeed, have our sacred texts: the Declaration of Independence, the Constitution, and perhaps a few others such as Adam Smith's *The Wealth of Nations.* We even have an august judicial body, a group of nine who wear black robes, who interpret these sacred documents for us. It would not be too far-fetched to say that our democratic creed is a consecrated creed that takes on the aura of a religious belief.

Americans are asked to believe in the democratic creed and to participate in its associated rites and rituals; this is part of what it means to be an American. During every election, for example, citizens are exhorted from every corner to get out and vote, whether they want to or not, and whether or not they are able to tell the candidates and parties apart. They are told it is their *duty* and their *obligation* as citizens.

Some members of a society can become cynical about its rites and rituals. It would be naive to suppose that all the "natives" who dance around trying to make it rain actually believe in what they are doing. After all, rain dances are great social occasions and are often accompanied by music, drinking, speech making, and other goings-on. Anthropologists usually do not ascribe cynical motives to those "natives" who may simply want to have a good time, or are there for reasons of social pressure. They are, after all, expected to be there, and it would not look good if they did not show up.

So too with American elections. There are those whose cynicism has reached the point of *alienation;* others may participate only because it is more or less expected of them; and some participate as true believers. If this cynicism occurred, for example, within a church group, it would be viewed as a disease to be eradicated. Certainly it is a symptom of the inability of some members to believe all that they are told. And it can produce low rates of participation in the rites and rituals of the society. Major scandals within the ideological framework (such as Watergate) can also have a major impact on the extent to which people continue to hold onto treasured beliefs. So too can poverty, unemployment, inexplicable wars, and police atrocities. An ideology is something very profound and very stable—but it, like anything else, operates within certain limits.

The major problem is that ideologies are, after all, matters of faith, and that faith can be abused. By themselves, elections and the democratic creed cannot serve as the initiators and makers of public policy. Something else is needed, and that something else in the United States is the corporate political system. But the disparity between what the ideology promises and what the actual political system produces cannot be so far out of line that people no longer keep their faith. Government must perform, at least minimally, in accord with the ideology.

## POLITICAL LANGUAGE

One of the factors that produces cynicism, alienation, and indifference within a political system is the wide gulf that exists between political language and political action. By *political language,* I mean language that individuals are exposed to in political campaigns on radio and television and in newspapers, and in other news sources. In order to understand this a little better, we need to know something about political language, of what it is composed, and the effects it has on individual citizens.

### Rational and Explanatory Models

The language we hear from politicians themselves is essentially the language of *action*— that is, it is cast in terms of goals and of means of arriving at those goals. In this sense, the language we hear is highly "rational" (that is, it specifies desired ends and ways of achieving them), even though the content of such rational talk tends to be enormously simple. Politicians give us some very abstract ends that we should be aiming for (justice, fairness, military strength, full employment, freedom), all goals that most of us would share, and then suggest very simple means by which we can achieve those goals (means that may simply be to elect into office those who are speaking). Our frame of reference, then, for understanding and evaluating political action and public policy is in terms of how well goals (abstract and ultimately unattainable goals in any pure and absolute sense) are being achieved.

There is, however, an alternative way to talk, an alternative that is, in some sense, in competition with the rationality model. This is the language of *explanation,* which tells us that events are "caused" by specific prior events. Freud, for example, tells us that our personalities are formed by our early childhood experiences with our parents. This idea of cause, of seeing an event as the result of a prior event, is different from seeing an event as the result of aiming at goals. The explanatory model looks to the past; the rational model aims for something in the future. The explanatory model tells us that events occur *because of* such and such; the rational, or active, model tells us that events should or will or do occur *in order to* accomplish such and such.

In addition, the language of action is often highly moral. The goals we are aiming for are "good." On the other hand, the language of explanation (which is, by the way, the language of science) is not necessarily moral—at least not inherently moral. Although real language tends to be a mixture of the two, the predominant mode of political language is to encourage the acceptance of public policies in order to achieve goals, and that of scientific language is to help us understand events in terms of what motivates them or what has produced them.

Now, let us take a particular public policy and see what this distinction between political language and scientific language produces. Let's assume that, as at present, our economy is not performing well. We can all agree that we would prefer an economy that is performing well. We can therefore make improvement in economic performance a goal. Let us then propose that in order to improve the state of the economy we need to give a large tax cut to corporations. The latter is the means by which we will achieve the goal we seek. On the other hand, we do not want to emphasize a *corporate* tax cut, since corporations do not fit neatly into the democratic model of individual politics. We therefore combine this tax cut with one for individuals as well (with an emphasis on benefits that will go mainly to the wealthy).

## PUBLIC POLICY AND POLITICAL CHANGE

Let us now look at this same public policy (corporate and individual tax cuts) from the point of view of explaining what is going on. However, instead of goals, we shall look for causes. We shall look at what the tax cut proposes and then try to figure out why those who are proposing it are doing so. Since the largest tax breaks will go to corporations (and to wealthy individuals), we would naturally look into the corporate political system as a motivating cause of the proposal. But this, of course, is exactly what political language attempts to steer us away from when it casts the problem in active, goal-seeking language. We are to see the event of a tax cut as a means to a goal that we can all share in common, and not as an event that is caused by anything else, including the corporate political system.

From the point of view of active language, stated in terms of the *purposes* of a tax cut, an analysis of a tax cut in terms of its causes is *inherently cynical*. That is, we are analyzing an event in a way that is different from—and outside of—the way in which we are being asked to look at it. It is inevitable, of course, that we are likely to read about or hear something (if only from the opposition) that encourages us to see the event in terms of its explanation rather than in terms of its purposes. And *any* explanation is likely to be at least morally neutral (in the sense that scientific language is not, like active language, by its very nature moral). In the context of juxtaposing such a morally neutral explanation (although the explanation itself may obviously be looked at morally) against an explicitly moral argument (the active language of politics), it will appear to be more or less *immoral* even if it is only *amoral*. It has this flavor of immorality simply because it does not fit into the same moral metaphor as the active language itself, which talks of good purposes. Rather, explanations of causes may talk simply of prior factors that are motivating the event.

This problem of the difference between the active, moral, purposeful talk of politicians who are proposing courses of action, and the explanatory, causal, and perhaps even morally neutral talk of those who are analyzing events (even if these analyzers are the political opposition) becomes especially serious when the policies that are proposed and adopted do not achieve the goals they set out to attain. If we are promised a world safe from some outside threat and enter into a war that fails to attain the goal, or if we are promised a better economy through a corporate tax cut and we do not get it, or if poor people are promised a higher standard of living that is not achieved, then we begin to distrust political language. The problem, however, is that most of us have never been taught an explanatory language that will help us understand how the political process really works. We are left to think that the present "ins" are simply incompetent, perhaps even "bad," and that they should be replaced through the only means available—i.e., elections—by the current "outs." Political change occurs then, essentially through replacing one set of people with promises and goals with another set of people with promises and goals. The process is never explained in a scientific way, a way that would analyze what the political system is really all about, and what motivates public policies.

The mass media, in general, do a very good job of reporting what politicians actually say. They cover political activities as news and report the goals and aims of political figures as they state them. The mass media, however, also analyze the news; they explore some of the possible causes of events and sometimes delve into the motivations behind political activities. In addition, of course, newspapers, magazines, television, and radio also report events that occur outside of what politicians say. They report on current happenings and activities. Sometimes these analyses and reports are congruent with what we have been led to expect by political talk—that is, the events and the talk may be consistent with each other. On the other hand, analyses often veer away from political language and search for causes; and thus reported events are often not consistent with what was promised. The number of such stories that are reported in any major newspaper or news magazine—stories of corruption, fraud, special arrangements between business and government, and attempts to keep information away from the individual citizen—is quite high. Such stories are bound to trouble us, given the fact that we have been led to expect moral actions. The prime example of this is Watergate, the largest political scandal in American history. Many of us assume that these stories are exceptions, and that they can be explained on moral terms. We are not likely to regard them simply as daily fare, unless we have a better understanding of how American politics actually works.

For this reason, then, such stories are likely to leave many people cynical, alienated, and indifferent. However, these events can also be explained as being normal, everyday political events that we can expect to happen if we have a reasonably realistic idea of what politics is all about (and all we really have to do, in this regard, is to take Madison at his word and see politics and government as concerned with the protection of property).

Although the individual political system is an inadequate method for making public policy, although its major function is to celebrate the democratic creed, and although its language of rational action is incapable of explaining how government and politics actually function, this does not mean that what it *does* do is trivial and without consequences—at least in the short run. Because "ritual" elections are competitive (in the sense that there are competing candidates) and therefore determine which particular people will take office, the winners and their appointees will often take measures, assuming the cooperation of the corporate political system, to insure their ability to continue in office. Let me give two examples.

## Political Change and the Corporate System

1982 was a congressional election year, and President Reagan's program was in serious difficulty. The unemployment rate had soared to over 10 percent (12 percent if those who were so discouraged that they were no longer searching for jobs are taken into account), the budget deficits were the highest in the nation's history (*twice* that of any previous administration), interest rates continued to be high, and the Gross National Product was falling. If the country was not actually in a depression, it was the most serious recession since the Great Depression of the 1930s.

President Reagan, with the cooperation of the business community, was able to lend support both to his program and to his fellow party members facing elections in two important ways. First, the Federal Reserve Board, which had been pursuing an extremely tight money supply policy, began to permit the money supply to grow (by 10 percent—a significant proportion) over a three-month period. This was well above its own stated guidelines for controlling the money supply. The expected effect of this policy occurred within three weeks of the election: interest rates fell several percentage points, and the stock market gained 25 percent in value. President Reagan then convinced NBC and CBS (ABC refused) to carry a nationwide economic address in which he informed the American public that this recent fall in interest rates and surge in the stock market clearly indicated that the economy was on the road to recovery.

Readers should not assume, by the way, that Republicans are the only party with the support of the business community, or that this analysis applies only to Republicans and not to Democrats. The corporate political system operates effectively with either party in control of the government. Policy-planning groups do not even endorse political candidates (their concern is with broad public policy, regardless of which party is in office). Financial support for both Democrats and Republicans comes mainly from the business community; and the roles of government advisory committees, interest groups, and the practice of appointing business people to government positions do not change when the party that controls the government changes. The only major difference between *some* Republicans and *some* Democrats in Congress is the fact that Democrats tend to have a larger percentage of the poor within their constituencies and hence—i.e., in order to compete effectively for office—must pay more attention than Republicans to them.

As we saw earlier, elections are competitive rituals involving two large, but quite variable, "totems," that claim to represent the general interests of everyone, as they see them, and symbolically represent two different clans. In practice, however, they differ only marginally in that, *in addition to business interests,* Democrats also tend to speak out more forcefully in favor of the interests of the unorganized potential voters who make up the least-advantaged elements of society. (Even this generalization must be qualified, however, since a significant number of Republicans are more "liberal" than many Democrats.)

Outside of the policy-planning groups (who concern themselves very little with strictly partisan politics), and with the exception of the historic concentration of Democrats in the South (many of whom are as conservative as many Republicans), *smaller and medium-sized businesses* support the Republican party more often than the Democratic party. We have already seen that part of the reason for this is that smaller businesses are more likely to find themselves in competitive markets and hence are much more likely to take the economic ideology of free enterprise and competition seriously. But this fact should not obscure the close relationships that Democrats as well as Republicans maintain with the 200 or so largest corporations, nor the fact that close relationships also exist between all representatives and the business interests within their constituencies.

Congress is not the institution in which broad public policy is formulated. This function is reserved for the executive branch. Members of Congress are mainly concerned with the local interests within their own districts, to which because of the political way in which congressional districts are drawn ("gerrymandering"), tend to be highly oriented either toward Republicans or Democrats (the poor tend to be concentrated in a small number of districts). Only about *10 percent* of all congressional districts are internally competitive; and fully *90 percent* tend to be, in effect, one-party districts. This fact explains why the tenure of most members of Congress is very long, why the corporate and interest-group system tends to support incumbents more strongly than challengers (regardless of party affiliation), and why all members of Congress, whether Republicans or Democrats, maintain close ties to the business interests within their districts.

## Government Aid to Business

The second example, occurring only a few days after President Reagan's nationwide political speech, makes it very clear that not only do politicians attempt to influence election outcomes in favor of the "ins," but that government officials assume a major role as spokespersons for major business interests as well. President Reagan announced the tripling of the amount of wheat available for sale to the USSR, much as the public relations director of a large firm might announce a special sale with the intent of taking customers away from the opposition. This announcement was coupled with two others: the United States would begin to subsidize farm exports; and the signing into law of a new export bill would permit American companies to form joint export trading companies (cartels) that would be exempt from antitrust laws. The export bill would also allow bank holding companies to own export trading companies, thus bringing together banks and competitive firms into the same organization.

The two political parties do compete with each other over who will win the small number of marginal seats that can go either way in an election, but they are primarily battling over matters of personnel, not over questions of fundamental policy (which are decided elsewhere). The rhetoric in an election may, at times (but only at times), make it appear as though the two candidates differ on certain issues; but these differences tend to be personal and moral in nature and almost never concern issues such as abortion, law and order, nuclear weapons, military preparations, busing, and the like. It is not that these are not important issues. It is simply that they are, first, largely outside the economic area, and second, are highly emotionally charged and are likely to be handled, in any case, either by the executive branch or the courts. Even the major component of Franklin D. Roosevelt's economic recovery program (as well as those of Kennedy and Reagan) was designed to aid the corporate system. In spite of obvious violations of antitrust laws, Roosevelt's program encouraged businesses to form cartels that would be designed to control supply, price, and profit. The similarity of Kennedy's economic program to Reagan's is even more striking and included large tax deductions, primarily for corporations. All three administrations illustrate the fact that the corporate system, the economy as a whole, and the government are inseparably linked. A great concentration of assets, sales, employment, and important products are within the scope and control of a small number of very large corporations; and *no* important government official thinks or acts without taking these interests into account.

If elections and political parties, the mainsprings of the individual political system, do not explain policy outcomes, the corporate political system certainly will. In the next three chapters we shall explore, in detail, how the economy and government are linked together. If power is in some way an expression of getting what one wants, then we would expect most government outcomes to favor the corporate political system and those who benefit from it. We shall see the extent to which this is true.

In order to study these relationships we shall need to know something more about the economy, about the role of government in economic affairs, and about the role of economic affairs in government. It is to these questions that we now turn.

# CHAPTER NINE
# DEMAND-SIDE
# GOVERNMENT

The size of the Gross National Product and how fast it is growing or declining are the major indicators of how well any country is doing economically. Nearly everyone appreciates the value of economic growth. It is, indeed, the *only* way in which the standard of living of a country's population can be improved over the long term. Economic growth frees up sufficient capital to increase expenditures for education, housing, transportation, food production, manufacturing, health, and the myriad other signs of material well-being. It has a major impact on the goods and services that the "average" citizen can afford, depending upon how the wealth and income it generates are distributed among the general population.

However, there are many things the GNP does not tell us. For example, it doesn't tell us what we may be doing to the environment and to the ecosystem of our planet, or what we may be doing to the lives of people who must "fit in" to the economic structure as presently constituted, with all its dehumanizing, boring work (both blue-collar and white-collar). It does not say anything about the alternative life styles of smaller communities, about sharing property in common, or about living closer to nature. In other words, not all of the features of *quality* of life are covered by economic comforts. Some of us may believe that "happiness," or "internal peace," or what may be in store for us after we die, are—or should be—more important than material well-being or the time we pass on this earth.

There is, however, no way in which we can agree on the value of psychological or religious states, on the value of alternative live styles, or on what is the *best* way for people to live. We *can* agree, however, that it is more pleasant to be rich than to be poor, and to live in a country that is able to generate great material well-being than to live in a country where most of the population lives just to survive. And, since we do live in the United States, which, along with all industrialized countries, stresses the importance of living well, we have few economic alternatives available other than trying to get some share of what the country has to offer. Indeed, our economic ideology places great value on doing just that. In this chapter, then, we shall concentrate on the ways in which government is involved in factors related to economic well-being and the generation and maintenance of wealth, and the ways in which government aids the economy and contributes to the size and growth of the GNP.

Measuring the *direct* impact of government on GNP is only one of the ways in which we can assess the significance of the role of government in American society and in the economy. Not only, as we shall see, are many government expenditures not calculated into the Gross National Product, but government also performs a number of important functions that are difficult to evaluate by dollars and cents alone. For example, government has a monopoly on the legitimate use of force in the society and has the responsibility of maintaining internal law and order and national defense capabilities. Government is responsible for the establishment and maintenance of a number of other "public goods," the most important being education, roads and highways, a retirement system, and the post office, among others. It also plays a key role in the support and regulation of a large number of economic, social, and political activities, such as the regulation of interstate commerce, communications, banking, subsidy programs to agriculture, the health sciences, industry, transportation, and small businesses; it actually owns a very small number of water, electric, and other utilities (the largest being the Tennessee Valley Authority).

But an analysis of the government's contribution to the Gross National Product (in large measure through these other functions) will give us an idea of the magnitude of the largest part of its economic and social role. I stress largest *part* of its economic role because a number of governmental programs, indeed some of its most controversial, involve what are called *transfer payments* (Social Security, servicing the public debt, welfare, and various "tax expenditures," to both individuals and corporations, being four of the most important), which do not figure into Gross National Product because they are expenditures that transfer money from one sector of the economy and the society into another and do not directly, except in their administrative costs, involve purchases of goods and services. Examples of such transfers include those from the less well-off to the more well-off, from the more well-off to the less well-off, from corporations to individuals, from individuals to corporations, from one set of corporations to another, from small business to big business, and so on. We shall, then, supplement the discussion of government's effect on the GNP with a description of some of these other programs as well.

## SUPPLY, DEMAND, AND PRICE

Before we begin to analyze the GNP and the role of government in the economy, we should first discuss three other concepts that will help us understand the relationship between economics in general and government.

Two of the most important economic concepts are *supply* (quantity of goods and services produced) and *demand* (what consumers buy). The most famous "law" of economics can be stated quite simply using these two concepts: in general, if demand rises, there will be pressures on the economy to increase supply. Conversely, if demand falls, the amount supplied will also tend to fall. This is the basic law of supply and demand; under this law, the *demand-side* of the equation determines output. This basic principle has been superseded in the Reagan administration by an emphasis on what is known as *supply-side economics* (a very old principle, formulated as Say's Law in 1803), which essentially has it that an increase in production will have the effect of increasing demand (by providing jobs, thereby generating income in the hands of consumers). Hence, government can intervene in the economy in two ways: by enforcing policies that will affect demand, or by enforcing policies that will affect supply.

The third concept that concerns us is *price,* one of the factors that links supply and demand. In the simplest case, if demand goes up and supply does not, then prices will rise. If demand goes down and supply does not, then prices will fall. Stated from the supply side: if supply goes up faster than demand, prices will fall. If supply goes down faster than demand, prices will rise.

These three concepts yield the following important generalizations:

### DEMAND-SIDE

1. If demand increases, *either* supply will also increase (and prices will remain level), *or* supply will not increase (and prices will rise).
2. If demand goes down, *either* supply will decrease (and prices will remain level), *or* supply will not decrease (and prices will fall).

### SUPPLY-SIDE

3. If supply goes up, *either* demand will increase (and prices will remain constant), *or* demand will not increase (and prices will fall).
4. If supply goes down, *either* demand will go down (and prices will remain constant), *or* demand will not go down (and prices will rise).

**PRICE-SIDE**

5.  If prices up up, demand will fall, producing pressures to lower supply.
6.  If prices go down, demand will rise, producing pressures to increase supply.

These generalizations will give us additional leverage in understanding the ways in which the government can influence demand, supply, and price. They also tell us how important it is to be able to influence these basic economic factors, since not only is the general health of the economy dependent upon their interrelationships, but the ability of individual firms to make money is as well. Some governmental policies, for example, attempt to *prevent* these economic generalizations from working. For example, with respect to proposition 3 (the effect of an increase in supply on demand and price), $4 billion a year is spent by the Department of Agriculture through farm price supports to insure that an increase in supply of farm products is met by sufficient *government* demand (the buying of excess production and storing it) so that it does not result in falling farm prices.

## Oligopolistic and Monopolistic Markets

We should not think, however, that government's ability to influence supply and demand is unlimited. Indeed, government plays a much more constrained role. Recall that oligopolies and monopolies are in a market position to control supply. Hence, in those sectors of the economy where a few firms control the amount produced (that is, nearly all of the major sectors of the economy), an increase in demand may *not* result in an increase in supply but rather an increase in price (proposition 1). Similarly, since those in a position to control supply are also in a position to control price, increases in prices may occur even in situations where demand is falling (a *reverse* effect of proposition 2 for oligopolistic markets).

Recall also that these factors of supply, demand, and price operate within a framework of *profit making*. To the extent that firms are able to manipulate supply, demand, and price, they may be expected to do so in a way that will maintain or increase profits, growth, and the stability of the market structure, none of which firms in competitive markets can control very well, but *all* of which firms in monopolistic and oligopolistic market structures are in a position to do. As we have already discussed at length, the market position that insures the highest profits is that of a monopoly or an oligopoly. These are positions where profit, price, and supply (and to some extent, even demand), are, at least in part, under the control of the firms themselves. Government, then, will be able to play some role in the matters of supply and demand, usually involving efforts to increase both, since the size of the GNP—and hence the general economic welfare of everyone—depends upon increases in supply *and* demand. But government will play a limited role in this process since it is the firms themselves that have the major share of influence over these matters. That is, to a large extent, the economy is *independent* from government (although, as we have seen, the reverse is not true). Corporations in oligopolistic market structures are much better able to affect their own interests through control of supply, price, and demand, than is government.

## Government Intervention

To the extent that government does play a role, however (and what it does is not insignificant), we can expect that role to be one of general support of the business community. It would, indeed, be silly to think otherwise, since the general economic well-being of the country is dependent upon the economic well-being of the business sector. In addition, since the corporate sector of the economy carries the most "clout" in political matters, governmental interventions in the economy are supported by at least *some* segments of the corporate political system, although, given the fact that specific actions may benefit some economic interests more than others, not necessarily by *all* segments. There will, on many matters, be competition for governmental support *within the business community itself*. On the other hand, some general governmental policies, such as across-the-board corporate tax breaks, for example, will have the support of everyone in the business community.

Many of government's interventions, however, are on the demand-side of the equation—that is, getting money into the hands of consumers (instead of business). Some of these interventions will not be supported by the business community in general, especially by smaller businesses. The most "enlightened" of those in the corporate system, however, see the necessity and value of these types of government interventions (welfare, for example), since level of demand is obviously an important dimension of the economic equation. (Furthermore, it would not look good if people in the richest country in the world were dying from hunger and resorting to crime; these would be compelling facts to those who have responsibility for overall policy planning). Since very large firms can control to a significant extent their own profit levels (through their control of supply and price), they can pass on any costs incurred by governmental policies to stimulate consumer demand (e.g. taxes) in the form of higher prices. Large corporations have economic factors on their side that permit them to take a larger view. Smaller businesses, as we have already seen, are much more vulnerable to increases in costs; they exist in more competitive markets where they are less able to control profit levels and hence are more resistant to government demand-side efforts to get money into the hands of consumers. We shall discuss this problem further when we come to particular governmental programs.

The seeming "conflict" between demand-side economics and supply-side economics, then, is much less an economic conflict than it is a *political* one. Increased production (*if* money for investment is available, interest rates are reasonable, businesses are confident they can sell what they produce, and sufficient funds are in the hands of consumers to insure that the demand is there) increases the number of jobs and perhaps raises wages. Increased demand (putting money into the hands of consumers) can produce an increase in production (although it can also lead to higher prices). *Both* an increase in supply *and* an increase in demand are necessary for a growing economy. Politically, however, the more conservative elements of the business community (small business in general) are likely to favor supply-side policies that directly benefit themselves; and liberal elements of the business community (mostly those in giant corporations) are likely to favor *both* supply-side and at least a minimum number of demand-side interventions by government as well.

With this additional information, then, let us now analyze the component parts of the GNP and the government's role in stimulating both supply and demand.

## THE COMPONENTS OF THE GNP

Recall that Gross National Product is equal to: the sum of all expenditures for newly produced goods (at the point at which they are sold in final form, avoiding the problem of "double-counting"); and the sum of all services performed for which there is no tangible product (banking, education, and medical services are three examples), represented by the amount of wages and salaries paid to those performing the services.

The major sectors of Gross National Product are the following: consumer spending (for goods and services); business spending (purchases of capital equipment and plant, called *investment*); government spending (for goods and services); and the difference between the value of exports and the value of imports (net foreign trade). These are essentially the same categories, by the way, that comprise Gross National Wealth.

In 1981, the United States had a Gross National Product of $2 trillion, nine hundred twenty-five billion ($2,925,000,000,000), placing it first in total GNP for all countries, and eleventh in terms of GNP per capita population among the industralized nations. Switzerland, Denmark, Sweden, West Germany, Luxembourg, Norway, Belgium, Iceland, France, and The Netherlands all have Gross National Products per capita which exceed that of the United States. That is, although the United States is the leading country in *total* GNP, it has fallen behind most of the other industrialized nations when the size of the population is taken into account. In other words, it can no longer be so easily argued that the U.S. population has the highest standard of living in the world.

Of this sum of $2.925 trillion total GNP in 1981, personal consumption accounted for 1.858 trillion (64%); business spending (gross private domestic investment) $451 billion (15%); government spending for goods and services (federal, state, and local) $591 billion (20%); and net foreign trade (the value of exports that exceeds the value of imports) $26 billion (1%). The 1982 GNP was over $3 trillion, most of the increase being due to the large inflationary rise in prices—9.4 percent in 1981, and 12.9 percent in 1980. The economy has essentially been stagnant in terms of *real* GNP growth during the past few years (−0.3% in 1980, +0.7% in 1981, and −1.8% in 1982). Since we will be discussing GNP and its relationship to other sectors of the economy, especially to governmental expenditures and taxes, and since the last year for which these figures are final at the time of writing this book is 1981, most of the data we shall use in this chapter will be for 1981. The *percentages* reported here, however, will be very close to those for earlier and later years (the GNP percentages by sector given above, for example, are identical with those for 1980).

## Consumer Spending

By far the largest component of Gross National Product, then, stated in terms of demand, is determined by what individuals in the society purchase. It is interesting to note what individuals bought for the $1.858 trillion they spent in 1981, as these figures will help us understand something about the nature of demand in the United States. Durable goods accounted for $232 billion, nondurable goods for $743 billion, and services for $883 billion. Table 9–1 gives a breakdown of these categories.

**TABLE 9–1  Consumer Spending in 1981 (billions of dollars)**

| | | |
|---|---|---|
| *Durable goods* | | $232 |
| motor vehicles and parts | $ 98 | |
| furniture & household equipment | $ 93 | |
| other | $ 41 | |
| *Nondurable goods* | | $743 |
| food | $382 | |
| clothing | $116 | |
| gas & oil | $ 94 | |
| other | $151 | |
| *Services* | | $883 |
| housing | $307 | |
| household operation | $126 | |
| electricity & gas | $63 | |
| other | $63 | |
| transportation | $ 69 | |
| other | $381 | |
| Total | | $1,858 |

SOURCE: Department of Commerce (Bureau of Economic Analysis), *Survey of Current Business,* 62, No. 6 (June 1982).

The fact that individual consumers purchase 64 percent of the value of the Gross National Product is important for a variety of reasons, but ultimately because economic growth depends upon both what is produced *and* the ability of consumers to buy goods and services. This is why anyone who is seriously concerned with the present state of the United States economy has to consider both supply-side and demand-side economics. It is also the major reason why many economists and others, including many corporate leaders in policy-planning groups, are greatly concerned about insuring that sufficient funds get into the hands of individual consumers. We shall discuss this point at greater length in the section on government spending; but for the moment, many of the programs that involve transfer payments are serving an *economic* function in the society as a whole as well as keeping people alive and permitting them at least a minimal standard of living. If people do not have money to spend, production will, by necessity, slow down and even decrease.

## Savings and Business Investment

If, on the other hand, consumers have sufficient buying power, they can use their money (or at least the major part of it—the rest going to savings) to purchase goods and services, creating demand, and thereby encouraging business to increase the supply available. Low wages, high unemployment, and high inflation will impede the demand-supply relationship and produce a stagnant economy for two reasons. First, consumers have less money to spend (or, in the case of inflation, when prices are rising, what money they do have is worth less). And second, consumers have less money to save. It is to be noted that saving is done by those people who have something to save—that is, by those whose income is sufficiently high that they need not spend all of it on present consumption. This excludes the bottom 25 percent of the population.

The importance of having sufficient funds to purchase goods and services speaks for itself. Production, as we have already indicated, is useful only to the extent that what is produced can be purchased. Savings are important because the amount of investment (e.g., business spending to replace worn-out machinery, buy additional machinery and plant, or start new businesses) depends to some extent on the amount that consumers can save. Firms must frequently borrow money from banks for investment; and that money comes, in part, from consumer saving. However, most business investment comes from the money business itself saves, in the form of retained earnings from profits, which account for approximately 75 percent of the funds used for business investment (and for noninvestment activities such as mergers).

The kind of "investment" that individuals engage in, the buying of already issued stocks and bonds, for example, is not really investment at all in the sense in which the word is used in economics, but rather is an alternative form of savings, similar to placing one's money in a savings account, though perhaps with somewhat more risk (and more return). *Investment,* as the word is used here, has to do with the purchase of new capital equipment, and is an activity of businesses, not of individuals, although some of the funds that businesses use for investment come from the money saved by individual consumers. Hence, both personal consumption *and* savings are important economic activities that stimulate the economy. Inadequate funds in the hands of consumers will both reduce demand (personal consumption) and reduce savings, thereby decreasing the amount of money earned by business in terms of sales, and decreasing the amount of money available for business investment.

## National Income

The total amount of money available to consumers, businesses, and government for the purchase of goods and services is known as the *National Income*. This figure represents the sum total of payments earned in the production of the Gross National Product (wages and salaries, rent, interest, and profits) and is arrived at by taking the Gross National Product ($2.925 trillion in 1981) and subtracting from it the amount businesses spend to replace worn-out machinery, for example called *capital consumption,* or *depreciation,* and indirect business taxes (such as property taxes) that are included in the costs of doing business and hence are already built into the price level. Total National Income available for purchases of goods and services in the GNP in 1981 was $2.347 trillion. Of this sum, $1.772 trillion was in the form of compensation to employees (of which $1.483 trillion was in wages and salaries and $289 billion in the form of supplements to wages such as Social Security paid by the employer), $135 billion was income from proprietorships (small businesses), $192 billion from corporate profits (after adjustments), $34 billion from rental income, and $215 billion from interest (savings accounts, for example). It is from these sources that purchasing power and savings are generated; and as is clear from these figures, individual consumers constitute the bulk of this buying power.

## The Distribution of Demand

The problem of demand is greater in a highly industrialized country like the United States, which depends upon a high level of mass consumption of what is produced, than it is in an agricultural economy. As is clear from Table 9–1, for example, consumer spending involves much more than the purchase of simple necessities (as would be true of an agricultural economy). Industrialized nations depend upon the sale of their products (automobiles, appliances, energy products such as gas, oil, electricity, and so on) to as large a proportion of the population as possible. In an economy in which most people grow their own food, and purchases of other than the bare necessities are reserved for only the very wealthy, the problem of demand for manufactured products hardly arises. Industry and the related banking, wholesale, retail, packaging, advertising, and transportation that go along with the production of goods and services are dependent for their own success on the ability of consumers to purchase those goods and services. A drop in demand, due to unemployment or to a general lack of consumer funds because of inflation or extremely low wages—as is the case for millions of Americans who work for the minimum wage or less—will result in fewer sales, unused productive capacity, and lower profits for the business community. Recessions and depressions do not hurt only the poor (although they are hit hardest, since they have no savings and are the first to lose their employment). A fall in demand affects the entire economic structure and results in increasing bankruptcies, falling revenues, and lower profit levels for business. The question, then, for industrialized nations, is not simply the *level* of demand (which may be concentrated, for example, in the hands of a small proportion of the population), although overall aggregate demand is very important. The problem is also the *distribution* of that demand in the population as a whole, since the products that are produced by industry are designed to be consumed by everyone.

## ECONOMICS AND THE PROBLEM OF DEMAND

Government programs that affect both the total level of demand and the distribution of that demand are numerous and varied in the means by which they operate, whom they benefit, and how they are financed. They are also classified under several headings, some of which include the same programs: *automatic stabilizers* (programs that automatically increase overall level of demand during periods of economic decline and put a break on growing demand during periods of general prosperity); *transfer payments* (expenditures, either in cash or in kind, that are not directly earned by those receiving them); *entitlements* (payments that go to all individuals who qualify under the law and include several of the automatic stabilizers; they are open ended and do not involve a fixed, legislatively predetermined allocation of funds); and *tax expenditures* (deductions and tax credits given to individuals and corporations for a specific or general purpose). In the following section I shall discuss the major governmental programs that influence both overall demand and the distribution of demand. I shall also classify them in a simpler, more descriptive fashion.

Before doing this, however, let me briefly sketch the *economic* reasons that lie behind the general problem of demand, and why government is called upon to play a major role in its regulation.

Let us take a period of general prosperity as our starting point. Gross National Product is growing (3 to 5 percent per year, in constant dollars), unemployment is low (2 to 3 percent, which reflects those who are in transition from one job to another), inflation is low (1 to 2 percent), savings are about 5 to 7 percent, interest rates are between 5 and 7 percent, and the amount produced (supply) is about equal to the amount demanded. The fifteen-year period between

1952 and 1967, with the usual ups and downs that are characteristic of any economic period, was one in which many of these conditions prevailed (except for unemployment, which was between 3 and 6 percent). It must also be remembered, however, that like all periods in American history, about 20 percent of the U.S. population lived in extreme poverty. It was not until 1964 and President Johnson's War on Poverty that the situation of the very poor in this country was clearly brought to the public's attention.

## The Problem of Supply

The chronic problem of the American economic system (and of other free-market industrialized systems as well) is that it is enormously successful on the supply side. If there is a demand for goods and services, the American economy seems quite capable of filling that demand (and shaping it as well). Indeed, the problem may be stated even more strongly: the American economy has a problem of being able to supply too much. Now, at one level, this hardly seems like a problem. As supply increases, prices should fall, demand should increase, and everyone should be better off (the classic supply-side economic thesis). The problem is, *producers* are not necessarily better off. For them prices are falling, they are working at or near capacity, and some of their factors of production are less efficient and cost them more, per unit of production, than the revenues warrant. That is, although producers make more money using these less efficient factors of production (less skilled workers, and older machinery and plant being the primary ones), their rate of profit falls. In economic language, their *marginal revenues* (what they gain by adding or keeping less efficient factors of production) drop in relation to their *marginal costs*. Hence, their overall rate of profit falls, a circumstance that they must not allow to happen if they want to insure a maximum level of profit. If, for example, their rate of profit by using more expensive factors of production is lower than it would be by investing their money elsewhere (in government bonds, for example), it would be more profitable for them to get rid of these less efficient factors and use their money to invest in something that brings them a greater rate of return. Hence, producers *restrict* supply (those producers who are able to—that is, producers in oligopolistic market structures who can control total output), to a point at which they receive the highest rate of profit. This point (in economic terms, the point at which marginal costs do not exceed marginal revenues) is a point *before* their overall profits go down (since their overall revenues still exceed their *average* costs); but business people are as interested in their rate of return as they are in total revenues.

However, in placing restrictions on supply to maintain a desired rate of profit, prices do not fall (and may even rise), profits do not fall, demand does not increase (or if it does, given restrictions on supply, inflation occurs), and the total work force becomes *underutilized*. Unemployment goes up, demand goes down (or grows more slowly), production is stifled, and the problem arises of getting money into the hands of consumers (attempting to increase the level of demand in the face of underemployment of the labor force). From the supply side, productive capacity is underutilized (because it is more costly, on the average, to utilize full plant, equipment, and labor). In 1982, for example, *fully 31 percent* of the total plant capacity of the U.S. economy was not being utilized (the figure for the steel industry was 60 percent).

Not only is productive plant underutilized, so are people. According to government figures, unemployment in 1982 was over 10 percent, which did not include the approximately 2 to 3 million Americans who had given up looking for work, a figure that would bring the total to over 12 percent, and if those working part-time instead of full-time were included, the underemployment rate was closer to 14 percent. This means that one out of every seven Americans was either out of work or was working fewer hours than he or she would like. *This* is the demand problem. Stated in its simplest form: in an economic system that defines an acceptable profit level in terms of a certain rate of return, supply will tend to be restricted. This, in turn, will have a negative effect on demand because firms will cut those costs (including labor, plant, and equipment) that take them below what they consider to be an acceptable rate of profit. This also helps to explain why firms seek oligopolistic market structures: in controlling supply, they are able to control price and profit levels. That this has a negative influence on demand is simply an inherent consequence of the profit-seeking behavior of firms in the economic system.

## Alternative Investment

Interestingly, then, few alternative solutions to this problem exist except government intervention, an intervention that will be sought by both consumers and business. If demand falls, the entire economy is hurt, and business is as anxious as consumers that the level of demand be maintained. One could ask corporations not to restrict supply, but individual corporations are profit-making organizations whose rational strategy is to maximize their rate of return, *even if this means lower overall profits within the firm.* That is, an individual firm would prefer to make $900,000 profit within the firm and $100,000 by holding government bonds (both, say, at the profit rate of 9 percent), than to make $950,000 within the firm (at an overall profit level slightly below 9 percent).

Hence, instead of using somewhat less efficient means of production that increase supply (but also reduce its overall rate of profit), a firm will invest in something that brings a higher expected return. A horizontal merger will be an attractive form of investment because it not only might bring in the expected rate of return, but also add to the company's size and market position, thus enhancing its ability to control supply, price, and profit. But even conglomerate mergers can be attractive to business firms as an alternative to further investment in their own companies. For example, one of the most significant mergers in 1982 was the conglomerate merger of Xerox, the world's largest manufacturer of copying machines, and Crum & Forster, one of the nation's largest property-casualty insurers, at a cost to Xerox of $1.6 billion. Xerox decided that using its funds to take over a company in a completely unrelated industry would bring a higher rate of return, in the long run, than using the funds to increase its own production of copying machines. U.S. Steel's decision to buy Marathon Oil was of the same type. Corporations will seek an acceptable rate of profit; and if this means going outside of the company rather than staying within it, then they will do so. One cannot expect individual corporations to take positions in the general economic interest that go against their own individual interest of maximum profit-making.

### Consumer Credit

There was, however, one decision that the business community did make to stimulate demand, a strategy supported by all sectors within the economy and that worked with outstanding success. Through various mechanisms of consumer credit (such as bank credit cards and retail credit systems), consumer debt rose from $44 billion in 1960 to $328 billion in 1981. What consumers could not buy with current income, they were encouraged to finance with expected future income. There was a limit, however, to this practice. As the economy worsened, and unemployment spread to people in better-paying blue- and white-collar jobs, the expected income presumed by credit extension was no longer forthcoming, and many individuals found themselves in debt without employment or with reduced income. Mortgage foreclosures, automobile returns, and small business bankruptcies were all a natural consequence of these credit problems.

## GOVERNMENT PROGRAMS THAT AFFECT DEMAND

There are three major ways through which government programs affect consumer demand (we will consider separately government actions that affect supply, and government programs that affect demand in general): (1) transfer payment programs that are indirectly earned by the recipients; (2) transfer payment programs that are unearned (frequently called welfare); and (3) tax expenditure programs (various income tax deductions and credits that leave more money in the hands of certain consumers for general or specific uses). We shall explore the major government programs in each of these three categories.

Recall that transfer payments are government expenditures paid to individuals that are *not* given for specific services or to purchase goods (it is for this reason that they are not considered a part of GNP). These payments, however, can come from two different sources. It is important to keep this distinction in mind, because one of the sources is the general treasury (tax revenues collected for general governmental purposes), and the other has a completely different form of financing. Transfer payment programs paid for out of general revenues are, for the most part, "welfare" programs. The second category of transfer payment programs includes those in which individuals who receive the benefits have made a financial contribution. In the case of one program (unemployment insurance), contributions are collected in the form of a business tax (like an excise tax) that is treated as a cost and is recoverable by the business in its pricing practices. We shall call transfer payment programs to individuals that are indirectly earned *contributory transfer payment programs,* and those that do not involve separate contributory financing *general revenue transfer payment programs,* indicating that these latter are funded through the general revenue budget.

## Contributory Transfer Payment Programs

By far the largest single contributory transfer payment program is Old-Age, Survivors, and Disability Insurance (OASDI), the major program in Social Security which, in 1981, paid out $139.6 billion to 36 million recipients (retirees, widows, and the disabled); 31.6 million pension checks were paid out to those who have retired. The OASDI is *not* a welfare program. Its benefits go to everyone who contributes (almost all working Americans must belong, and in 1981 Social Security had 116 million individual contributors). OASDI is essentially a *retirement* system (it also includes disability insurance, which amounted to $17.3 billion of the $139.6 billion total) to which individuals contribute one-half and employers contribute one-half of the special tax that is collected to pay for it (6.7 percent of wages or salary for each in 1981). Neither the 6.7 percent that individuals pay, nor the 6.7 percent that business pays, is taxable income, but is treated as a cost that is deductible *before* income taxes for individuals and corporate income taxes for business are figured.

Begun in 1935, the major purpose of OASDI is to insure that retirees have sufficient income on which to live, and in this sense is clearly a program designed to stabilize consumer demand. It is generally acknowledged that the Social Security program is financed in a "regressive" fashion—that is, the contributions are collected in such a way that those of lesser income pay a higher proportion than those of higher income. The major reasons for this are that the 6.7 percent collected from individuals includes earnings only up to $29,700 (in 1981)—income beyond this amount is not taxed; and the 6.7 percent collected from business is added to the price of items sold (as a cost of doing business) and hence is very much like an excise or sales tax that takes a higher percentage of income from the less well-to-do.

OASDI, then, is not financed through general taxes, and its benefits go to rich and poor alike. In fact, the Social Security System does not even belong in the federal budget, and was not until recently, since it is not a general revenue program. It is there now because President Johnson thought he could hide the growing expense of the Vietnam War by merging Social Security with the general revenue budget, thereby making the federal budget appear larger and military expenses a smaller proportion of the total, expanded budget.

In 1965, Medicare (which pays the medical expenses for those over 65) was added to the Social Security program; it is financed in the same fashion, so that the Social Security program now includes OASDI and Medicare ($42.5 billion in payments in 1981), for a total of $182.1 billion.

Social Security, although the largest of the contributory transfer payment programs, is not by any means the only one. Federal employees have their own retirement and disability program; in 1981 the payments amounted to $30 billion ($17.7 billion for civilian employees, and $12.3 billion for the military). The railroads also have a separate retirement system ($5.3 billion in contributory transfer payments in 1981), as do disabled coal miners (nearly $2 billion). In addition, unemployment compensation is financed separately (by a state and federal tax on businesses) and amounted to nearly $20 billion (the federal contribution) in 1981. The total for all of these indirectly earned contributory transfer payment programs (which, because of their separate means of financing could easily be taken out of the general revenue budget, except for the government contribution to federal employee retirement), amounted to $239.4 billion in 1981.

## General Revenue Transfer Payment Programs

The federal government funds a number of transfer payment programs to individuals that *do* come out of general revenues. To the extent that these programs are aimed at giving aid to the poor (and most, but by no means all, of these programs are designed to help the poor), they may be considered as welfare programs. Their purpose is to insure that those with insufficient incomes have enough money to purchase needed goods and services. There are no indirect contributions by those receiving them, except to the extent that recipients may pay taxes that go into the general revenue fund. Hence, these transfer payments directly affect the distribution of demand; they take money from general revenues and transfer it to selected individuals.

The major general revenue transfer payment programs that help the poor (dollar figures are for the 1981 federal budget) are Medicaid ($16.8 billion), food stamps ($11.3 billion), Aid to Families with Dependent Children ($8.5 billion), Supplemental Security Income (aid to the blind, the aged, and permanently and totally disabled—$7.2 billion), housing assistance ($7 billion), school lunch and other child nutrition programs ($5 billion), and Energy and Emergency Assistance ($1.5 billion). The total dollar value of these programs was $57.3 billion.

The largest single general revenue transfer payment program, however, is not specifically designed to aid the poor. This program is for veterans and in 1981 amounted to expenditures of $20 billion. Although *some* veterans may be poor, not all of them are. In any case veterans' benefits are not considered to be welfare payments and are designed to benefit a particular group of people who are considered to have performed an especially meritorious service.

The 1981 total of all individual transfer payments, then, was $316.7 billion, of which $239.4 billion was in contributory transfer payment programs (76% of the total), and $77.3 billion was in general revenue transfer payments (24%). Of the general revenue transfer payments, however, only $57.3 billion (18% of the total $316.7 billion in transfer payments to individuals), were welfare payments. I emphasize this point simply to illustrate that 82 percent of all transfer payments are either indirectly earned and involve individual contributions and special forms of taxing, or are designed for veterans and do not involve welfare. Among the industrial nations of the world, the United States ranks next to last (before Japan, which has an income security system quite different from other countries) in terms of total transfer payments to individuals as a percentage of GNP.

## Tax Expenditures for Individuals

There are, essentially, three ways in which government can influence the level and distribution of individual demand in the economy. We have already described two of them: contributory transfer payments that maintain overall demand, and general revenue transfer payments, many of which are directed toward the poor and hence affect the distribution of demand within the population. What these programs have in common is that they collect money—either through special contributory taxes, as in Social Security, or through general revenues—and then transfer this money back to the population. In the case of general revenue transfer payment programs, the payments involve a redistribution of funds from general taxpayers to particular categories of people (veterans and the poor).

The third way in which government influences individual demand is *not* to collect taxes in certain particular instances, thus leaving them in the hands of the designated group of taxpayers. This mechanism, although identical to welfare in that it involves a transfer of money from one group to another, is handled quite differently from the mechanism that collects taxes and then transfers them. For one thing, such a system does not show up as a budget entry, since these items are neither actual revenues nor actual expenditures. Rather, they are deductions, credits, exclusions, and exemptions from the general tax laws that involve a loss of revenue that would ordinarily have been collected by the government had the special tax exemptions not been in force. The name given to these exemptions, exclusions, deductions, and credits is *tax expenditures,* presumably because they "spend" tax revenues by not collecting them and therefore actually involve a government subsidy to certain designated groups. (They are also called "tax loopholes" by those who do not like them.) Fundamentally, they are revenue losses from the general treasury, since they are exceptions to the general tax laws.

Another feature that makes these tax expenditures different from welfare payments (beside being at least partially hidden), is the nature of the groups who benefit from them. As everyone knows, our federal income tax system is thought of as being progressive—that is, the wealthier one is, the higher the percentage of income taxes one pays. In part this is true. The federal income tax is mildly progressive (at least until one reaches the very top, where it becomes regressive—that is, the very wealthy pay a smaller actual percentage than do the middle groups). But one of the consequences of tax expenditures is that, because these revenue losses benefit wealthier groups they greatly modify the income tax structure, making the proportion paid by all tax-paying groups, rich and poor, much more equal. In addition, tax expenditures are one of the major programs that benefit corporations, a point we shall discuss in the next chapter.

It is probably not by accident that benefits designed for the poor are highly visible (that is, they show up in the federal budget, both as taxes and as expenditures, and are given such names as "transfer payments," "entitlements," "public assistance," and "welfare") and that advantages given to the nonpoor are hidden (that is, they are not a part of the federal budget and are called "tax expenditures"). Americans, in general, are made very aware of the money that is spent on the poor. In fact, very frequently Social Security and other contributory transfer payment programs are erroneously put on the list of "welfare" programs, thus making the list look larger than it really is. The same is not true, however, for what some people have labeled "wealthfare"—those government programs that give advantages to middle- and upper-income Americans. As we shall see, the amount of money involved in tax expenditure programs that aid wealthier Americans *vastly exceeds* the $57.3 billion spent on welfare.

In 1981, there were 104 federal tax expenditure programs that involved revenue losses of $228.6 billion. Of this sum, $179.8 billion (79%) went to individuals, and $48.8 billion (21%) were corporate tax expenditures. The following is a list of the major deductions, exemptions, credits, and exclusions that make up the $179.8 billion in tax expenditures to individuals.

Exclusion from taxable income of pension-plan contributions and earnings: $25.7 billion

Preferential tax rate on capital gains: $21.3 billion

Deductibility of home mortgage interest payments: $19.8 billion

Deductions for state and local taxes (other than the property tax on owner-occupied homes): $18.4 billion

Exclusion of employer contributions for medical insurance premiums and employee health care: $14.2 billion

Exclusion of Social Security benefits from taxable income: $11.1 billion

Deductibility of property tax on owner-occupied homes: $8.9 billion

Deductibility of interest on consumer credit: $5.3 billion

Exclusion of interest on life insurance savings: $4.0 billion

Investment credit for individuals: $3.1 billion

These ten tax expenditures for individuals represent nearly 75 percent ($131.8 billion) of the total $179.8 billion in tax expenditures for individuals. Some of them are very broad in their application (exclusion of Social Security benefits as taxable income, for example) and benefit the poor who receive Social Security as well as the wealthy, although even here the wealthy benefit more since presumably their tax rate would be higher. Most of them, however, provide much larger benefits to middle- and upper-income groups (interest on home mortgages, property taxes on owner-occupied homes, and capital gains, for example). In their totality they certainly cannot be said to be directed toward helping the poor. Indeed, one would have to conclude just the opposite: that tax expenditures for individuals advantage primarily middle- and upper-income groups. Two-thirds of all people in the United States live in owner-occupied homes, for example, which leaves one-third who do not. And very few of the 14 percent of the population under the poverty line own their own homes and thus benefit from these income tax exclusions. Those who benefit from the lower tax on capital gains represent almost exclusively the upper 5 percent of the total population. Compared with the $57.3 billion in general revenue transfer payments that may be called welfare, this $179.8 billion in individual tax expenditure programs that are primarily for wealthier Americans clearly outweights the amount given to the poor (over three times as much). Indeed, if we took only nine of the *smaller* individual tax expenditures that go almost entirely to middle- and upper-income groups [employer contributions for medical insurance premiums and medical care ($14.5 billion), deduction of interest on consumer credit ($5.3 billion), interest on life insurance savings ($4.0 billion), investment credit ($3.1 billion), interest on state and local bonds ($3.1 billion), oil exploration and depletion allowances to individuals ($2.4 billion), exclusion of premiums on group-term life insurance ($1.9 billion), dividend and interest exclusion ($1.3 billion), and exclusion of income earned abroad ($.6 billion)], and combined them with the losses on the preferential tax rate on capital gains ($21.3 billion), the total would exactly equal the amount that is spent on welfare ($57.3 billion). *The total amount of individual tax expenditures (which go mainly to the well-to-do) is more than three times the amount of money spent on welfare.*

In this chapter we have limited ourselves to a discussion of how government affects individual demand, the 64 percent of GNP ($1.858 trillion in 1981) that consumers spend on goods and services. In the next chapter we shall discuss the relationship between governmental programs and the business community: what government does, in terms of subsidies and tax expenditures, to aid business. The major rationale for government aid to business is in terms of supply-side economics rather than demand-side economics—that is, these programs are presumably designed to encourage production instead of demand, or, stated in more classical supply-side terms, to encourage production in order to stimulate demand. Whether these programs accomplish what their rationale says they are for, or whether they are simply subsidies and tax advantages to the very wealthy that perpetuate and at times even increase the inequalities in income and wealth we have already discussed, will be something that individual readers will have to decide for themselves. Once again, the *language* of politics when used to justify the issues and programs in the individual political system, and the *causes* for events that occur, must be clearly separated and examined for their possible congruities and incongruities. We have already seen that the sums that government provides to wealthier Americans to stimulate demand easily exceed the sums provided to the poor for the same purpose. It might not be unhealthy, then, to bring a little skepticism to this discussion of supply-side economics, especially since we have already seen that it is essentially the corporate political system that is responsible for general and specific policy making in the United States anyway.

# CHAPTER TEN
# SUPPLY-SIDE
# GOVERNMENT

In the last chapter we discussed the government's influence on consumer demand. This chapter will concern another component of Gross National Product, investment: the amount of money spent by business on new capital equipment and plant, either to replace worn-out existing capital goods, or to purchase additional capital equipment and plant. This, by and large, is the major focus of supply-side economics because it is concerned primarily with government programs that increase the amount of money at the disposal of business (and the well-to-do) for possible investment and hence, theoretically, encourage growth in the production of goods and services.

The Reagan Administration has been particularly associated with supply-side economics, although, as we have seen, the idea that demand follows production (rather than vice versa) is a very old one. But supply-side economics has been a feature of every administration in this country, whether Republican or Democratic. Since growth in the GNP is such a highly valued goal, it is not surprising that government would be called upon to play a role in its development. During the nineteenth century, for example, the government offered enormous subsidies to railroad developers involving billions of dollars (both in terms of cash and land) to encourage the building of the railway system. The major component of President Franklin Delano Roosevelt's administration was incentives of all kinds (including cash and exemptions from antitrust laws) to encourage business to expand. Presidents Kennedy, Carter, and Johnson as well as Eisenhower, Nixon, and Ford, have also vigorously acted on the belief that government ought to help stimulate production as well as demand.

Supply-side economics—the idea of stimulating business investment and production in order to create jobs and put money into the hands of consumers (the so-called *trickle down theory*)—appeals to many during stagnant economic periods. This theory would be especially appealing if it were also combined with the idea that government activities to stimulate demand should be prohibited (as is the case in a "conservative" philosophy). What is missing here, however, is another theory that might explain—rather than justify—the current emphasis on aiding businesses instead of individuals.

When periods of economic growth do occur, *nearly everyone* (except, perhaps, the very poor) does better. More people are employed, wages are likely to increase, business sales and profits rise, and, in general, more money is available to a larger proportion of the American population. This is simply a "natural consequence" of the economic pie getting bigger.

## THE ZERO-SUM HYPOTHESIS

Now, what of a period of zero growth? The pie is not getting any larger—in fact, it may even be shrinking. The only way for *some* people to do better is to take things away from others. We become, in Lester Thurow's words (and book by the same title): a *zero-sum society*. When the total amount to be shared is fixed, what anyone "wins" as an increase in his or her share must be counterbalanced by an equivalent "loss" by someone else. Politics, in other words, gets tougher and meaner. And if we view the fight as between the individual political system (represented, in part, by demand-side economics) and the corporate political system (represented by supply-side economics), then we do not have to be told who is likely to win.

Indeed, the data from a study by the Congressional Budget Office already show who the winners have been. The effect of the Reagan Administration's tax changes for the single year of 1982 has been to redistribute income *from poor to rich*. Those earning less than $10,000 have suffered an average *loss* of $240; those earning between $10,000 and $20,000 have gained an average of $220; those earning between $21,000 and $40,000 have gained an average of $810; those earning between $40,000 and $80,000 have gained an average of $1,700; and those earning over $80,000 have gained an average of $15,130. The figures clearly show a net loss of $240 for the very poor, and a $15,130 net gain for the very rich.

Whatever the status of this zero-sum hypothesis, however, which predicts a greater assertion of business power and more conflict-laden politics between the wealthier and less wealthy and between business and consumers during periods of economic stagnation, public debate is likely to be over whether government should give incentives to business to increase production or initiate consumer programs to stimulate demand. It is obvious to supply-siders that what is needed is more production. It is just as obvious to demand-siders, however, that an increase in supply will produce an increase in demand only if consumers have the wherewithal to puchase what is supplied. But, more important, business firms will in fact increase investment, and hence increase production, only if they see a profitable market for what they produce.

When a large proportion of an economy's existing plant and equipment is not being utilized (about 31 percent in 1982), then programs to stimulate the building of even larger capacity seem doomed to failure. Indeed, the figures clearly indicate that very little of the increased money going to businesses by way of corporate tax deductions and incentives is being spent for investment. In spite of the large tax deductions for corporations that began in 1981 and 1982 ($180 billion worth over a five-year period), investment, measured in real dollars, actually *declined* in 1981 and 1982, leading Secretary of the Treasury Donald T. Regan to comment: "It's like dropping a coin down a well. All I'm hearing is a hollow clunk." Capital investment for plant and equipment is projected to fall an additional 5.2 percent in 1983, after a 4.8 percent drop in 1982. Corporate mergers, however, increased by over 27 percent in number, and by nearly 100 percent in dollar value. In other words, when one takes money away from consumers and gives it to business for investment purposes, business will not necessarily use it for supply-side purposes—that is, investment in new plant and equipment.

It is a good deal easier for government to influence demand than to influence supply. Government can directly influence demand by increasing the amount of money in the hands of consumers for spending or saving, both of which are important for production and investment, or by increasing its own spending. It can influence supply only indirectly by increasing the *opportunities* for business to invest the extra money it is given *if business chooses to do so*. The only way in which government could affect supply directly would be to take on the role of supplier itself (as in the Tennessee Valley Authority, for example), a prospect that is certainly *not* a part of free-enterprise supply-side economics, nor demand-side economics for that matter.

## CORPORATE INVESTMENT

In 1981, purchases of capital goods by business amounted to $451 billion, or 15 percent of GNP. Table 10–1 gives the breakdown of these capital purchases. Business investment is divided into two major categories: *fixed investment* (the amount of expenditures on capital equipment and plant, by far the larger figures), and *inventory* (the amount of goods produced that are left unsold at the end of the

**TABLE 10–1    Business Investment in 1981 (billions of dollars)**

| | | | |
|---|---|---|---|
| *Fixed investment* | | | $435 |
| Nonresidential | | $329 | |
| structures | $126 | | |
| producers' durable equipment | $203 | | |
| Residential | | $106 | |
| nonfarm structures | $100 | | |
| farm structures | $   3 | | |
| producers' durable equipment | $   3 | | |
| *Change in business inventory* | | | $  16 |
| Nonfarm | | $  14 | |
| Farm | | $   2 | |
| Total | | | $451 |

SOURCE: Department of Commerce (Bureau of Economic Analysis), *Survey of Current Business,* 62, No. 6 (June, 1982).

year). Although changes in business inventories can be an important indicator of short-term business activity, it is sufficient to note here that a large positive change in business inventories (from the previous year) is an indication that supply is greater than demand (due either to overproduction or underconsumption, depending upon whether one looks at inventory levels from supply-side or demand-side). A negative change in business inventory indicates just the reverse, that consumers are buying more than is being produced, or that business is producing less than is being consumed.

## Residential Investment

Two components of fixed investment (accounting for over 90 percent of total business investment) concern us: residential and nonresidential. Residential investment is the indicator for the housing industry in this country and is an extremely important sign of how well the domestic economy is doing. In 1981 the housing industry accounted for just slightly less than 25 percent of total fixed investment.

In recent years the home-building industry has run into a great deal of difficulty. The number of new housing units has dropped precipitously. In 1977, for example, the percentage of first-time home buyers was 36.3 percent. In 1981 the figure had dropped to 13.5 percent. The average price of a home is now approximately $75,000, with monthly payments of about $850. Not only have the home builders been hurt, however, but also the building trades, the real estate industry, and the banking community, especially the savings and loan associations, which deal primarily in home mortgages. The two major causes that are cited for the housing slump are the rising initial prices of homes and the high interest rate, which affects the ability of people to take out mortgages.

Government has been called upon to help the housing and related banking industries in a number of ways, the two major ones being to adopt policies to both decrease the rate of inflation and to lower the interest rate. Unfortunately, however, the two policies seem to work at cross-purposes. A tight money policy carried on by the Federal Reserve Board is designed to make money difficult to come by (which has a negative influence on demand and thereby a negative influence on supply); it makes economic growth difficult but cuts the rate of inflation (from 12.9 percent in 1979 to 9.4 percent in 1981). This same policy, however, also drives up interest rates (hovering between 14 percent and 17 percent in 1981) because the money supply is restricted. The unemployment rate has also risen very quickly over the same period. Hence, although the inflation rate has been decreased (but is still quite high), interest rates continue to make it difficult for potential homeowners, as do high rates of unemployment. The upshot of this is that the federal government has been able to do very little to help the housing industry and has, instead, directed its attention to the ailing banking community.

*Government aid to the banking industry.* Since the banking industry, especially the savings and loan associations, is so closely associated with the question of home ownership, a decline in the housing industry has produced a serious strain on this sector of the financial community; and a number of governmental programs have been developed to aid banking interests.

In 1981 and 1982 the federal government passed several new laws designed to aid banks and savings and loan associations:

1.  Deregulation of interest rates on deposits (to begin in 1986 or sooner), to help banks and savings and loans compete with the new money market funds;
2.  The creation of new seven-day savings certificates with interest rates tied to the ninety-one-day treasury bill (14.1% in 1981);
3.  Restriction on the transfer of old mortgages (which were issued at lower interest rates) when homes are sold, requiring the new buyer to take out a new mortgage at the higher prevailing rates;
4.  Permit the sale of money market fund accounts, with no limit on the rate of interest (money market funds had grown to over $220 billion by 1982);
5.  Permit savings and loan associations to make business and commercial loans;
6.  Provide aid to ailing banks and savings and loans in the form of net worth certificates (an artificial form of "paper" money), issued by the federal insurance funds for banks and savings and loans, increasing their assets. In 1981, 220 banks were considered to be in financial difficulties by the Federal Deposit Insurance Corporation, and 100 more were added to the list in 1982.
7.  Permit across-state mergers, even between banks and savings and loan associations. One of the first banks to take advantage of this possibility was Citibank of New York, the second largest bank in the United States, which acquired the Fidelity Federal Savings and Loan Association of California (with $2.9 billion in assets). This merger will undoubtedly move Citibank ahead of Bank of America as the nation's largest bank. Another large mer-

ger was announced in 1983, between Financial Corporation of America and First Charter Financial Corporation, creating the nation's largest savings and loan association (to be called American Savings). The combined assets of American Savings would be $20 billion, placing it well above Home Savings of America, the current leader with assets of $15 billion. There were, in total, 217 savings and loan mergers in 1981 alone;

8. The establishment of other special accounts, such as the new IRA's (tax free individual retirement accounts).

All of these actions had the strong support of the banking and savings and loan community. It asked the government to take these steps, and the government put them into legislation. So, although the housing industry itself is in a severe slump, the spillover effects on the financial community are being remedied through federal legislation. It is not irrelevant to point out, in this regard, that home building is very decentralized, composed of many local companies, whereas banking is highly concentrated, dominated by a few giant financial corporations.

## Corporate Tax Deductions

But by far the largest category of fixed investment is in the nonresidential sector (accounting for slightly over 75 percent of all investment in plant and equipment). This includes all investment outside of the housing industry and is centered primarily in manufacturing and industry. The single largest component of this investment is in equipment. It is this component, amounting to $203 billion in 1981, which is at the heart of supply-side efforts to increase business investment (along with other programs designed to increase corporate profits).

The federal government has encouraged business investment mostly through tax expenditures for corporations (exemptions, exclusions, deductions, and credits from corporate income taxes). Recall that of the total revenue losses of $228.6 billion in tax expenditure programs in 1981, $48.8 billion (21 percent of the total, *and a dollar figure that is only slightly less than total welfare payments in 1981 of $57.3 billion*) was granted to corporations. The following eight major revenue losses from corporate tax deductions, credits, exclusions, and exemptions, account for $44.4 billion of the total $48.8 billion in corporate tax expenditures (over 91%).

—Direct credits for investment in capital plant and equipment: $17.3 billion (35% of the total)

—Reduced rates on the first $100,000 of corporate profits: $7.4 billion

—Exclusion of interest on bonds: $6.6 billion

—Asset depreciation (including depletion allowances for oil and other fuels): $4.7 billion

—Deferral of income of domestic international sales corporations, controlled foreign corporations, and tax credits for corporations doing business in U.S. possessions: $3.1 billion

—Research and development: $2.0 billion
—Exploration and development costs for oil and gas: $1.9 billion
—Capital gains (other than agriculture, iron ore, and coal): $1.4 billion

Several corporate tax expenditures included in President Reagan's Economic Recovery Act deserve special attention. One was simply a 10 percent tax credit for capital investment—that is, for every $1,000 spent on equipment, $100 could be subtracted from corporate income taxes. (Revenue losses from investment tax credits in 1981 were $17.3 billion, 35 percent of the total tax expenditures for that year.)

Another enormous tax break for corporations was the Accelerated Cost-Recovery System, which permitted corporations to deduct the cost of capital investments faster than the equipment they buy wears out. This was a capital depletion allowance and worked in the following way. If a company bought machinery worth $1,000,000, it was able to deduct the cost of this machinery over a five-year period ($200,000 each year) from its taxable income, even if the machinery were to last ten, fifteen, or twenty years or more. Smaller equipment could be deducted even faster (three years), and most buildings could be depreciated over a fifteen-year period. The revenue losses from the Accelerated Cost-Recovery System were expected to be, by U.S. Treasury estimates, $10 billion in 1982, $53 billion in 1986, and a total of $500 billion (one-half trillion dollars) by 1990, a figure which represents *one-half* of the current national debt! Furthermore, a company that bought, say, $1 million in new machinery, would not only be able to deduct its cost over five years, but would *also* be able to reduce its tax bill by an additional 10 percent or $100,000 in the first year. Tax deductions were subtracted from taxable income. The investment credit was subtracted from the total tax bill *after* the deductions had already been made.

Still another tax expenditure for corporations in President Reagan's Economic Recovery Act, even more controversial than accelerated depreciation, was a provision that permitted corporations to sell tax credits which they themselves could not use (because their taxes were already zero) to other companies that could use them. The estimated revenue loss from this provision alone was put at $3.8 billion in 1982 and would total $28 billion by 1986. For example, the General Electric Company had profits of $2.5 billion in 1981; but through the buying of tax credits from other firms that had too many, General Electric not only paid no taxes that year, it actually received a *refund* of nearly $100 million on its taxes from previous years that had been affected by its acquisition of 1981 tax credits.

Through the new system of 10-percent tax credits, *plus* the Accelerated Cost-Recovery System, *plus* the selling of tax credits, it is expected that an ever-increasing number of corporations (the figure has already reached 50 percent) will have zero or close to zero taxes in the near future.

But perhaps the most unusual corporate tax deduction of all, trivial perhaps in size but important as an example of how far these matters can go, was a provision that allows U.S. corporations to deduct bribes to officials of foreign governments in order to make a sale. The justification for this action is that bribes are an essential part of doing business with certain foreign governments. When the provision was attacked on the floor of the Senate, Senator John H. Chafee, Republican from Rhode Island, rose to its defense: "Those payments are to make things move faster, and it all translates into jobs for Americans. This is a bill that favors the working men and working women of America." Apparently this was too much for even the Senate of the United States, which is well known for accepting strange arguments, and the whole chamber burst into laughter. Among other things, however, one of the inherent difficulties of corporate tax deductions for bribes is how to account for them. Bribes, after all, are not something for which one normally receives a signed receipt. But in its rush to get the entire tax bill through Congress, little time was spent discussing this undoubtedly minor problem.

## CORPORATE TAXES AND GOVERNMENT REVENUES

As a consequence of the ever-increasing number of tax exemptions, exclusions, deductions, and credits, the tax rate and percentage of total taxes paid by corporations has dropped significantly over the past thirty years. (Recall that it is not only the Reagan Administration that has engaged in supply-side economics, but every administration. It is simply that the Reagan Administration has made something of an ideology out of it and is going faster and farther with such policies.) In 1980, the International Telephone and Telegraph Corporation earned $803 million in profits and paid 1.1 percent in corporate income taxes; the United Technologies Corporation had profits of $787 million and paid 1.4 percent; Bank of America made more than $1 billion and paid 3 percent; American Telephone and Telegraph made $8.6 billion and paid 8 percent. The official corporate tax rate is 46 percent on profits over $100,000. During the 1950s the effective rate paid by corporations averaged 38 percent, *declining to 18 percent* by the end of the 1970s. And these are tax rates *before* the Reagan Administration took office. Senator Dole, chairman of the Senate Finance Committee, pointed out in 1983 that the eighteen largest banks in the United States have been paying a tax rate of 0.03 percent (three one-hundreths of one percent) in recent years!

It is also interesting to observe the effect that the increasingly large number of corporate tax expenditures has on the total revenues collected by the United States to pay for its many activities. As a function of the more than halving of the effective tax rate for corporations over the past thirty years, due to the addition of more and more tax deductions, exemptions, credits, and exclusions, the percentage of the national budget funded by corporate income taxes has fallen precipitously, from as high as 33 percent in 1952, to 8 percent predicted for 1983. Federal revenues in 1981 were $599.3 billion. Of that sum, corporate income taxes accounted for $61.1 billion, or just slightly over 10 percent. The official estimate for 1982 is 9 percent, falling to 8 percent in 1983.

The most important consequence of this reduction in the percentage of the national budget paid for by corporate taxes is that a larger percentage is obviously being paid for by someone else. Since the 1950s the federal tax burden has shifted from corporations to individuals; the tax load has been redistributed. And, at the same time, the concentration of assets and sales revenues among corporations has increased to the point that almost 50 percent of all corporate assets are now in the hands of approximately 200 giant corporations. This concentration of economic power has given corporations a firmer control over supply, and with that, a firmer control over prices and profit rates. That is, much of this shift from corporate taxes to individual taxes has been used to subsidize an increasingly oligopolistic market structure within the United States. The same phenomenon can be seen in 1981 and 1982: an unusual amount of merger activity within the corporate world that has left giant corporations larger still.

The effect on individual taxpayers has been just the opposite: they now have a smaller percentage of their wages and salaries to spend on consumer items because they now bear an increasingly larger share of the tax burden. Part of the increase in taxes is due to the larger role of government in the economy and in society. But a large percentage is also due to the fact that individual taxpayers have had to make up for the smaller pecentage contribution by corporations. And, as a consequence of these deep corporate tax cuts, the shift of the tax burden to consumers will increase at an even faster pace. A 1-percent drop in a corporate contribution of 10 percent is a 10 percent reduction. A 1-percent drop from 9 percent to 8 percent is a reduction of over 11 percent. In other words, from the corporate community's point of view, the percentage share of the total tax burden that they have to pay fell by over 20 percent between 1981 and 1983.

## THE JUSTIFICATION FOR TAX EXPENDITURES

There are two explanations why the effective tax rate for corporations fell from 38 percent in the 1950s to 18 percent in the late 1970s (and even lower in the 1980s), and why corporations were funding an increasingly smaller proportion of the total tax burden—from 33 percent in 1952, to 21 percent in 1962, to 17 percent in 1972, to 9 percent in 1982. We can look at the data just presented and *justify* these very large tax expenditures for corporations as supply-side economists and politicians do: they are needed as *incentives* for the business community. More money left in the hands of business means, potentially, more money available for investment in new plant and equipment. Or, we can look at the questions *causally*: this country's corporations have enormous economic and political power. It should not be surprising that governmental policies are designed to give them more money for whatever purposes they may have.

These are alternative explanations, not only in content but also in *kind*. Justifications are cast in the language of rationality and specify actions to be taken in order to accomplish goals: in order to have a productive economy, one must put money in the hands of business. Justifications of this sort speak to intentions and to the future, of goals that will pull us toward something better. Money is given to corporations now in order to improve the economy at some future time.

Causal explanations are quite different. They suggest that policy is *pushed* by certain factors (in this case, wealth and power) rather than being pulled (by good intentions, for example). In causal language, money is given to corporations because the corporations ultimately control the political process, and not in order to accomplish some goal. Causal explanations seek to explain events in terms of the prior conditions that are linked to them, rather than future goals that people say they are aiming toward.

## The Allure of Justification

Justifications can be very powerful arguments. They are inherently more acceptable than are causal explanations (not only to those who are predisposed to take them at face value but to most of us who want to believe in rationality and good intentions). Justifications are "nicer," for one thing. Causal explanations often turn out to be not so nice, to show the seamier side of life. Justifications in terms of intentions *never* do. Most of us prefer to believe that humans are driven by selfless, rational motives and not by forces of power and interest. For this reason, justifications are tailormade for the political language in the individual political system. Politicians who want to get elected and those who believe that the wealthy deserve their wealth are overwhelmingly tempted to talk in terms of justifications rather than causes. Scientists will talk in terms of causes, but they rarely run for office. And even scientists will employ the language of justification when they want to justify long-held beliefs or to defend the business community. For example, most economists ignore much of the data in this book not because the data are not true or are not generally available—most of it comes from government sources—but because they are trained to talk about the business sector, just as most political scientists are trained to talk about the government sector. Few economists or political scientists talk about the relationship between the one and the other. Hence justification, as an explanation, is likely to predominate over causality—at least in discussions concerning the relationship between the economic community and the political community.

## An Examination of Incentives

We can, however, examine the scientific basis for using justifications as explanations; in fact this has been done with respect to the question of incentives. Does it help, as an incentive to work, to give people more money? Do they work harder and longer as a consequence of being better paid?

First, however, let us clarify how this question applies to the kinds of business incentives we are discussing. The problem is not: if you work harder, you will be given more money. The question is, if you are given more money, will you work harder? That is, the money comes before the work, not after. It is generally agreed that the *prospect* of earning more money will induce many people to work harder. In fact, the conclusions we shall cite in this section suggest that as well. But that is not how the business incentives we have been describing here work. The money is given first. The question is, then: *after* people are given more money, will they work harder?

We might, at the outset, question whether the justification for tax expenditures as *incentives* really involves incentives at all. What most of us understand to be an incentive is that we shall be given more money if we work harder. The practice of giving money first is not what is usually meant by an incentive. Nevertheless, the justification for corporate tax expenditures to spur investment activity is stated in just these terms: that such tax advantages are given as *incentives*. We have no choice, then, but to investigate the truth of the justification as stated, even if, on closer inspection, "incentive" does not mean what it ought to mean.

The problem, then, of justifying large tax expenditures for corporations turns out to be a very interesting one—and for a number of reasons. On the one hand, supply-siders would be the first to say that one should not put more money into the hands of poor people (in the form of welfare, for example, but also in the form of contributory transfer payments such as Social Security) since it is likely to have a *negative* effect on their incentive to work. Why work harder, or even work at all (assuming you have a choice—that is, that you are not unemployed in an economy in which 12 percent of the work force is unable to find work), if someone is going to give you money no matter what you do? On the other hand, why should business people work harder if the government is going to give them money no matter what they do? Why should corporation managers respond any differently from workers in the labor force? The question of the wisdom of giving money to people through tax expenditures and government subsidies may depend upon whether one is talking about the wealthy or the poor, corporations or individuals. In any case, it is unfair to use the question of incentives *against* one group of people and *for* another group. There is certainly *no* evidence whatsoever that people respond differently to incentives depending on whether they are machine operators or corporate directors.

Part of the answer to this question, of course, lies in the fact that business investment has *not* increased as a consequence of the tax advantages given to corporations in the last two years. (On the other hand, the number and dollar assets of business mergers *have* increased enormously.) That is, the purpose for which the tax advantages were given to corporations has not been realized, although other purposes are being served by placing an increased proportion of the national wealth in the hands of corporations. But what of the larger question of prior money incentives producing more and harder work?

## The Substitution Effect and the Income Effect

Studies have been done on this question and they show that, in fact, people are likely to work harder if you *take money away from them* (in the form of taxes, for example) than if you *give them more money*. In general, if people are given more money, they are likely to spend more time in leisure activities than in working; this is called the *substitution effect*. If you give people less money, or take more of what they have away from them, then the incentive to earn more (and work harder and longer) is increased; this is called the *income effect* (Thurow and Lucas, 1976; Fusfield, 1982).

The following are citations from two economists who have paid attention to the link between government and business: Lester Thurow and Daniel Fusfield. Both summarize the available literature on the relationship between income and the effect on incentives to work harder.

> Most of the existing literature on work incentives focuses on the activities of high income managers and self-employed professionals. These are the working individuals who are thought to have the capability of altering their work habits. Such analysis found that high income individuals with the capability of altering their work habits seemed to work harder or longer as a result of higher marginal tax rates. Economic analysis of labor force participation rates confirms this result for the general population. For the labor force as a whole, income effects seem to dominate substitution effects. When taxes are raised and incomes fall, individuals work more not less (Thurow and Lucas, 1976, pp. 14–15;[1] see also Thurow, 1971, p. 23).

> This conclusion is quite significant. It tells us that one of the benefits of economic growth (rising real incomes) is increased leisure. Economic growth makes it possible for people to work less and do other things with their time. Our conclusion also suggests that higher taxes are likely to get people to work more rather than less. We often hear the argument that high income taxes on large incomes reduce work incentives. Yet if the income effect of lower earnings after taxes dominates the substitution effect of reduced rewards for work, which is what the data tell us, people will work harder if taxes take a larger proportion of their income. (Fusfeld, 1982, p. 277).[2]

Justifications, of course, need not be true to be effective. People must merely *believe* they are true—or at least believe that they have a certain logic to them. It certainly seems sensible and logical to say that giving people more money would be an incentive to their working harder. My guess is almost everyone believes it. The trouble is, the data do not support it, at least not if incentives are given first and people already have the money that is suppose to spur them on

[1]Reprinted by permisison of North-Holland Publishing Co., American Elsevier Publishing Co.

[2]From *Economics: Principles of Political Economy* by Daniel R. Fusfeld. Copyright © 1982 Scott, Foresman and Company. Reprinted by permission.

to greater activity. What most of us believe, however, is that the *promise* of more money will make us work harder, at least up to a point; and we are led to think that tax expenditures for corporations are incentives of this sort. When, in addition, there is very little competition with the justification given, then it is even more likely to stick as the legitimate and authorized explanation that most everyone will accept. No one, to my knowledge, argues that we should take money *away* from corporations in order to encourage them to work harder and to earn more money. Yet that is exactly what the data indicate should be done.

Since, however, the notion that increased prior monetary incentives result in greater work productivity is, according to the best available data, not true, and since there are no other justifications (the accepted one having withstood the test of time, if not of fact), we are still left with the question of why corporations are being treated so advantageously. The answer must therefore be found in the causal explanation that increased rewards go to corporations because corporations simply want them and are powerful enough to get them. This answer may not justify what is happening, but it at least has the virtue of being true, if not very nice.

## OTHER FORMS OF GOVERNMENT AID TO BUSINESS

Tax expenditures, although a major form of direct government aid to business, are not the only way in which the government attempts to assist business. The federal government, for example, spent $4 billion in 1981 on direct subsidies to agriculture ($2 billion for the dairy industry alone, with an additional $50 million for storage of surplus milk, butter, and cheese), $1.5 billion on agricultural research and services, and an additional $10.9 billion on various agricultural credit programs. (In 1982, farm price support programs cost over *$11 billion,* including supports for wheat, corn, sorghum, rice, soybeans, dairy products, peanuts, and tobacco.) Other programs providing economic aid and financial assistance, mainly through the Export-Import Bank and the Small Business Administration, amounted to $5.9 billion. And these figures do not even begin to tap the economic programs scattered throughout the remainder of the federal government. (We shall discuss some of these direct subsidy, financial aid, and service programs in more detail in the next chapter.)

Frequently, however, government aid comes in a form that is not directly related to cash payments, tax deductions, or even services, but through special legislation permitting a particular industry to engage in otherwise illegal activities. For example, in the building of the natural gas pipeline from Prudhoe Bay in Alaska, through Canada, to the West and Midwest, the federal government has granted the utility companies permission to pass on their costs to consumers in the form of higher utility prices as each segment of the line is being built, no matter how high the eventual cost may become, and even if the pipeline is never completed. What this amounts to is a guarantee that the funds invested by the utility companies will be repaid under *all* circumstances, making the pipeline a totally *risk-free* undertaking for its financial backers. Many government actions of this kind are designed to reduce the risks of investment as well as to provide tax deductions, subsidies, and service.

## FOREIGN TRADE

There is another component of the Gross National Product that is concerned with business activities. Recall that the GNP is made up of four components: consumer spending, business spending (investment), government spending, and net foreign trade. We have already discussed consumer spending (demand), and business spending (investment), and will discuss the government's contribution to the GNP in the next chapter. Here, then, we shall consider the role of foreign trade in the nation's economy and its relationship to government.

The contribution of *net* foreign trade is a very small percentage of the GNP, accounting for only $26 billion of the total $2.925 trillion (just slightly less than 1 percent of the total). This minimal contribution to GNP, however, masks the importance and total value of imports and exports since net foreign trade is arrived at by subtracting the value of imports from the value of exports. In 1981, the total value of exports purchased by other countries from the United States was $341 billion, and the value of goods and services imported into the United States was $315 billion, making a total dollar value of the import-export trade $656 billion, with a favorable balance to the United States of $26 billion.

What these figures tell us right away, then, is that the United States is both a supplier and a customer in the international economy, and is therefore interested in foreign countries both as *markets* for goods produced in the United States and as *suppliers* of raw materials and other goods, which contribute both to our productive capacity and our standard of living.

World trade in terms of markets for finished products and the importation of raw materials has been a concern of industrialized countries since the eighteenth century, with trade building up as the Industrial Revolution progressed. The impact of international economics on both domestic policies (protective tariffs, for example) and foreign policies (colonialism and imperialistic policies, for example) have been enormous. In recent years, however, the number and dollar value of business ventures abroad has increased significantly, producing a large growth in multinational corporations and an increased competition for both raw materials and markets for finished products. For example, the total assets of U.S. companies abroad have tripled over the last fifteen years and are now well over *$2 trillion*. Eleven of the fifteen largest multinational industrial corporations are United States companies: Exxon, General Motors, Texaco, Ford Motor, Mobil Oil, Standard Oil of California, International Business Machines, Gulf Oil, General Electric, Chrysler, and International Telephone and Telegraph. The same pattern of internationalization can be seen in the financial and communications sectors as well.

It is difficult to overemphasize the importance of international trade, investments abroad, and multinational corporations as determining factors in any nation's governmental policies, whether we are speaking of industrialized nations or less-developed countries. Industrialized countries seek markets for their products; and foreign markets have become an increasingly larger source of sales, revenues, and profits for the United States and other countries as well (Japan is as good an example as any). The European Economic Community, composed of the major nations of Europe, coordinates and facilitates economic exchanges, both within the community itself and with outside nations. OPEC, a consortium of the major oil-producing countries of the world outside of the major powers, is another example, in this case composed of less-developed countries.

Corporations are obviously vitally concerned with their investments abroad, the profits that they make there, and the supply of raw materials that they need for the productions of goods to be sold both at home and abroad. More than 20 percent of all U.S. corporate profits, for example, are earned abroad. Almost half of all loans made by our largest banks (Bank of America, Citibank of New York, and Chase Manhattan among them) have been to foreign countries. Over 50 percent of the twenty-three most important minerals used in manufacturing are imported, mostly from Third World countries. (These minerals include strontium, cobalt, manganese, chromium, platinum, aluminum, asbestos, mercury, tin, nickel, gold, silver, zinc, tungsten, and potassium.) Indeed, these economic concerns are considered to be in the national interest to preserve and protect; vitally, they are considered to affect the economic, political, and military security of the United States.

It is difficult to specify exactly what proportion of government expenditures are directly related to the encouragement, maintenance, growth, and protection of our economic interests abroad (such matters are complicated by military security considerations). However, many U.S. military and international relations programs directly benefit U.S. economic interests and help them expand. The United States has, for example, more than 3,000 military bases abroad, and an army, navy, air force, and marine corps capable of arriving quickly at any spot on the earth where our national interest (however defined) is threatened. The United States is also strongly committed to the economic, political, and military security of many foreign countries (approximately 75); and it expends over $11 billion, *outside of the military budget,* on economic, military, financial, and internal security assistance.

Although clearly not as influenced by international economic matters as is foreign policy, our domestic economy is also significantly affected by the problems of imports and exports and by what occurs in international markets. Wheat sales to the USSR (and whether and when to place an embargo on them), automobile imports, arms sales, disputes between economic sectors having large export markets and those relying heavily on imports, unemployment (to the extent it is related to imports that displace American-made products), the value of the dollar in the world economy (which affects both the prices we pay for imports and the prices we receive for exports), the price of oil (almost 50 percent of our oil is now imported), and other matters all ripple through the U.S. economy and affect the lives of all of us. The United States, for example, has recently concluded agreements limiting the importation of Japanese automobiles and Western European steel. Such trade restrictions, designed to protect the sales of domestic industries, also have the effect of raising the prices that American consumers pay for these products. Because of the 1981 agreement with the Japanese on automobile imports for example, it was estimated that Americans spent an additional $400 for every compact car they bought in 1982. The price of imported steel items also rose and had a strong impact on the automobile, construction, and military equipment industries. President Reagan also announced the payment of an export subsidy for agricultural products and considered a program that would severely restrict the importation of machine tools from Japan, which are about 10 to 15 percent cheaper than those manufactured domestically. In addition, a bill was passed in 1982 that permitted U.S. corporations to form joint export trading companies, a practice that, before passage of the bill, was in violation of U.S. antitrust laws. This same bill also permitted bank holding companies to own export trading companies (also a prior violation of antitrust laws), thus allowing financial institutions and corporations that export goods to work together more closely.

Foreign trade is very big business. Investments, sales, and profits abroad are a significant feature of our economy and are continuing to grow rapidly. As we gain markets abroad, however, we may also lose markets at home to foreign competition. As we rely more heavily on the importation of raw materials from abroad (most notably oil), we also expand the concept of our own national interest and become involved in the protection of that interest throughout the world. And as U.S. corporations become more multinational, their interests clearly transcend our own borders. Indeed, most of our foreign policy, and an increasingly larger percentage of our domestic policies, are becoming more and more related to that misleadingly small sector of the GNP known as net foreign trade.

# CHAPTER ELEVEN
# GOVERNMENT
# SPENDING

Up to this point we have accounted for 80 percent of the Gross National Product of the United States. The largest item was consumer demand (64%); business investment in plant and equipment comprised 15 percent; and the smallest but most important item, in terms of our role in world affairs, was net foreign trade (1%). We have also investigated the manner in which government is involved in each of these components of our national economy: the effort to stimulate consumer demand through contributory and general revenue transfer payments, and through tax expenditures and subsidy programs to stimulate the supply side of the economy (business investment); and economic, military, financial, and security foreign aid programs to encourage and protect international markets and the sources of raw materials abroad.

In this chapter we shall investigate the direct, overall contribution to GNP of government itself: the amount of money ($591 billion in 1981) that government at all levels (national, state, and local) spends on goods and services (what it buys in terms of tangible products and labor). We shall also discuss what government *does* with its goods and labor—that is, what functions it performs in the economy and society beyond those that we have already described.

## THE ROLE OF GOVERNMENT IN THE U.S. ECONOMY

There are approximately 80,000 separate governmental units in the United States: 1 national government; 50 state governments; 3,000 counties; 18,500 municipalities; 17,000 townships; 16,000 school districts; and 24,000 special districts. These governmental units, combined, account for 20 percent of all purchases of goods and services as calculated in the Gross National Product. It is interesting to note, in this regard, that although the national government is responsible for the largest single component of the total $591 billion spent by all governments ($230 billion, or 39%), the other governmental units combined significantly outspend it in terms of purchases of goods and services ($361 billion, or 61%). Remember, however, that only the purchase of goods and services is counted in the GNP. Those government expenditures that do not involve the purchase of tangible goods or labor, such as transfer payments and the payment of the interest on the national debt, although counted in the budget, are not a part of the GNP.

There are two initial points, then, to emphasize about the role of government, particularly the federal government, in the U.S. economy and society. First, government itself, at all levels, is the second largest buyer of goods and services in the nation (after individual consumers). What this means is that government is a large component of the demand for goods and services, and therefore has a significant effect on the level of production in the economy. As we shall see, the government also has an important influence on *what* is produced as well as how much is produced. However, the federal government ranks behind state and local governments in terms of its contribution to that demand.

Second, in 1981 the federal government's budget was $657.2 billion. We already know that $230 billion was spent on goods and services. That leaves $427.2 billion that does not represent the buying of goods and services, but is simply the amount of money that was *transferred* from one place to another. In terms of federal government expenditures, this means that 65 percent of all federal outlays serve functions *other than* making a direct contribution to the GNP.

We have already described two of these functions: contributory transfer payments ($239.4 billion), involving primarily the Social Security System ($182.1 billion) and other retirement, disability, medical insurance, and income security programs ($57.3 billion); and general revenue transfer programs ($77.3 billion), involving welfare ($57.3 billion) and veterans' benefits ($20 billion). The sum total of these two transfer payment programs is $316.7 billion, which leaves $109.6 billion in non-GNP budget items still unaccounted for.

The largest item in this $109.6 billion is interest on the national debt. In 1981 the federal debt surpassed the $1-trillion mark ($1,003,941,000,000), and interest payments were $82.5 billion. Because government agencies hold $209.5 billion of the total debt, however, the *net* interest paid out to those outside of government agencies was $68.7 billion. The other $40.9 billion of the $109.6

billion in additional transfer payments was distributed among various agencies and programs.

To summarize, then, nearly 60 percent of the $657.2 billion spent in the federal budget is involved in three major transfer payment programs: Social Security and other retirement and income security programs (36.4% of the total budget); welfare and veterans' benefits (11.5%); and interest on the national debt (10.4%). In other words, most federal spending goes toward running retirement systems, which cover nearly *all* older Americans; assisting poor people and veterans, which include the unemployed, those who receive wages at or below the minimum wage, and those who have served in the military; and paying off the national debt, owed mainly to financial institutions, other institutional investors (private pension funds, for example), and middle- and upper-income groups.

Another major activity of the federal government that affects both demand and supply but does not figure in the budget itself, is the vast program of tax expenditures to individuals and corporations. In 1981 this lost federal revenue amounted to $228.6 billion, of which $179.8 billion (79%) went mainly to middle- and upper-income individuals, and $48.4 billion (21%) went to corporations. In terms of the percentage of the federal budget which these revenue losses represent, the total is 35 percent, of which 27 percent is for individuals and 8 percent went to corporations.

## FEDERAL SPENDING ON GOODS AND SERVICES

But what of the $230 billion (35% of the federal budget) that is spent on goods and services? What does the federal government buy in the form of tangible goods and in wages and salaries to employees?

### Military Expenditures

The answer to this question is rather surprising. Of the total $230 billion spent by the federal government on goods and services, $154 billion (or 67% of the total) was spent for military equipment and the salaries of military personnel. And if one includes the $11.9 billion spent on various programs for foreign aid (economic and military) and for the conduct of foreign affairs, and the $4.9 billion spent on the space program, the total is 75 percent. In other words, federal purchases of goods and services turn out to be overwhelmingly related to military operations.

There is also another surprising feature of this military expenditure. Approximately 4,161,000 employees work for the federal government. Of these, 2,000,000 are military personnel, and nearly 1,000,000 are civilian employees in the Department of Defense. Of the total number of federal employees, then, nearly three-fourths are working for the military, which leaves only about 1,000,000 working in purely civilian functions. Since we hear a good deal about attempting to cut the number of employees who work for the federal government, it should be noted that there are not all that many to cut if one excludes military personnel from the list.

## Grants to the States and Other Federal Programs

Of the approximately $76 billion remaining in the federal budget for the purchase of goods and services outside of direct military expenditures, and the approximately $41 billion in miscellaneous transfer payments that are scattered among various federal agencies (for a total of $117 billion), the breakdown of these expenditures by function falls into two main categories: grants to the states ($54.8), and other federal programs ($57.4). The category "other federal programs," includes $88.6 billion in actual expenditures, and $31 billion in miscellaneous federal receipts that must be subtracted from the total for this category.[1]

In the category "grants to the states" ($54.8 billion) are such programs as highway construction ($9.1 billion), community development ($4 billion), elementary, secondary, and vocational education ($6.6 billion), training and employment ($8 billion), social services ($6.2 billion), and general revenue sharing ($5.1 billion).

In the category "other federal programs" ($88.6 billion in expenditures minus the $31.2 billion in receipts) are all of the other functions of the federal government: energy programs ($11 billion); natural resources and environment ($10.8 billion); education, training, employment, and social services ($4.2 billion); agricultural programs ($14.5 billion); international affairs ($11.9 billion); the space program (4.9 billion); and the other administrative functions of the federal government (administration of justice, general government, and so on).

Let us briefly summarize this analysis of federal spending: The total federal budget in 1981 was $657.2 billion. Of this total, 65 percent was in the form of various transfer payments (mainly, in the order of the amount of money expended, retirement programs, payment of the national debt, welfare, and veterans' benefits), and 35 percent was for the purchase of goods and services. Of this latter ($230 billion), 67 percent ($154 billion) went to the military, an additional 8 percent went to international affairs and the space program, and 25 percent went to the purchase of goods and services for purely domestic programs. Of this 25 percent, $55 billion was given as aid to state governments, and $72 billion went toward domestic federal programs.

[1]These figures add up to $112.2 billion, not $117 billion, due to the fact that the total military budget was $159.8 billion, of which $154 billion was for goods and services; the approximately $5.8 billion of the $41 billion was used up in miscellaneous transfer payments. There is also an "error" of about $1 billion, but I am, apparently, no more able to balance the budget than is the federal government.

## STATE AND LOCAL GOVERNMENTS

Of the total $591 billion in Gross National Product attributable to government, state and local governments accounted for $361 billion, or 61 percent. In terms of total expenditures, however, the federal government outspends state and local governments because of the large share (65%) of the federal budget that is devoted to non-GNP items (transfer payments, which do not involve the purchase of goods and services). State and local governments also out-employ the federal government by a considerable margin. Of the approximately 17 million government employees in the United States (16.2% of all those employed), nearly 13 million work for state and local governments (approximately 75% of all government employees). The major reason for this is that all public-school teachers are employees of state or local governments, and school teachers make up over 50 percent of combined state and local government employment. About 50 percent of combined state and local government budgets are also devoted to education.

In addition to education, state and local governments have primary responsibility for highways and roads, health, police and fire protection, sanitation, and recreation. They also participate in various transfer payment programs (unemployment benefits, for example, which are funded by a special levy for this purpose on corporations), and help distribute some federal transfer payment programs ($39.9 billion was distributed to the states in 1981 for allocation in transfer payment programs), as well as receive federal funds in the form of block grants and general revenue sharing for such purposes as highways, community development, education, training and employment, and social services ($54.8 billion in 1981).

## FEDERAL REVENUES

In order to pay for its $657.2 billion budget outlays in 1981, the federal government collected $599.3 billion in revenues, running a deficit of $57.9 billion in the process.[2] Of this $599.3 billion, $285.9 billion came from personal income taxes (48%), $182.7 billion (31%) came from income security taxes and contributions (mainly Social Security), $61.1 billion came from corporate income taxes (10%), $40.8 billion (7%) came from excise taxes (mainly on gasoline, liquor, and cigarettes), and $28.7 billion (4%) came from custom duties, estate and gift taxes, and other incidental taxes.

[2]In 1982, the budget deficit was approximately $110 billion, making it more than one and one-half times as large as the previous deficit high ($65 billion) under President Carter, and was projected to be approximately $190 billion in 1983. The total national debt is now over the $1.15-trillion mark, with payments on the national debt slightly in excess of $100 billion.

### Regressive Taxation

We have already discussed how individual income tax deductions, credits, exclusions, and exemptions have a leveling effect on the progressive income tax, and how corporate tax expenditures have reduced the total tax burden carried by corporations. We need only add that if one takes into account total taxes paid by individuals, including state taxes, which rely heavily on the regressive sales tax, and local government taxes, which rely heavily on the regressive property tax, there remains very little difference in the overall tax rate for individuals of whatever income level. In fact, some economists have argued that, when sales, excise, and property taxes are taken into account, the entire tax-rate schedule is somewhat *regressive*. According to Thurow: "In the U.S. the pre- and post-tax distributions of income are not noticeably different. When all of our taxes (local, state, and federal) are added together, progressive taxes seem to be cancelled by regressive taxes leaving a proportional tax system" (Thurow and Lucas, 1976, p. 16).[3]

### The Tax Burdens of the Middle Class

One of the major consequences that the large reduction in corporate income taxes has had on U.S. society—along with the leveling of the progressive income tax that permits wealthier Americans to pay about the same percentage in taxes as everyone else, and the virtual elimination of inheritance taxes as a method of recovering funds from the very wealthy—is that the broad middle class of the United States finds itself shouldering more and more of the total tax burden. These policies have had two major effects on the political behavior of the middle class.

First, since the middle class has traditionally been a large source of total savings in this country (which are then lent out by banks to corporations for investment and to individuals for home mortgages), there has been a significant downturn in the percentage of income that middle-class Americans can save. A smaller percentage of incomes going to savings has, in turn contributed to higher interest rates (since banks have less money to lend for investment or any other purpose), although the Federal Reserve's tight money policy has also been very important in this regard. Reduced levels of savings have also led to successful pressures on the government by corporations to provide further tax incentives in the form of deductions, credits, exemptions, and exclusions for the ostensible purpose of filling the investment gap left by decreased savings. What has resulted, instead, is a significant further decrease in the share of the tax burden paid by corporations (8 percent in 1983), and a great expansion of merger activity as these investment incentives are diverted in order to increase the size and power of our major corporations.

[3]Reprinted by permission of North-Holland Publishing Co., American Elsevier Publishing Co.

Second, the middle class is also the major source of overall demand in the economy. However, as it rapidly becomes the major provider of tax revenues, its disposable income for the purchase of goods and services declines. Further, with the increase in inflation during the late 1970s and early 1980s to as high as 13 percent, and the fact that most members of the middle class work for fixed salaries, it has suffered a noticeable loss of buying power. These factors have produced a two-pronged reaction: a growing reluctance on the part of the middle class to contribute further to public spending; and a number of tax revolts, most notably in California with Proposition 13, an overwhelmingly successful referendum to cut property taxes by over 50 percent. Similar tax revolts have occurred in other parts of the country as well.

The economic difficulties of the middle class have been even further compounded by the fact that as the unemployment rate goes up, federal spending automatically increases (unemployment insurance and welfare being the most important), and federal revenues automatically decrease (because of fewer taxable incomes). It is estimated that a rise in unemployment of 1 percent increases federal spending and decreases federal revenues by a combined total of $4.5 billion. With the official unemployment level nudging 11 percent, and the actual unemployment level pushing 13 percent (when the category of "discouraged workers" is included—that is, those unemployed who have given up trying to find work), there is little the middle class can do but feel the pinch.

In addition, rising inflation, rising interest rates, rising unemployment, falling tax contributions by corporations, and a tax structure that places the greatest percentage share of the tax burden on the middle class are certain to produce increasingly insistent demands by this large group to redistribute income advantages in their favor (the protection of Social Security benefits, for example, and perhaps even tax cuts). But such aggressive efforts, as discussed earlier, have been directed neither toward the corporations nor the wealthy, but toward the poor, primarily in the reduction of welfare programs. That these programs comprise such an insignificant proportion of the federal budget ($57 billion) and do not therefore represent a very promising source of possible savings (not to mention the fact that welfare is frequently the only source of income for many) is actually unknown to most of the middle class, having been told time and time again that it is "welfare" spending that is causing all of their difficulties.

The outcome of this redistribution struggle among corporations and the very wealthy, the middle class, and the poor, compounded by a stagnant economy, is yet to be completely played out; but the future does not look bright for the unemployed, those family heads working full-time and earning $6,700 per year on a minimum wage, and other less fortunate Americans. And other types of difficulties may also be in the offing, especially since the unfortunate in America are disproportionately blacks, Hispanics, women, single parents, and the young.

It is also to be noted, as we push to higher and higher levels of military spending (the Reagan Administration has put into motion a five-year $1.6-trillion program) that this sector, which in 1981 already accounted for 67 percent of the federal government's contribution to the GNP, will increase to perhaps 75 percent or higher. Contrary to the production of most goods and services, military production is not consumable by the general population (at least, let's hope not). That is, the production of military hardware, unlike the production of houses, automobiles, or medicines, adds *nothing* to the standard of living of anyone, other than in salaries and profits for what even President Eisenhower has warned us against, the "military-industrial complex." But even in terms of wages and salaries, military production is an industry that is enormously *capital* intensive instead of labor intensive, meaning that fewer workers per total expenditure are employed than in most other industries. Every dollar spent in the production of military equipment is equivalent, in terms of employment, to about fifty cents spent in other industries.

Not only, then, does the military budget produce goods that are not consumable by the general public, but their production calls for high levels of capital investment (thus taking money away for investment purposes in other sectors of the economy), and employs fewer workers than other sectors of the economy. Higher military expenditures also further increase the national debt and convert the economy to one of guns rather than butter, both of which will result in even greater attempts to attack the $57 billion currently being spent on welfare programs. But the aggressive attacks on the income of others is not likely to stop there. There may very well be designs on the much larger government subsidies and tax expenditures that benefit the middle class, since even the total elimination of welfare would not have much of an effect on overall government expenditures and on balancing the budget, not when the budget deficit for 1983 is expected to be $190 billion. Indeed, the crisis of the 1980s may not be entirely the plight of the poor (although this will be serious enough). It appears that the middle class, and especially the lower middle class (those with incomes of between $15,000 and $25,000—an income level in which over 50 percent of the American population falls), is also likely to be seriously affected.

We have pointed out before that the middle class tends to side with the corporate political system and with the wealthy against the poor, even when it is demonstrably *not* in its interests to do so (for example, it has favored the elimination of even nominal inheritance taxes, leveling the progressive income tax, and increasing the level of tax expenditures to the business community). Whether the middle class, as it sees its own benefits being eroded, will continue to look downward for the source of the problem rather than upward is a matter of conjecture. Traditionally, its acceptance of the business creed has always placed it primarily with the corporate community. As the middle class learns more about its own interest, however, and as these interests become increasingly jeopardized by further "winnings" going to the corporate world, to the very wealthy, and to the military, a new American Revolution could be a consequence. On the other hand, given the power of the ideology that binds them to the corporate political system, and their lack of knowledge of what is actually happening, the conjecture that such a turnabout could take place may be misdirected. The middle class has been told too loudly and too often that their problems are caused by poor people who are inherently lazy and that welfare is likely to keep them that way to lose faith in the idea that the corporate world is the free-enterprise, competitive system they have been led to believe it is, and to believe that corporations may have private interests that transcend even Adam Smith's "invisible hand." But the resolution of this conflict, if indeed it ever becomes one, is still in the future—your future, my future, and the future of our children already born and yet to come.

# CHAPTER TWELVE
# 131 SUMMARY
# PROPOSITIONS

In this concluding chapter I would like to summarize briefly the major findings and conclusions presented in the preceding pages. I shall simply list them, by chapter. This summary will then be followed by an epilogue in which I shall discuss some of the consequences for individual citizens of this description and analysis of the two American political systems.

### Chapter 1: *Politics and Property: An Introduction*

**1.** There are two kinds of persons in the Unitd States: individual persons and corporate persons.

**2.** Since politics is concerned with the relationship between governmental institutions and persons, there are two political systems in the United States: the individual political system and the corporate political system.

**3.** Politics cannot be studied in a vacuum. One cannot know much about political processes unless one knows what motivates these processes—this is what politics is all about.

**4.** Politics, as James Madison informed us long ago, is about the ownership and control of property.

**5.** The principle function of government is to protect the unequal distribution and control of property.

**6.** The form of government established in the Constitution is a republic, not a democracy.

**7.** The governmental institutional structure of the American republic makes it impossible for majorities even to form, let alone rule.

### Chapter 2: *Society, Property, and Politics*

**8.** Property is anything that can be owned and controlled. The most tangible forms of property are economic in nature and are treated as wealth and income.

**9.** What the winners win in politics, and how they win it, can be either justified or explained. Justification and explanation should not be confused with each other.

**10.** Ideologies are established and used, in part, to justify the political, economic, and social activities of winners, and the unequal distribution of those winnings. But these justifications are frequently confounded with explanations for those activities and unequal distributions.

**11.** Societies are organized around the relationships of persons to property: its use, distribution, and control.

**12.** Societies have two broad methods of control over their members: voluntary compliance and forced compliance.

**13.** One of the major functions of a society is to socialize its members into its ideology in order to insure voluntary compliance with its rules, regulations, and laws.

### Chapter 3: *Corporate Wealth and Economic Power*

**14.** About 40 percent of the nation's wealth consists of business assets.

**15.** Business ownership and control of economic assets is highly concentrated.

**16.** Corporations, comprising 15 percent of all business establishments, account for 88 percent of all sales.

**17.** Approximately 200 giant corporations (0.0014% of all business establishments) control over 50 percent of all business assets.

**18.** The ownership and control of property permits a few people to have a disproportionately large share of the world's material goods.

**19.** Most American corporate production is organized into oligopolistic market structures (that is, markets in which a few sellers control a high percentage of the total business).

**20.** Oligopolies strongly influence supply, price, and profit.

**21.** Business will, wherever possible, tend toward oligopolistic markets.

**22.** Markets are becoming increasingly concentrated in oligopolies; and economic assets are becoming concentrated in the hands of an increasingly small number of giant corporations.

**23.** This increase in concentration of business assets has been due primarily to mergers that are largely financed from the retained earnings of the corporations themselves.

**24.** Control over such a large proportion of business wealth by a relatively few corporations organized into oligopolies results in enormous economic power, a redistribution of business wealth from small business to big business, a redistribution of wealth from consumers to producers, underproduction, ineffficient allocation of resources, chronic unemployment, and inflation.

### **Chapter 4:** *Individual Wealth and Income*

**25.** Individuals in American society own about 40 percent of Gross National Wealth.

**26.** The lowest 25 percent own zero wealth; the next 32 percent own 6.6 percent; the next 24 percent own 17.2 percent; the next 18.5 percent own 50.4 percent; and the top 0.5 percent own 25.8 percent.

**27.** The bottom 57 percent of the population, then, owns 6.6 percent of the wealth.

**28.** The bottom 81 percent of the population owns 23.8 percent.

**29.** The top 19 percent owns 76.2 percent.

**30.** The top 0.5 percent owns more than the bottom 81 percent.

**31.** Fifty percent of the very wealthy inherit their wealth.

**32.** Income is also very unequally distributed. The lowest 20 percent receive 1.7 percent, and the highest 20 percent receive 48.1 percent.

**33.** Working income for the lowest 20 percent has fallen and has been replaced by transfer payments and double incomes (working wives).

**34.** If one reduces the amount of transfer payments to the poor, one will have to increase the amount of money they will be able to earn by working.

**35.** Twenty-nine percent of the American work force works for less than the minimum wage ($3.35 per hour).

**36.** A full-time worker with a family of four working for the minimum wage will earn $6,700 per year, will be below the official poverty level, and will be on welfare.

**37.** Poverty is more closely related to low wages than to unemployment.

**38.** Twenty percent of Americans live in poverty or near-poverty as these terms are defined by the government.

**39.** If unearned income (e.g., capital gains, interest and dividend income) is included in income, inequality in the distribution of income rises even higher.

**40.** The top 5 percent of the population owns 86 percent of all stock.

**41.** Most large income earners are connected to the corporate sector, providing a close relationship between individual wealth and corporate wealth.

### Chapter 5: *The Corporate Economic System*

**42.** The corporate economic system has great influence over the quantity, quality, and price of goods, even without government help.

**43.** The control of most large corporations is in the hands of a relatively few corporate executives, not the stockholders nor the boards of directors.

**44.** There is a good deal of overlap and contact between the top executives of the largest corporations through various forms of interlocking, joint ventures, horizontal, vertical, and conglomerate mergers, trade associations, and government advisory boards.

### Chapter 6: *The Difficulties of Demonstrating What Is Inherently Impossible to Prove*

**45.** Power relationships are impossible to prove and must be inferred from other data, much of which, like the concepts of wants and interests, must also be inferred.

**46.** The idea that the individual political system governs America is just as impossible to prove as the idea that the major source of public policy making in this country is the corporate political system.

**47.** With no possibility of absolute proof, readers will have to make their own determination on the basis of the data presented for each idea.

**48.** One of the major functions of the American ideology is to foster the belief that the individual political system determines public policy.

**49.** Capitalism, as an economic ideology, encourages belief in a competitive market system in which supply, demand, price, and profit are determined by competitive market forces.

**50.** This economic ideology is also belied by data indicating that oligopolies characterize the corporate structure, and that this structure permits significant control over supply, price, profit, and even to some extent demand (through advertising).

**51.** The ideological justification for the presumed power of the individual political system is often confused with the explanation for how the political process actually functions, just as the ideological justification for the presumed power of competitive markets is often confused with the explanation for how the economic process actually works.

**52.** The problem of access to data for studying the corporate political system poses special difficulties. Much of the data are secret and kept hidden from the public.

**53.** Those who study the power of corporations also face another difficulty: that of going against the prevailing belief that the "will of the people" determines public policy.

**54.** One of the consequences of the democratic ideology is that economics and politics are rarely studied together. Politics is seen as a democratic process, as an independent force unconnected to any dominant content, let alone to property.

**55.** One can know very little about politics if one does not also know something about economics.

**56.** There is a large amount of data showing the relationship between the corporate and governmental sectors. These data are usually ignored since the democratic ideology separates politics from economics.

**57.** One does not have to be a ''leftist'' to study the connections between the economic and political spheres, although the ideology encourages this view.

### Chapter 7: *The Corporate Political System*

**58.** Most of what people understand about politics is based on the democratic ideology.

**59.** To learn what actually takes place, one must go beyond the ideology.

**60.** There are three goals of politics: to control the general policy-making process in its broad outlines; to control the details of specific policies; and to control the personnel who will be making, interpreting, and enforcing the policies.

**61.** The corporate political system is well structured to perform each of these three activities; it controls the great bulk of material resources with which to carry them out, and it is sufficiently motivated to do so.

**62.** Beside controlling policy making and those who make policy, the corporate political system also controls the ideology (and hence the methods and institutions of voluntary compliance) and the law-enforcement system (forced compliance).

**63.** Supracorporate policy-planning groups are closely linked to large corporations, universities, foundations, and major research centers.

**64.** Auxiliary planning groups, which provide much of the research for the corporate political system, are also closely linked to large corporations, universities, and foundations.

**65.** Most lobbying groups are business oriented.

**66.** The electoral process, in both the selection of candidates and their election to office, is largely financed and controlled by the corporate political system.

**67.** Most high-level government officials, in both the legislative and executive branches, have direct interests in business.

### Chapter 8: *The Individual Political System*

**68.** The individual political system, organized principally around political parties and elections (which are already largely controlled by the corporate political system), is incapable of making public policy, either in general or in particular.

**69.** Relationships involving individual citizens, political parties, elections, and policy outcomes show very weak support for the argument that the individual political system determines public policy.

**70.** The disparity between what the democratic ideology says and what actually occurs is likely to produce frustration and cynicism in the general population.

**71.** Not only is much of the corporate political system hidden and secret, Americans are often lied to by government and corporate officials; and there is a good deal of fraud and corruption.

**72.** The individual political system inadequately represents the American political system because it does not specify what politics is all about—i.e., property. Indeed, it specifies no content at all, but rather an idealized description of a process.

**73.** A two-party system, as opposed to a multiparty system, provides a very weak organization of interest representation among the general public.

**74.** Election laws, and especially single-member districts and plurality voting, promote a two-party system and impede the development of a more representative multiparty system.

**75.** Voter turnout in American elections is very low. Only about 50 percent of those eligible vote in presidential elections, and about 35 percent in congressional elections.

**76.** Party platforms do not express clear policy differences. They tend to be similar on broad goals and imprecise with respect to specific policy.

**77.** Voters, to the extent they are concerned with issues, either have no choice or a very blurred choice.

**78.** Multiple issues make it difficult, if not impossible, for voters to determine which issues they are voting for or against.

**79.** If specific public policies are going to be made, they will have to be generated elsewhere. That elsewhere is the corporate political system.

**80.** The individual political system is incapable of explaining political outcomes. Its major use is to justify those outcomes arrived at by other means.

**81.** Elections are essentially an American symbolic ritual celebrating the democratic ideology as expressed in its texts and documents.

**82.** Symbolic political language is the major characteristic of the individual political system.

### Chapter 9: *Demand-Side Government*

**83.** The power of the corporate political system is reflected in the governmental programs that benefit it.

**84.** Consumer demand not only affects the general standard of living of all Americans, it also has a direct relationship to production.

**85.** Even the corporate political system has an interest in the overall level of consumer demand.

**86.** The amount of money that consumers have to spend affects not only demand for goods and services but the rate of savings as well.

**87.** Falling demand can cause unemployment, underutilization of plant, falling production, and bankruptcies.

**88.** Government will take steps to bolster demand for products and services.

**89.** Since oligopolies control supply, price, and profits, prices can remain stable or even increase during periods of falling demand (stagflation), and prices and profits, but not supply, can rise during periods of rising demand.

**90.** There are three major ways in which government programs affect consumer demand: (1) contributory transfer payment programs that are indirectly earned by the recipients, the Social Security System being the most notable example; (2) transfer payment programs that are unearned (welfare); (3) and tax expenditure programs (i.e., various income tax deductions, exclusions, credits, and exemptions) that leave more money in the hands of selected categories of people.

**91.** The total of all individual transfer payments in 1981 was $316.7 billion, of which $239.4 billion was in contributory transfer payment programs (mostly Social Security, representing 76% of the total), and $77.3 billion was in general revenue transfer payments (24%), of which $57.3 billion (18% of the total of all transfer payments) was welfare. Eight-two percent of all transfer payments were made to programs other than welfare.

**92.** Tax expenditures, which go mainly to the well-to-do, significantly reduce the progressivity of the federal income tax.

**93.** In 1981, $179.8 billion worth of tax expenditures went mainly to well-to-do individuals.

**94.** The amount of tax expenditures which went to the mostly well-to-do was more than three times the amount of welfare paid to the poor.

## Chapter 10: *Supply-Side Government*

**95.** The amount of goods and services produced in the economy affects the standard of living of all Americans.

**96.** The federal government provides economic "incentives" (tax expenditures for corporations), direct subsidies, and indirect subsidies to business that business may use to increase supply if it chooses to do so. The government, however, cannot force business to increase supply; and business can use these increased resources for mergers or simply retain them as profits.

**97.** The conflict over the distribution of wealth and income between the rich and poor becomes particularly severe during bad economic periods; during these periods the wealthy try to increase their wealth and income at the expense of the poor.

**98.** In 1982, as a consequence of President Reagan's tax changes, those earning less than $10,000 suffered a net loss of $240, while those earning more than $80,000 reaped a net gain of $15,130.

**99.** In spite of the large tax deductions granted to corporations in 1981 and 1982 in order to stimulate investment, business investment actually declined.

**100.** The number of corporate mergers during the same period, however, increased by 27 percent, and the dollar value of mergers increased by 100 percent.

**101.** Many laws were changed and new ones passed in 1981 and 1982 to aid the banking industry.

**102.** Tax expenditures for corporations amounted to $48.8 billion in 1981, nearly the total value of welfare payments in the same year.

**103.** Large increases in tax expenditures benefiting corporations were also enacted in 1981 and 1982; these were predicted to produce revenue losses to the federal government of one-half trillion dollars by 1990.

**104.** Fifty percent of all corporations pay no income taxes.

**105.** The eighteen largest banks in the United States pay a tax rate of 0.03 percent.

**106.** Corporations paid only 8 percent of all federal revenues in 1983, down from 33 percent in 1952.

**107.** The tax burden has shifted more and more to individuals.

**108.** Data indicate that tax breaks do not provide an incentive to work harder.

**109.** If one were going to provide incentives for corporations to work harder, one would tax them more, not less.

**110.** The capitalist ideology justifies political actions that help the well-to-do without either being correct or explaining the real reasons for such actions.

**111.** In 1982, direct subsidies to farmers amounted to over $11 billion.

**112.** U.S. foreign and military policy is directly linked to American investment abroad ($2 trillion), American imports ($315 billion), and American exports ($341 billion).

**113.** Eleven of the fifteen largest multinational corporations are U.S. owned.

**114.** More than 20 percent of all U.S. corporate profits are earned abroad.

**115.** Almost one-half of all the loans made by the largest U.S. banks have been made to foreign countries.

**116.** The United States has more than 3,000 military bases abroad.

**117.** The United States spends over $11 billion, outside of the military budget, on economic, military, financial, and internal security assistance to foreign countries.

## Chapter 11: *Government Spending*

**118.** Government at every level (national, state, and local) accounts for 20 percent of all spending on goods and services in the United States (GNP). Government, then, is an important part of the total demand for goods and services and plays a significant role in U.S. society as an economic unit.

**119.** The federal government accounts for 39 percent of all government expenditures on goods and services, state and local governments accounting for the other 61 percent.

**120.** In terms of the federal budget, 65 percent of all federal outlays do not involve the purchase of goods and services, but are, rather, various transfer payment programs—a very small proportion of which are welfare payments.

**121.** The two largest federal expenditures outside of the purchase of goods and services are contributory transfer payment proograms (e.g., Social Security), and interest on the national debt.

**122.** Interest payments on the national debt, which are now above $100 billion a year, go almost entirely to a very small number of institutional and individual holders. Interest payments now amount to almost double the sum spent on welfare.

**123.** Tax expenditures to individuals and business represent 35 percent of the total national budget. These deductions, exclusions, credits, and exemptions go mainly to the well-to-do and are more than four times the amount spent on welfare.

**124.** Of the 35 percent of the national budget spent on goods and services, two-thirds is devoted to direct military expenditures. If various foreign aid programs (both military and economic) and the space program are included, the total is 75 percent. In other words, what goods and services the federal government does purchase are overwhelmingly related to military operations.

**125.** Nearly 75 percent of all federal government personnel work for the military and the Defense Department.

**126.** When one takes into account all taxes—federal, state, and local—the combined effect is neither progressive nor regressive. All Americans, regardless of income, pay about the same percentage rate.

**127.** The middle class is now shouldering more and more of the tax burden.

**128.** The disposable income of the middle class is declining.

**129.** In spite of the increased economic pressure on the middle class, it continues—against its better interests—to side with the corporate political system.

**130.** In a stagnant economy, the corporate political system puts increasing pressure on the middle class to give up some of its wealth and income.

**131.** Whether this pressure might cause a new "American Revolution," in which the middle class opposes the corporate political system, is a matter of conjecture.

# EPILOGUE

It is commonplace, in a book of this sort, to offer suggestions for change and improvement for what has been discussed. Certainly the nature of the material cries out for proposals for change. I am not going to do this, however, and I feel I owe the reader an explanation as to why.

Offering policy proposals is something those outside of the corporate political system are frequently prone to do. These proposals are usually offered in good faith and with good intentions, and because they make a certain sense. They have a kind of logic, given the material presented. But their logic is not that of the corporate political system—nor even that of the individual political system for that matter. They come from a different sort of reasoning, a kind of intellectual logic; they represent an attempt to figure out, in the abstract, what might be done. The difficulty with these proposals, however, is that they are suggested in a political vacuum, as though the two political systems did not exist. Politics has little room for intellectual solutions. Politics is based on self-interest and power, and the participants in politics are not interested in playing intellectual games. They are after something very real; and they will fight very hard to get what they want, using the considerable resources at their disposal. In order for the proposals of intellectuals to carry any weight, they themselves must become involved in politics. And obviously the most effective political arena to become involved in is the corporate political system.

Some intellectuals, especially economists, and occasionally political scientists, do indeed become involved in politics—even at the corporate political level. Henry Kissinger, for example, chief foreign-policy advisor and secretary of state for Richard Nixon and Gerald Ford, was a political scientist at Harvard and a member and active participant of the Council on Foreign Relations before he assumed his governmental positions. The president's Council of Economic Advisors is composed of economists who usually have some practical experience in politics. These people speak for the interests of the corporate political system—in fact, they have become part of that system. Proposals that do not reflect the interests of the corporate political system or the interests of a wide group of people in the individual political system, will be nothing but more or less interesting, worthwhile, but vacuous suggestions.

## TWO MODEST PROPOSALS

Let me offer two such proposals. One has been bandied about many times by others: confiscatory inheritance taxes. The other I dreamed up myself: a proposal to get the economy back on its feet again. Both will have a certain intellectual appeal. They will make a certain sense. But neither will be acceptable to either the corporate or the individual political system.

### Confiscatory Inheritance Taxes

In Chapter 4 we discussed the large inequalities in wealth in the United States. We have also seen that much wealth is passed on through inheritances, a mechanism that obviously perpetuates inequalities. In addition, it has also been shown that inheritances provide no economic benefits to the society as a whole.

Our democratic creed seems inconsistent with large inequalities, and especially with respect to passing on those inequalities from generation to generation. We claim to be a society in which there is equality of opportunity. For this to be true, however, we should certainly all start more or less equally. Few would argue that someone starting out with a million dollars and someone starting out with nothing would be starting from the same place. Resources are important—they do, in fact, provide people with opportunities.

Let us do the following, then. Let us say that people will still be allowed to make as much money as they can during their lifetimes. But at the end, the state will confiscate all that they themselves have not spent. Let us look at some of the consequences this would produce.

1. People would start on a more equal footing in the economic and social system.
2. They would have more incentives to work for themselves.

3. Everyone but a small, but highly significant, minority (the top 19%) would benefit from redistribution of wealth, although the middle class, being a majority, could keep it all for itself if it wanted to.

4. It would raise a great amount of government revenue.

5. Taxes could be cut significantly, including income taxes.

Of course, all of the problems of inequality would not be solved by such a proposal, just the worst. Clearly children of wealthy parents would still benefit enormously while their parents were still alive, and would be treated to all the educational, social, and cultural advantages that such wealth provides. Also, people would still vary in how much wealth they could accumulate over their lifetimes, except, in this case, they *really would* have earned it.

But the reasons why such a proposal would never be adopted are equally as clear. No matter how much the majority middle class might benefit, it is doubtful they could ever be persuaded to give up their middling accumulations in order to take away the quite sizable wealth amassed by the top 19 percent. In addition, the top 19 percent and corporations are clearly not going to be very keen on the proposal. In other words, the proposal will fly neither with the individual political system nor with the corporate political system. It would take something of a revolution for such a scheme to be adopted—a middle-class revolution at that—and I am certainly *not* proposing a revolution. Too many people get hurt, not to mention the fact that the middle-class revolutionaries, in the unlikely event that they would fight against the wealthy, would undoubtedly lose.

So, although this suggestion makes good economic sense and would modify political power more nearly in line with the democratic ideology, it remains a more or less interesting, perhaps worthwhile, but vacuous proposal. The corporate political system would find it against its interests; and the middle class, which would benefit most, does not yet understand how this would be so. The middle class sees its self-interest as aligned with the wealthy, however mistakenly; and unless *that* is changed, then nothing—absolutely nothing—will happen. In fact, just the opposite has happened: the Reagan Administration and Congress passed inheritance tax legislation that for all practical purposes reduced what few inheritance taxes there were to zero.

## Turning Missiles into Mustangs: A Proposal by a Maverick

The second proposal, which I alone will take responsibility for (and when you read it you will see why!), has to do with how one might, in President Reagan's phrase, "turn the economy around." Gross National Product has fallen, real income has fallen, unemployment is up, nearly one-third of our productive plant is idle, and 14 million U.S. families live below the poverty line of $9,000 per year.

This proposal starts with the fact that the automobile and steel industries are two of the country's major centers of industrial production. In addition, a large sector of the rest of the economy (e.g., rubber tires and highway construction) depends on how well the automobile industry is doing. Let's take Eisenhower's secretary of defense, Charles Wilson (former president of General Motors), at his word when he said: "What's good for General Motors is good for the country."

At a conservative estimate, the MX missile program will cost at least $70 billion. As with all money spent for something, there are what economists call *opportunity costs;* these represent alternatives foregone, what isn't bought instead with the same amount of money. Moreover, almost everyone agrees that the MX missile program is worthless.

Instead, let us give each family in poverty $5,000 for a new car ($5,000 × 14 million = $70 billion). However, they cannot have this $5,000 unless they use it to buy a new U.S.-built car within the next three years.

All U.S. car manufacturers would develop models in the $5,000 range to compete for these funds. The automobile and related industries would be booming. Unemployment would go down. Incomes would go up. Industrial production would go up. GNP would go up. Idle plant would be reduced. Those in poverty would have a new car.

But, those in poverty don't want a new car. They want money instead. They could turn around and sell their new cars at a discount (say $4,000) to the middle class. The poor would then have an extra $4,000, the middle class would have new cars very inexpensively, and the economy would take off!

Whether you like this idea or not, rest assured that it will not work. It, too, is an intellectual proposal. It would have to be adopted by the corporate political system (which has its own ideas about such matters), and the individual political system would have to be persuaded that giving all that money to the poor is a good idea that would be of benefit to it. Not to mention the fact that anyone proposing such a scheme would have the military, and what even President Eisenhower warned us about, the military-industrial complex, to contend with. As Kurt Vonnegut would say: "Hi-ho."

## THE VIRTUES OF CYNICISM

Aside from pointing out that viable public policy alternatives are generated by the corporate political system, that this system sets the policy agenda among other things, and that therefore policy proposals must take into account its realities and be tailored to its needs, I have consistently refused to offer solutions to the problems I have raised. My purpose is not to tell readers what to do, but to tell them what is happening so that they can figure things out for themselves. I am a describer and analyst of U.S. politics, not a policymaker. There are many possible "solutions" to the issues that have been raised in this book, and it has not been my intention to lead a crusade on behalf of any of them.

Besides, almost all the readers of this book belong to the individual political system, and they will have to rely on it in order to change anything. However, this political system inherently avoids the facts we have discussed here. It avoids these facts because it is controlled, both in terms of money and in personnel, by those who have strong connections to the corporate political system; and actual political power, as opposed to ritual celebrations of the democratic creed, lies outside of it.

I hesitate to tell you what ought to be done, therefore, because there isn't, frankly, much those in the individual political system can do. It is the corporate political system that dominates public policy making in this country—not the electoral process. And to the extent that the election process has any effect, it is merely to determine which particular set of office-seekers—and, occasionally, which conflicting business interests (most notably large corporations vs. medium-sized ones)—are likely to predominate. President Carter was an example of a representative of the larger corporations, President Reagan of the next size down. And it is those in the group below the giant corporations that are the more conservative of the two.

My purpose in this book, rather, has simply been to make certain you know enough about how the system actually works so that you will not be easily led astray by what you read and hear from government spokespersons and others who have a stake in telling you what they want you to hear. If I have even partially fulfilled my duty as a Political Scientist to describe and analyze politics as it is, then I will have accomplished my purpose as a researcher and teacher.

Knowledge *can* lead to action—but it can also lead to cynicism. It may be that what I have told you will be a source of great frustration for you. There is not much you can do at the action level, since the only activity open to you—an activity that has frustrated countless people—is participation in the individual political system. Beyond that, cynicism is not such a bad alternative. At least it will immunize you to the inanities that you will hear constantly from political spokespersons. It may even eventually lead to a wider exposure of the realities of the U.S. political process.

But I doubt that also. There are strong pressures in any society to present a *positive* image of itself and its political institutions and practices. This, after all, is much of what politics in the individual political system and the democratic ideology is all about. One is trained in school to *admire* our system, not to criticize it or to say bad things about it, *even if they are true*. What I have told you will not contribute to that positive image, nor will it make you very proud of the two-tiered political system in which you live. I am sorry for that. My justification is that there is little I could do about it, other than to describe it and let the chips fall where they may. I didn't make it that way, and you didn't either.

The problem of what to do, then, is yours. It is not an easy one, and I can only wish you luck. I can say, however, that sometimes getting caught up in the politics of the individual system is like not being able to see the forest for the trees. One overemphasizes the efficacy of the actions one is engaged in. On the other hand, it may also be true, from my vantage point as a member of academia, that I cannot see the trees for the forest; I may be overemphasizing the difficulties and underemphasizing the possibilities of concerted action in the individual political system. But I don't think so. I think I have, in fact, left you with the very serious problem of whether any type of action will be efficacious. After all, those with whom you will be contending are the very people and institutions I have been describing here, and they are very powerful indeed.

But *my* task is finished. You now know what the two U.S. political systems are like. Go do what you think best—assuming it's even something in which you want to get involved. There is no easy answer. But if there is a solution, we shall certainly never arrive at it if we are ignorant about how the two political systems actually function.

# BIBLIOGRAPHY

## CHAPTER 1

JAMES MADISON. "No. 10: The Size and Variety of the Union as a Check on Faction." In *The Federalist Papers*.

## CHAPTER 3

PHILLIP I. BLUMBERG. *The Megacorporation in American Society: The Scope of Corporate Power*. Englewood Cliffs, N.J.: Prentice-Hall, 1975.

THOMAS DYE. *Who's Running America? The Carter Years*. Englewood Cliffs, N.J.: Prentice-Hall, 1979.

JACK FARKAS AND DEBORAH S. WEINBERGER. *The Relativity of Concentration Observations*. The Conference Board, no date.

DANIEL R. FUSFELD. *Economics: Principles of Political Economy*. Glenview, Ill.: Scott, Foresman, 1982.

ROBERT L. HEILBRONER AND LESTER C. THUROW. *The Economic Problem*. Englewood Cliffs, N.J.: Prentice-Hall, 1981.

_____. *Economics Explained*. Englewood Cliffs, N.J.: Prentice-Hall, 1982.

JOHN W. KENDRICK. *The National Wealth of the United States*. The Conference Board, 1976.

## CHAPTER 4

*Forbes* magazine. "Who Gets the Most Pay" (June 7, 1982), pp. 74–100.
———. "THE FORBES FOUR HUNDRED" (September 13, 1982), pp. 99–172.
ROBERT L. HEILBRONER AND LESTER C. THUROW. *Economics Explained*. Englewood Cliffs, N.J.: Prentice-Hall, 1982.
ROBERT J. LAMPMAN. *The Share of Top Wealth-Holders in National Wealth*. Princeton: Princeton University Press, 1962.
DOROTHY PROJECTOR AND GERTRUDE S. WEISS, *Survey of Financial Characteristics of Consumers*. Federal Reserve Board, 1966.
JONATHAN H. TURNER AND CHARLES E. STAINES. *Inequality: Privilege and Poverty in America*. Pacific Palisades, Calif.: Goodyear, 1976.
LESTER C. THUROW. *The Zero-Sum Society*. New York: Basic Books, 1980.

## CHAPTER 5

PHILIP I. BLUMBERG. *The Megacorporation in American Society: The Scope of Corporate Power*. Englewood Cliffs, N.J.: Prentice-Hall, 1975.
THOMAS DYE. *Who's Running America? The Carter Years*. Englewood Cliffs, N.J.: Prentice-Hall, 1979.
EDWARD S. HERMAN. *Corporate Control, Corporate Power*. Cambridge, Eng.: Cambridge University Press, 1981.

## CHAPTER 6

ALLAN PARACHINI. "Tape Reveals Nixon Move to Suppress Air-Bag Rules." *Los Angeles Times* (November 29, 1982).
ELEANOR RANDOLF. "Burford Problems Reflect Reagan Ecology Approach." *Los Angeles Times* (March 10, 1983).

## CHAPTER 7

DAVID ADAMANY. "Money, Politics, and Democracy: A Review Essay." *American Political Science Review*, **71**, No. 1 (March, 1977), 289–304.
*Congressional Quarterly* (September 2, 1978, and September 1, 1979).
KENNETH M. DOLBEARE AND MURRAY J. EDELMAN. *American Politics: Policies, Power, and Change*. Lexington, Mass.: Heath, 1981.
THOMAS DYE. *Who's Running America? The Carter Years*. Englewood Cliffs, N.J.: Prentice-Hall, 1979.
———. JAROL B. MANHEIM. *American Politics Yearbook, 1982–83*. New York: Longman, 1982.
*National Journal* (August 7, 1982).
HARRELL R. RODGERS, JR. AND MICHAEL HARRINGTON. *Unfinished Democracy: The Ameican Political System*. Glenview, Ill.: Scott, Foresman, 1981.

## CHAPTER 8

ROBERT A. DAHL. *A Preface to Democratic Theory*. Chicago: University of Chicago Press, 1956.

THOMAS R. DYE. AND L. HARMON ZEIGLER. *The Irony of Democracy*. Belmont, Calif.: Wadsworth, 1981.

MURRAY EDELMAN. *The Symbolic Uses of Politics*. Urbana: University of Illinois Press, 1964.

## CHAPTER 9

CONGRESSIONAL BUDGET OFFICE. *An Analysis of the President's Budgetary Proposals for Fiscal Year 1983*. Washington, D.C.: GPO, 1982.

————. *Balancing the Federal Budget and Limiting Federal Spending: Constitutional and Statutory Approaches*. Washington, D.C.: GPO, 1982.

————. *Reducing the Federal Deficit: Strategies and Options*. Washington, D.C.: GPO, 1982.

————. *Tax Expenditures*. Washington, D.C.: GPO, 1981.

DEPARTMENT OF COMMERCE (Bureau of Economic Analysis). *Survey of Current Business*, **62,** No. 6 (June, 1982).

DANIEL R. FUSFIELD. *Economics: Principles of Political Economy*. Glenview, Ill.: Scott, Foresman, 1982.

OFFICE OF MANAGEMENT AND BUDGET. *Budget of the U.S. Government*. Washington, D.C.: GPO, 1983.

## CHAPTER 10 (Same as Chapter 9)

DANIEL R. FUSFELD. *Economics: Principles of Political Economy*. Glenview, Ill.: Scott, Foresman, 1982.

LESTER C. THUROW. *The Impact of Taxes on the American Economy*. New York: Praeger Publishers, 1971.

————. *The Zero-Sum Society*. New York: Basic Books, 1980.

———— AND ROBERT E. B. LUCAS. "The Distribution of Earned Income." In Otto Eckstein, ed., *Parameters and Policies in the U.S. Economy*. Amsterdam and Oxford: North-Holland, 1976. Pp. 11–75.

## CHAPTER 11 (Same as Chapters 9 and 10)

# INDEX